Anglicanism in Ecumenical Perspective

DUQUESNE STUDIES

Theological Series

4

ANGLICANISM IN ECUMENICAL PERSPECTIVE

by

WILLIAM H. VAN DE POL, S.T.D.

DUQUESNE UNIVERSITY PRESS

Pittsburgh, Pa.

Editions E. Nauwelaerts, Louvain

1965

Henry J. Koren, C.S.Sp., S.T.D., Leonard A. Bushinski, C.S.Sp., M.A., S.T.L., Leonard J. Swidler, Ph.D., S.T.L., editors.

Volume One—*Albert Dondeyne*, FAITH AND THE WORLD. XI and 324 pages. Price: $5.00 cloth.

Volume Two—*Peter Schoonenberg, S.J.*, GOD'S WORLD IN THE MAKING. IX and 207 pages. Price: $3.95 cloth.

Volume Three—*Leonard J. Swidler, editor*, SCRIPTURE AND ECUMENISM. VII and 197 pages. Price: $4.95 cloth.

Volume Four—*William H. van de Pol, S.T.D.*, ANGLICANISM IN ECUMENICAL PERSPECTIVE. X and 293 pages. Price: $6.75 cloth.

In preparation
J. H. Walgrave, *Person and Society*
Henry Fries, *Bultmann-Barth and Catholic Theology*

Imprimatur
✠ Bernard Cardinal Alfrink
Archiepiscopus Ultraiectensis
Ultraiecti
1 Julii 1964

Library of Congress Catalog Card Number 65–10053

Contents

v

Preface

DR. WILLIAM H. VAN DE POL is professor of the phenomenology of Protestantism at the Catholic University of Nijmegen, Netherlands. He has published, in addition to other works, half a dozen books about ecumenical topics, which have appeared in Dutch, German, English and Italian editions.[1]

Born in 1897 and baptized in the Dutch Reformed Church, the author worshipped in this church and the Lutheran Church until, in 1919, he was confirmed by the Anglican bishop of North and Central Europe. For twenty years he remained a regular communicant of the Church of England. In 1940 he was received into the (Roman) Catholic Church, of which he became a priest in 1944.

[1] The following is a list of the author's books:
Liturgie, Zeist, 1931.
De Kerk in het leven en denken van Newman, Nijkerk, 1936; German ed., *Die Kirche im Leben und Denken Newmans*, Salzburg, 1937.
Het Christelijk Dilemma, Roermond, 1948; English ed., *The Christian Dilemma*, London and New York, 1952.
Wegen tot Geloof, Roermond, 1952.
Karakteristiek van het reformatorisch Christendom, Roermond, 1952; German ed., *Das reformatorische Christentum*, Zürich, 1956; Italian ed., *Il Cristianesimo della Riforma*, Rome, 1958.
Het Wereldprotestantisme, Roermond, 1956; Italian ed., *Il Protestantesimo nel Mondo*, Rome, 1959; German ed., *Der Weltprotestantismus*, Essen, 1960; English ed., *World Protestantism*, New York, 1964.
Het Getuigenis van de Reformatie, Roermond, 1960; German ed., *Das Zeugnis der Reformation*, Essen, 1963.
De Oecumene, Roermond, 1961; German ed., *Probleme und Chancen der Oekumene*, München, 1962.
Het Anglicanisme in oecumenisch Perspectief, Roermond, 1962; English ed., *Anglicanism in Ecumenical Perspective*, Pittsburgh, 1965.

After studying geography at the University of Utrecht from 1915 to 1920, he studied Greek, Latin and Hebrew and in 1925 became a student of the Theological Faculty of the same university until 1933. Three years later he obtained his doctorate in theology with honors on his dissertation, *The Church in the Life and Thought of Newman.* From 1941 to 1944 he studied Catholic theology at the University of Nijmegen. These studies were followed by four years of pastoral work until in 1948 he received his appointment as professor at Nijmegen.

Born in a "typically ecumenical" family, and active in ecumenical work as early as 1928 at the Anglican Church Congress of Cheltenham and at the Edinburgh Conference on Faith and Order of 1937, Father van de Pol's unique background eminently qualifies him to speak with authority on ecumenical matters and especially on Anglicanism.

The text of the present book has been translated by Father Walter van de Putte, C.S.Sp., and carefully revised by the undersigned. Subdivisions of the chapters have been added to facilitate reading. A few slight changes have been made to incorporate events of the past two years and to bring the bibliography up to date. Indexes have been added for easy reference.

HENRY J. KOREN, C.S.SP.

Duquesne University, Pittsburgh, Pa.

CHAPTER ONE

Why Anglicanism?

1. THE NEED FOR UNITY

THE apostle St. Paul repeatedly sums up, in a few short words
of his epistles, what constitutes the chief content of the message
the world and until the end of time in the name and in virtue
of salvation that must be proclaimed to all men throughout
of the command of Christ. We have an example of it in a
passage of his letter to Titus which begins with the words: "The
grace of God our Savior has appeared to all men," or, according
to a recent translation, "The grace of God, source of salvation for
all men, has appeared."[1]

In the epistles of St. Paul the grace of God means God's
mercifulness and readiness to pardon which spring from His
infinite love and rest on His eternal fidelity. This grace of God
appeared in the dark world of our human existence by the coming, apparition, the word and work of salvation of Christ; and it
has manifested, revealed, made itself known amidst the situation
of our human existence. This grace is destined for all men; it is
the "source of salvation" for all men who believe in Christ.

It is because the grace of God shines in the world in and
through Christ that Christ is simply called "the light of the

---

[1] Titus 2:11.

1

world," the only "true light that enlightens every man who comes into the world."[2]

It is because the grace of God is a "source of salvation for all men" in and through Christ, that Christ is simply called "the Savior of men," the only true Savior, whose Name is the only "name under heaven given to men by which we must be saved."[3]

Scripture is concerned with the broadest possible ecumenicity and at the same time professes the most absolute exclusivism. On the one hand, it is concerned with all men all over the world and of all times and, on the other, proclaims the only true Light and the one and only true Savior.

Ecumenicity and exclusivism in the Christian message of salvation not only do not exclude each other but they necessarily belong together, presuppose each other, and are immediately and most closely interlocked.

The exclusivism of the Christian message does not rest on an arbitrary human claim. On the contrary, it is necessarily implied by the universal validity and sufficiency of God's act of reconciliation that was manifested once for all in the salvific work accomplished by Christ for all men of all times and the whole world. This salvific work is concerned with nothing less than the salvation of all mankind from an existential distress that afflicts all men: namely, the distress and evil of sin and death.

The pronounced ecumenical character of the Christian message is based upon the absolutely exclusive character of its essential content. That is why ecumenicity and exclusivism are two fundamental and mutually complementary characteristics of the one and indivisible Church of Christ.

The salvific work of Christ and the Church's proclamation of salvation are concerned with nothing less than the ultimate incorporation of the whole of mankind into the Body of Christ.

---

[2] John 1:9.   [3] Acts 4:12.

Only in and under Him will the *Ecumene* attain its complete unity, cohesion and communion.[4]

The first, most important and essential task of every Christian, therefore, consists in this, that as God's associate, he be a witness of Christ the one true Light and the only true Savior. This he should be in all his conduct, by word and deed, in his whole attitude of life, in every respect and circumstance. The first, most important and essential vocation of every Christian is being a roadsign in the world, pointing to the "source of salvation for all men," that is, to the grace, love, fidelity, mercy, readiness to forgive and actual reconciliation which God has revealed in Christ.

This revelation of Christ the Christians are called to manifest in the world. It is principally for this reason that they are called "Christians." The attitude of Christians toward one another and toward all fellow men and, not in the least, the way Christians belonging to diverse denominations meet and converse with one another, ought to be determined and ruled in every respect by that primary vocation.

Just as Christ is "the one Mediator between God and men,"[5] and "God . . . has reconciled us to himself through Christ,"[6] so does the Christian's primary function in this world consist in this that he take action as mediator and reconciler, even when his own interests are at stake. By daily prayer and daily penance he must try to overcome first of all his deep-rooted self-seeking, his eagerness to contradict and combat others, thereby developing a readiness to listen, ponder, serve, and cooperate with others. In short, the vocation of a Christian consists in this that, in all his relations with men and in all his actions and omissions, he purposively continues to build on the foundation of the peace

---

[4] "This his good pleasure he purposed in him to be dispensed in the fullness of the times: to re-establish all things in Christ, both those in the heavens and those on earth." Eph. 1:9–10.

[5] 1 Tim. 2:5.   [6] 2 Cor. 5:19.

and reconciliation which God has revealed and actually fulfilled in Christ.

The same applies above all to the Church. "Jesus Christ gave himself for us that he might redeem us from all iniquity and cleanse for himself an acceptable people, pursuing good works."[7] She has as her vocation in this world to be the herald of the Gospel of God's grace, the witness of the true Light and of the one true Savior, the dispenser of the gifts which she draws from the "source of salvation for all men," the mediatrix who appears everywhere in the world as reconciler and as the pattern of unity which binds all the faithful together in Christ.

Jesus said already to His first disciples: "You are the light of the world. A city set on a mountain cannot be hidden."[8] Now what are we to think of this after twenty centuries of Church and Christianity?

No doubt in every century and in all denominations there have been true Christians who in their thought and conduct were truly animated by the love of Christ and, on that account, corresponded more or less to their vocation as Christians, either openly in the wide world or hidden within a private circle.

But let us examine how we, Christians, frequently act toward one another in daily life or fail one another, how we treat one another in economic, social, political and even in ecclesiastical affairs as competitors and antagonists. Let us recall how Christian peoples have fought and plundered one another in the course of centuries. How can all that be reconciled with Christian charity, patience and the desire for reconciliation? How do such things harmonize with the vocation of the Christian in the world?

Add to that the innumerable theological quarrels, the ecclesiastical schisms, the mutual religious persecutions with their one-sided and often false accusations, the unchristian measures

---

[7] Titus 2:14. [8] Matt. 5:14.

4

and punishments, the unwillingness to understand and suffer one another, the unwillingness to confess one's fault and become reconciled. In short, how often have not Christians been sacrificing charity to so-called truth and justice?

Thousands in our own day no longer know what to think about the faith and are in the process of noiselessly falling away and turning their back to the Church and Christianity. Must not we ask ourselves whether all this has to be attributed solely to the blindness, selfishness, pride, indifference and bad will of those people? Is it not true that to a great extent the fault lies with ourselves, with individual Christians, with Christian churches and with peoples, who for centuries have passed for Christian peoples?

In today's world, there are innumerable persons who do not see the Light, do not recognize the Savior and do not understand the meaning of salvation. It is as if an impenetrable wall had been built between Christ and men. For centuries stones have been added and the wall has been raised higher and higher.

No doubt, Christian preaching and ecclesiastical practice are bent down under the ballast of antiquated situations and conventions, theological representations and teachings, devotional practices, worn-out forms and often incomprehensible language. But, over and above that, there is the great evil of Christian disunity, the result of antagonisms that arose in periods of error and decadence as well as in those of reformation and renewal.

It is not by accident that renewal and reunion are repeatedly mentioned in one breath.[9] There can be little hope for reunion if there is no renewal of the Church and theology, of faith and living one's faith. Without both renewal and reunion, there is little chance that the Gospel will once more get a hearing from the large mass of men of our time and that the Church will

---

[9] Hans Küng, *The Council, Reform and Reunion,* New York, 1961; cf. Visser 't Hooft, *The Renewal of the Church,* London, 1956; Kraemer, *A Theology of the Laity,* London, 1958, Chap. 3, pp. 74 ff.

witness the entry within her portals of the millions who now live outside her walls.

Without the renewal of the Church and the restoration of her unity, there will also be little chance that the world will take her voice seriously and that the Church will be able to exercise a beneficent influence on the course of things in the world. There exists a very direct and intimate connection between all these diverse facets of the situation in which we Christians find ourselves.

2. THE DESIRE FOR UNITY

That is why we can certainly consider it as one of the most gladdening phenomena of our time that Christians of the most various denominations and communities throughout the world are conceiving a sincere and strong desire for an actual and complete restoration of the unity of faith and church communion which were lost in the course of the centuries.

The ecumenical movement, which was born about half a century ago from that desire, is plainly growing in strength and extension. The faithful of practically all existing denominations are taking part, in ever increasing numbers, in ecumenical gatherings of every sort. And in ever widening circles prayers are offered for the restoration of unity, not for a preconceived type of unity, but for the unity that Christ Himself willed and for which we altogether are longing.

The growing generation especially has established its hope on renewal and reunion. It is of the utmost importance for the Church that the expectations of youth will not be disappointed.

The unexpected and striking rapprochement that is taking place between Christians should not be attributed to the threat of an atomic war or the thrust of communism. The writings of ecumenical pioneers and the reports of important ecumenical gatherings during the last fifty years show clearly that the cause lies much deeper and that it has an eminently religious character. The desire and striving for the reunion of Christians is the direct result of a return to the heart of the Gospel, a deepening of the faith and a new vision of all the Christians of their common vocation in the world.[10]

The centuries-old quarrel among Christians ought to belong definitely to the past just as colonialism and imperialism. We are now at a turning point in the history of Christianity. That which comes from God remains. What is a matter of faith, "*de fide*," is irrevocable. But on the level of human understanding and life, sweeping changes are coming, which, of ourselves, we would have been neither willing nor able to make.

We believe and profess that Christ is the Lord, the only true *Kyrios*, to whom "all power in heaven and on earth has been given,"[11] which means far beyond the limits of our small earthly reality. If so, it is perfectly certain that He has the power also in our own day to put to shame the wisdom of our frequently shortsighted logic and to "save (us) by the foolishness of preaching."[12]

There is no doubt then that He has the power, when He wills it and in the way He wills it, to gather once more the flock that is scattered and dispersed all over the earth. By the power of His Word and His Spirit, it will become one faith and one baptism, one bread and one body, one flock and one shepherd, one fraternal communion and one Church.

The joint longings, prayers and striving for the actual and complete restoration in faith and church order, of unity and

---

[10] Visser 't Hooft, *The Pressure of Our Common Calling,* London, 1959; Rouse-Neill, *A History of the Ecumenical Movement,* London, 1954, Chap. VIII, pp. 353 ff. and Epilogue, pp. 725 ff.

[11] Matt. 28:18. Cf. Dan. 7:14 and Phil. 2:9–10.

[12] 1 Cor. 1:21.

ecclesiastical community among Christians and Christian churches, are definitively on the march. The ecumenical leaders and representatives of the churches do not yet see clearly how the numerous existing difficulties and problems will be solved. But one thing stands out as certain for the believing Christian: it is no longer possible to hold back the process of unification; it is going steadily forward until the final goal shall be reached, namely, the restoration of the unity in the form and manner that have always been willed and intended by Christ.

What today is taking place among the Christians of the whole *Ecumene* is for the believer a clear manifestation of the *magnalia Dei*, the great works of God. This is not a human work. Humanly speaking, the actual difficulties and oppositions in the ecumenical field seem insuperable. And yet something is going on, something is taking place by which the conviction is growing in ever widening circles that God is at work in the Church and the churches, that He desires the restoration of the unity and communion and that He also can and shall bring it about. We on our part have the obligation of persevering in prayer in order that we may have a more true vision of faith, more openness, more docility and readiness, in short more "faith, hope and charity, these three; but the greatest of these is charity."[13]

3. THE ECUMENICAL SITUATION

It is not our intention to speak at length in this chapter about the origin, development and the problematics of the ecumenical movement.[14] However, by way of introduction to the content of the present book, it seems necessary to say a few words about the ecumenical situation of the churches at the present time.

---

[13] 1 Cor. 13:13.
[14] Concerning this matter see the author's *Probleme und Chancen der Oekumene,* München, 1962.

For a good many years the ecumenical movement has ceased to be the purely academic concern of specialists, who are interested in denominational, ecclesiastical and theological differences and who exchange ideas about them without believing in the possibility of bridging the gap between opposite camps and overcoming disunity. The situation of the churches all over the world has become too serious to indulge exclusively in such purely theoretical considerations as a way of passing the time in a scholarly manner.

We have now reached the "eleventh hour" in regard to the ecumenical question. We are in the midst of a religious crisis such as Christians perhaps have never known before. Many have the feeling that it is a question of to be or not to be. An ever increasing number are earnestly considering the possibility that the end is near.

In such circumstances it is no longer a matter of speculations and of words but of solutions and deeds. That is why the ecumenical movement makes sense only as a practical movement. It is a question of securing tangible results, a real reversal in church attitudes, and of making evident progress on the road to a complete reunion in faith and Church.

The formation of the World Council of Churches in 1948 takes a first place among the results which the ecumenical movement has been able to achieve. Toward the end of 1961 the third Assembly took place in New Delhi, and here the number of churches that had joined reached 198.[15]

Looking at the period from 1948 to 1961 we are able to see that in that short span there has taken place a not unimportant clarification and broadening of the ecumenical insight. There developed steadily a better mutual understanding of the churches' religious and ecclesiastical beliefs.

---

[15] *The New Delhi Report,* London, 1962. The first chapter (pp. 1–55) is written by the United States' ecumenist Samuel Cavert. It tells the story of the New Delhi meeting.

9

It appeared clearly, particularly at New Delhi, that the bond between the churches had become more real and close and that, once more, a number of prejudices and resentments had disappeared.

The way in which the Russian Church in communion with the patriarchate of Moscow entered the World Council and was able to create an understanding of her position; also the way the churches of the World Council received her in their midst; the cordial reception given to the first officially appointed Vatican observers; the personal conversations of the latter with the various delegates; all these are evidence that the laborious pioneer efforts of the first ecumenists have begun to produce visible and lasting fruits.

Many have also commented on the impression which the Anglican Communion Service made on representatives of the most diverse churches when Communion was offered to all whose conscience found the offer acceptable. Some, of course, had to abstain from the Communion on account of the beliefs of their particular church; but everyone must have seen in that service a foreshadowing of what, as we believe, hope and pray, will again become a reality for all Christians.

At the same time, many, beholding the Anglican liturgy with the elegant harmony of its elements born of classic Catholicism, Reformation and the present liturgical renewal, have, no doubt, seen in it the prototype that points to the future liturgy of the reunited Church. For precisely in the renovation of the liturgy that is taking place in almost all churches, it will be a question of synthesizing and reintegrating all that is true, good and beautiful in the diverse ways in which the as yet separated churches offer God praise, honor, thanks and adoration by the celebration of the Holy Eucharist.

All the reports of witnesses speak of the spontaneous cordiality with which the delegates, as well as the observers, and representatives of the press, conversed with one another during the third assembly at New Delhi. The reporters pointed out the cordial and open-hearted spirit that reigned among them and the interest and patience with which they listened to one another's ideas, experiences and aims.

This, of course, can also be said to a certain extent of earlier assemblies and ecumenical conferences. But many had the impression that at the assembly at New Delhi, more than ever before, everyone manifested a natural readiness to recognize and treat others as true Christians in spite of all differences or at least to suffer one another in cases where complete understanding had still to be attained.

The assembly of New Delhi will be remembered in the history of the World Council principally because of three events: the acceptance of a new basic formula that is extended in a Trinitarian sense; the integration of the International Mission Council into the World Council; and the entrance into the World Council of the Russian Church in communion with the patriarchate of Moscow. But besides that we shall have to consider as one of the principal gains at New Delhi the just-mentioned experience of the unity and communion in which all who believe in Christ and are baptized know themselves to be bound together.

There are some who express the fear that by attaching too great positive value to the unity already attained and to the cooperation with others, indifference regarding essential variations in belief will be generated. It seems to me that such fears have their source in a typically pre-ecumenical mentality. Of course, as the Archbishop of Canterbury pointed out to the Assembly, there is need of vigilance. For it is not a question of attaining any kind of unity in general, but very definitely of reaching "unity in truth and holiness."[16] This means a unity

---

[16] Ramsey, "Unity, Holiness and Truth," *The Ecumenical Review*, vol. 14, no. 2 (Jan. 1962), p. 188.

which does not neglect anything that is actually contained in God's revelation and in the word of Christ.

Keeping this reservation in mind, we can expect that every real and intense experience of Christian unity that is already achieved will make so much more painful the realization that the still existing disunity is a senseless situation which no one can ultimately wish to maintain. Christians who consider that situation unbearable will not easily be led to obscure the facts. On the contrary, they will be prompted to make a careful examination of the historical, psychological, theological and other numerous causes that are at the source of the disunity.

As a result of such studies, it is possible that eyes will be opened to particular essential elements belonging to the preaching, the church structure and practice of other confessions which might be missing in the preaching and the practice of one's own church. It will also become more and more evident that the church that will result from the complete reunion will not coincide with any of the existing churches, but it will rather embrace the riches of faith and life of all churches to the extent that they are in harmony with God's Revelation and Christ's intention. In this way the appreciation of the unity and communion that already exists will not tend to water down or obscure things, but it will stimulate a deepening and widening process.

We must still call attention to two remarkable changes in ecumenical thinking during the last years. A growing number of Christians everywhere have begun to realize that the present situation of the Church is an inheritance from the past. They regard it as something that has not merely to be cherished and accepted but also to be critically examined in the light of the demands made by the present and the future.

Despite the appreciation of Christians for the safeguarding function of tradition and the imperishable value of particular acquisitions inherited from the past by which the content of

Revelation has received a clearer expression, many have a growing conviction that the past is in many respects a burden under which, as a Dutch Roman Catholic bishop said in a sermon, "the Church would long ago have succumbed were it not that she is the Church."

However, the churches are not only weighed down by a heavy burden inherited from the past. Because of what happened in the past, centuries ago, they have reached an impasse of disunity from which they cannot be freed by any human power. And yet, as for every man who is weighed down by sin and guilt, there is the possibility of a new beginning and a new future. It can be found only in Christ who by His word of pardon and reconciliation removes the heavy burden from man's shoulders and makes everything be again as if this guilt had never existed. This liberation through the word and the spirit of Christ, all churches singly and together are in need of.

In this connection we appreciate more and more the need for a fundamental reconstruction of Church history. Every history is a construction of facts on the basis of more or less preconceived viewpoints. At the present there is a demand for a "Church history in an ecumenical perspective."[17]

In former years, on the contrary, not only historical but also phenomenological, theological and dogmatic studies of the Church were often undertaken for polemical and apologetic ends. Those studies also will have to be placed more and more in an ecumenical perspective, in order that the cause of the disunity and the road to unity may stand out in ever clearer ecumenical light, even from the theological standpoint.

Secondly, ecumenical circles more and more realize that the interior unification of Christians through love, understanding and cooperation need not wait for the final solution of the ecumenical problems which still remain difficult. The latter of

---

[17] Benz, *Kirchengeschichte in ökumenischer Sicht*, Leiden, 1961; Lortz, *Die Reformation als religiöses Anliegen heute*, Trier, 1948, pp. 217 ff.

course must also be achieved. But in the end such a solution will be possible only on the basis of the already discovered, experienced and real interior unity.

The meeting at New Delhi has, as we have said, contributed greatly to that interior unification. Very important is the fact that the whole assembly accepted and proposed, for further examination by the churches, the report of the third section regarding the actual ecumenical purpose and the course to be followed. The description of the ultimate ecumenical purpose is given as follows in the *Report:*

> We believe that the unity which is both God's will and his gift to his Church is being made visible as all in each place who are baptized into Jesus Christ and confess Him as Lord and Saviour are brought by the Holy Spirit into one fully committed fellowship, holding the one apostolic faith, preaching the one Gospel, breaking the one bread, joining in common prayer, and having a corporate life reaching out in witness and service to all and who at the same time are united with the whole Christian fellowship in all places and all ages in such wise that ministry and members are accepted by all, and that all can act and speak together as occasion requires for the tasks to which God calls his people.[18]

This principal paragraph taken from the *Report* about unity can properly be considered the *Magna Carta* of the ecumenical movement. It sums up the results of the deliberations concerning unity. It wishes first of all to give expression to the common vision of faith about the Church of the future, to a persuasion based on faith regarding the future restoration of the fully visible unity of all who already now form a real communion through faith and baptism, but who are still on the road toward a final complete and visible expression and manifestation of that communion in the One Holy Catholic and Apostolic Church.

The first part of the *Report* gives an explanation of the sense in which the main terms and expressions used in the principal

18 *The New Delhi Report*, p. 116.

paragraph must be understood. The second part contains a minute and detailed consideration of the concrete implications that are contained in the ultimate ecumenical goal as stated in the *Report*, both for the associate churches and for the World Council. A number of questions that still demand a solution are thus clearly indicated. There are also a number of suggestions regarding the manner in which the churches in concert can try to smooth the way for the attainment of the proposed ultimate goal.

The *Report* recalls that the mutual recognition of the validity of baptism has always served as the foundation-stone for every ecumenical encounter and discussion. Hence it is necessary to examine carefully and establish the consequences that follow for the partners in the dialogue from the fact that all the baptized are already received in the Catholic Church and are already bound together by a real bond in the mystical body of Christ. The unity and communion that already exists must be taken with perfect earnestness by all those who are involved.

On the other hand the *Report* also points out, as was done by the Encyclical *Mystical Body*, that the connnection in faith and baptism is of itself not sufficient to give full expression to the unity of the Church. The churches must examine together the question of what is still essentially and therefore necessarily required for the complete restoration of unity:

Our union with God is a mystery which passes our understanding and defeats our efforts to express it adequately. But as Christ has come visibly into this world and has redeemed men of flesh and blood, this union must find visible expression.[19]

The *Report* warns against lowering the vision of the ultimate unity by imagining the reunited Church, as was formerly done in history, as if it were a human organization or an institution in the juridical or legal sense. The Church is primarily an organism that arose from and lives through the operation of the

---

[19] *Ibid.*, par. 5, p. 118.

15

Holy Spirit. It is a dynamic reality, in which one speaks and listens, receives and gives. That is why those who wrote the *Report* preferred to describe the Church of the future by the term "fellowship" where one would have expected to find the word "church."

The ecumenical movement stands obviously at the beginning of a new phase of its development. Among other things, this is linked up with the fact that the two largest churches of the catholic type have clearly expressed their intention of cooperating henceforth with the other churches in an official and constructive way for the attainment of unity among Christians.

The Russian Church, when she became a member of the World Council, gave the assurance that it was not her intention to be merely a passive member; she hoped to be able to make a positive contribution to unification by taking part in the discussions and operations.

The Catholic Church in communion with the Apostolic See has not merely sent official observers to the Assembly of the World Council. By a "Secretariate for the fostering of unity among Christians," she has made it possible to maintain regular official relations with the World Council and eventually with individual churches. This secretariate is under the presidency of Cardinal Bea and the daily direction of Msgr. Willebrands.

In Holland there is a great improvement in the understanding between the Roman Catholic Church and the Reformation churches. The latter sent delegates to the meeting at which the new Roman Catholic translation of the New Testament was presented to Cardinal Alfrink, and also to the Cardinal's dedication of the ecumenical center "Den Eikenhorst" near Boxtel, in November, 1961.

The pastoral letters of the Dutch Episcopate and of individual bishops, the speeches of Cardinal Alfrink in 1960 and 1961 show most clearly how earnestly they study the ecumenical principles. They are perfectly convinced that the relations between the churches and between individual Christians must be rooted in charity. They realize that a true ecumenical consciousness and a genuine ecumenical way of thinking should produce a radical change in the conduct of Christians toward one another. They know what positive conviction is necessary in order that the ecumenical endeavor may receive powerful support and assistance.[20]

In the "Episcopal Directives concerning the limits and possibilities of religious communion between Catholics and Protestants," the Dutch bishops reject expressly as unecumenical a dialogue which is conducted in the purely polemical way of controversy or with the hope of converting the other party to one's own way of thinking because it simply considers its own way to be the pure and complete Christian way.[21]

The new phase which the ecumenical movement has now reached is characterized by an actual reversal of church relations.

The ecumenical pioneers on the Roman Catholic side are men like Pribilla, Congar, Lortz, Karrer, Couturier, Boyer, Sartory, Tavard, Leeming, and others, who by their writings have opened the way for that reversal. But the decisive push was given by the late Pope John XXIII, who is rightly considered to have been a "new" kind of pope. He was the first pope to stress the intimate connection between renewal and reunion. He repeatedly expressed the hope that the Second Vatican Council would, by means of a true renewal of the Church, also create an opportunity for a renewed and fruitful ecumenical contact with the other Christian churches.

Pope John on several occasions expressed his conviction that the Roman Catholic Church, considered in its human aspect, is also to be blamed for the origin and the permanence of Christian

---

[20] *Analecta v.h. Aartsbisdom Utrecht,* 34e jrg., no. 1, p. 7; see also no. 3, pp. 89 ff. and no. 11, pp. 239 ff. Cf. also the common pastoral letter of the Dutch bishops on the occasion of the New Delhi Assembly of the World Council of Churches, *ibid.,* no. 11, pp. 234 ff.
[21] *Ibid.,* no. 12, pp. 249 ff.

disunity. Meanwhile Pope Paul has publicly asked forgiveness for what other Christians have had to suffer from the hands of Roman Catholics.

When, according to plans, an investigation is made of the repeated claims by Protestants that they are persecuted or oppressed by Catholics in some countries, the Vatican will no doubt do everything it can to do away with such abuses. The Holy See desires all Christians throughout the world to live in peace and union in a manner that is in perfect accord with the demands of Christian charity. Protestants can feel perfectly certain about that.

In England there has been a good improvement in the relations between Roman Catholics and Anglicans as a result of the visit by the former Archbishop of Canterbury to the Pope, as was indeed desired. The Roman Catholic Archbishop of Westminister, then of Liverpool, John Heenan, called that visit "the most powerful gesture for centuries."

The same archbishop is himself a member of the above mentioned Roman Secretariate and he has created a similar secretariate for England. This secretariate can be considered the Roman Catholic counterpart of the Anglican "Council on Foreign Relations" that functions under the presidency of the Archbishop of Canterbury and the recently appointed commission on Roman Catholic relations.

The reversal in church relations is indeed a reason for new hope. However, this does not eliminate the fact that the road will be long and difficult and that it is necessary to be on one's guard against premature expectations and irresponsible adventures. If the necessary moderation, prudence, self-control and wisdom are made use of, there will be nothing but advantage to the ecumenical movement. The actual progress which characterizes the present phase of the ecumenical movement is chiefly of three sorts.

First of all, a marked change has taken place in the manner

in which the churches encounter, look upon and treat one another. The churches have become more modest in those interrelations. They have become aware of relative and defective human elements in the life of the churches. They are not as ready as formerly to pride themselves on possessing the truth because they have come to realize that it is at most the truth that possesses them. Even if the churches are still unshaken in their confession of the truth, they realize better than in the past that the other churches are not less sincere and firmly convinced of the truth of their beliefs.

God's Truth is absolute and immovable in its firmness. However, when the churches cannot agree about the content of God's revelation and the manner in which it comes to us, encounter and dialogue are meaningless unless all the partners have full freedom to express and defend their most profound convictions. All partners must also be ready to take one another's testimony seriously. They must be prepared to listen to one another in an existential manner and not merely *pro forma*, in a perfunctory way.

More and more is it considered unecumenical for partners in the dialogue to adopt a polemical method of discussion and to be merely intent on catching one another in inconsistencies. It is considered unecumenical when one church puts itself above the other churches, refuses to listen to the others, but decrees what the others should believe and do. The churches are ever more willing to go back to the Sacred Scriptures as "the starting point, the basis and the heart of the matter in all ecumenical dialogue,"[22] and to begin from there an open and frank discussion.

Secondly, during half a century of ecumenical encounter and dialogue, the churches have gradually come to realize that no actual reunion will take place as long as the churches think religiously that it is their duty to cling to a point of view that

---

[22] *Ibid.*, no. 3, p. 95.

was once adopted, to a character that was fixed once for all, and to their own never to be renounced tradition and church practice. If such a static concept of the Church persists, the churches can do no more than exchange views and be resigned to the *status quo*. Then things will remain as they were of old, and no change or progress will be possible.

There are indications, however, that the ecumenical movement has passed beyond its static and purely informational phase. It is possible, more and more, to speak of an ecumenical dynamics. A contributing factor for the change of mentality has been the fact that practically all churches realize that they must get rid of much conventional ballast, that they must reconsider their doctrine and life, liturgy and church structure. They must be open and ready to accept what has been acquired by modern exegesis, theology and related sciences; and they must pay more attention to the entire *Ecumene* than to themselves, be more interested in the growing Church of the future than in the particularism of the past.

The churches are also more and more on the move in regard to their own interior life. In almost all churches there is going on a revision of the church structure, the liturgy and the particular religious confession. In almost all churches we notice the influence of new theological insights. This mobility also makes it easier for the churches to look with more objectivity and detachment at what they have in proper when they deal with other churches. It also makes them able to leave more room for profound changes that would affect their teaching, structure and liturgy when such changes appear to be more in harmony with our time and favorable toward rapprochement and reunion. Without such mobility, without renewal and openness in the direction of the future, belief in reunion is but an illusion.

In the third place, it becomes increasingly evident that reunion stands or falls according to the churches' readiness not only to listen but, if necessary, to acknowledge one's one-sidedness and eventually even one's error, and their willingness to learn from one another and to accept from the other what is wanting in one's own church. Unification is a process of growth, a process by which all that is true, good and beautiful is integrated in the full riches of the future Church.

This does not mean that there should come about a rigid uniformity. It is merely a question of sharpening the eyes of faith so that the most vital distinction be made between, on the one hand, what truly belongs to Revelation and therefore necessarily pertains to the faith and, on the other, the many forms of expression that are purely accidental. The churches together must reflect upon that distinction. The question that must be kept in mind, with an eye to the Church of the future, is: which elements are *per se* indispensable because they are truly given with Revelation, and, on the other hand, which expressions of faith and life are accidental so that great freedom for differences is left to the judgment of communions and individuals?

As the churches progress on the dynamic road to integration, it will become increasingly clear that in the long run it will be a question of the right relationship between the Church and the Gospel. The Church herself has a place in the Gospel, in other words, her inmost nature cannot be understood except through the Gospel. On the other hand, the Gospel sounds only within the Church and it cannot be announced in all its purity and truth except in and through the Church. The Church and the Gospel postulate each other as the Word and the Sacrament postulate each other. The reunion of Christians will, to a great extent, come down to a new and complete integration of the Church and the Gospel.[23]

---

[23] Guitton, *L'Eglise et l'Evangile,* Paris, 1959; Tavard, *Holy Writ and Holy Church,* London, 1959; *The Lambeth Conference 1958,* London, 1958, Part II, pp. 3 ff., 13 ff. These pages contain the report of the committee on the authority and the message of Holy Scripture. Its president was Dr. A. M. Ramsey, then Archbishop of York. Cf. also Ramsey, *The Gospel and the Catholic Church,* London, 2nd ed., 1956.

4. THE SPECIAL POSITION OF THE ANGLICAN CHURCH

In the light of the ecumenical situation we have just described, it seems to me that it clearly makes sense and is even positively useful to pay particular attention to Anglicanism in our study of the ecumenical problem. For the churches that belong to the Anglican Communion have a special place and function on account of their nature and position. They seem, as it were, destined by their nature to play a special role in the process of unification of all Christian churches constituting the *Ecumene,* the world of Christian believers.

A first reason for this, it seems to me, lies in the simple fact that the Church of England and the other churches of the Anglican Confession have for three quarters of a century regularly occupied themselves with the examination of ecumenical possibilities. They have systematically investigated ecumenical problems and attempted the formation of ecumenical relations and dialogues in every direction. All this they had already done before the contemporary ecumenical movement was officially born.

It is customary in ecumenical circles to make the ecumenical movement officially begin with the international and interconfessional Mission Conference which, in 1910, was held in Edinburgh. But the first purposive ecumenical decisions and activities from the Anglican side date from the third Lambeth Conference, a gathering of bishops of the entire Anglican Communion, that was held in the year 1888.

Coupled with that is a second reason. The Anglican Communion had devoted many years to the study, examination and discussion of the ecumenical concept with representatives of other churches. For this reason it was able to present a carefully balanced ecumenical concept to the other churches for their consideration at a time when the great ecumenical conference

On Life and Work of Stockholm (1925) and the conference *On Faith and Order* of Lausanne (1927) had still to be held.

In the Lambeth Appeal, to which we here refer and that was made at its sixth Lambeth Conference, the Anglican Communion made an urgent call to all churches without any distinction, asking them to be earnest in seeking to restore church unity and communion.

Looking backward, we realize that the time for such an appeal for cooperation of all churches was not yet ripe. The churches were still too much estranged from one another and too much animated by a controversial spirit. It is sufficient to recall how hesitatingly and laboriously many participants in the conferences of Stockholm and Lausanne, and even later in those of Oxford and Edinburgh (1937), tried to find a path through the world of contradictions and misunderstandings with which they were suddenly confronted; how difficult it was for them to show understanding in the presence of the resistance, sensibilities and claims of the churches that were foreign to them. Thus it is not surprising that the Anglican Lambeth Appeal failed to attain the result which its authors had expected. This we shall deal with in more detail in a separate chapter.[24]

The third and at the same time the principal reason to give special attention to Anglicanism from the ecumenical standpoint is the nature, spirit and mentality that is proper to Anglicanism, and the particular position of the Anglican Church among other churches.

In an earlier, pre-ecumenical period which was characterized by a purely polemical attitude, it was difficult to reach such an insight. During the centuries-long struggle for the truth, every church was fully convinced that it possessed the truth and that error belonged to the other churches. The churches had become accustomed to entertaining a merely negative attitude toward one

---

[24] See Chapter Four.

23

another. They considered it true *a priori* that what they possessed was by far the best, while the others—although not understood—were *per se* condemned and rejected simply because they happened to be different.

In such a situation Anglicanism could not expect much sympathy from the non-Anglican churches. It was generally looked upon as a questionable phenomenon and one did not know what to make of it. Protestants of the Puritan-Calvinistic type usually saw in it a Roman danger. Roman Catholics considered it to be genuinely Protestant. Many took it for a product of the State and to be based on opportunism, or a stronghold of humanism, idealism and rationalism. Few had anything good to say about it.

At the present stage of ecumenism, however, the churches are less pretentious. They are more critical in respect to themselves. They no longer look upon the differences found in other churches as purely a result of error and decadence, but they see many things which they can positively appreciate as valuable. Through ecumenical contacts much self-satisfied misunderstanding and many prejudices have disappeared. For all these reasons the road is free for a better understanding of the religious, ecclesial and scriptural principles by which the Anglicans have been guided from the time of the Reformation. These principles are at the basis of the special and original character that marks the Anglican church structure and worship, its doctrine and theology, its spirituality and mentality.

This special and original character of Anglicanism owes its origin in the first place to the conscious striving of the bishops and theologians of the sixteenth century to preserve the equilibrium of the *Ecclesia Anglicana* amidst the severe ecclesiastical storms of that time. As is evident from the official church documents and the voluminous correspondence between Anglican and continental reformers, as well as from the works of Jewel, Hooker and many other classical Anglican theologians, it was not a question of reaching a compromise by which all parties could become united. It was on the contrary based on a principle accepted with full conviction, namely, the principle of moderation.

The first sentence of the prologue directed against the Puritans, in the *Book of Common Prayer* of 1662, states that: "It hath been the wisdom of the Church of England, ever since the first compiling of her Publick Liturgy [in 1549], to keep the mean between the two extremes, of too much stiffness in refusing, and of too much easiness in admitting any variation from it."[25]

Anglicanism had to wage a constant war on two opposite fronts from the death of Henry VIII in 1547 to the Restoration in 1660. It has, besides, consistently tested and compared all Roman teachings and practices with those of the undivided Church of the first ten centuries. With equal consistency it has compared all post-reformational, puritanical teachings and practices with the original intentions of the reformers; that is, with the original testimony of the Reformation which the Anglican Church has always accepted with no less conviction and resoluteness than the other reformed churches.

The *via media* of Anglicanism, therefore, is not a mean between the Catholic Church and the Reformation; but it is explicitly the middle between the extreme devotions of the late Middle Ages, on the one hand, and the post-Reformation extreme puritanism on the other. But at the same time it has refused to relinquish the Catholic Church.

It has always entertained the conviction that the Council of Trent accomplished only half of its task of purifying the Catholic Church of the medieval ideas, teachings, customs and practices which, according to Anglican conviction, are in conflict with pure, scriptural and at the same time early Christian Catholicism.

That is why the Church of England has always been deeply

---

[25] *Book of Common Prayer*, Preface.

convinced that it is truly the reformed prolongation of the Catholic Church in England. It has always attached great importance to a church structure and a liturgy in which the continuity with the pre-Reformation church is clearly expressed. At the same time, however, it fully agrees with the witness of the Reformation concerning the purity of the Gospel as it has been "rediscovered" in Holy Scripture.

The principal and most characteristic feature of Anglicanism is moderation. That feature must not be sought in Anglicanism's comprehensiveness, no matter how much the latter is praised as its strength—or decried as its weakness. This comprehensiveness is a characteristic of later times, although it is connected with the humanistic tendency which was always stronger in the Anglican churches than in the Reformed and Lutheran churches. At bottom, however, this comprehensiveness is the spiritual offspring of the latitudinarianism that arose in the seventeenth century and the liberalism and rationalism of the eighteenth century which were connected with the latter.

As late as the eighteenth century, the Church of England tried to maintain a certain uniformity, but it was not able to prevent later currents such as Methodism and Anglo-Catholicism from acquiring permanent recognition even till our own times. It is principally to this fact that Anglicanism owes its present comprehensiveness.

It is especially Anglo-Catholicism that has met with strong opposition. The Evangelicals, but also many modernistic Anglicans, are convinced that the Romanizing tendency of Anglo-Catholicism is in conflict with the character and position of authentic Anglicanism. Hence no greater mistake could be made than to judge Anglicanism according to Anglo-Catholicism and on this basis to classify Anglicanism with the "catholic" type of churches. We hope that the facts and examples we shall give in this book will prove that conclusively.

If the facts, circumstances and possibilities mentioned thus far are understood in their mutual coherence, they appear to offer us every reason to study and describe Anglicanism in ecumenical perspective. This is the reason why we have chosen to give this title to the present book.

In the meantime it will appear evident, I trust, that this choice of Anglicanism must not be conceived as having an apologetic or dogmatic nature. It is not our intention directly or indirectly to prove that the church that is in complete communion with the See of Canterbury is or is not the true Church and that Anglicanism is or is not the only pure and scriptural form of Christianity.

The intention of this book is strictly phenomenological. It aims at expressing, analyzing and clarifying Anglican characteristics, opinions, visions and suggestions so far as they are ecumenically important and can clearly be deduced from official and authentic data.

When the term "Anglicanism" is used in this book, it means expressly the official, authentic Anglicanism that is accepted by the greater number of Anglicans, although we shall from time to time deal with the more extreme evangelical, modernistic and Anglo-Catholic "modalities." However, these forms cannot be regarded as representative of Anglicanism as such.

A strictly phenomenological discussion can fulfill an important function in preparation for an ecumenical encounter and dialogue. It helps in making such an encounter and discussion possible, meaningful and fruitful. Most failures of ecumenical conferences are still the result of insufficient familiarity with the situation of the dialogue and of the difficulties and possibilities that are contained in such a situation.

One of the conditions which enable phenomenology to exercise a useful function is that it does not try to anticipate the results that may follow from the ecumenical encounter; it leaves them entirely to the parties in the dialogue. It is not the task of the phenomenologist to anticipate a solution.

The service which the phenomenologist tries to render presupposes that he goes to work objectively and impartially. It is unavoidable of course that he has a personal, specific, religious and denominational conviction. But he can render service as a phenomenologist only if he does his very best to interpret the "phenomenon" as conscientiously as possible in complete agreement with reality. However difficult it may be, he must try to abstain from giving his own personal testimony, so long as he is offering his service as a phenomenologist. Hence let no reader expect any approval or disapproval, and refutation or defense of Anglicanism, or a justification of the writer's personal belief.

It is the author's intention to approach and characterize Anglicanism on the basis of the contribution it has tried to make during the past century toward the solution of the ecumenical problem. He also wishes to evaluate and throw light upon this problem from the standpoint of the specific nature of Anglicanism. It is a question of dealing with the ecumenical problem in an Anglican perspective and with Anglicanism in an ecumenical perspective.

This method of approach is, of course, not the only possible one. It does not pretend to be the best or the only one that is correct. We merely wish to help in explaining the often disputed character of Anglicanism by means of that rarely used method. And, on the other hand, we wish thus to clarify the involved and many-sided nature of the ecumenical problem.

There exists an extensive literature emanating from Anglican authors regarding Anglicanism itself, the place and vocation of Anglicanism, and the ecumenical ideas and activities which have characterized it during the last years.[26]

On account of the almost unlimited comprehensiveness of Anglicanism, within which almost every imaginable sound can be heard, it is not always easy to determine what is typically

_____
[26] See the bibliography on pp. 288 ff.

Anglican. Nor is it always possible to know whether what individual writers say expresses representative ideas and suggestions which would meet with the approval of official ecclesiastical authorities.

That is why a method had to be chosen that guarantees the greatest objectivity and, as a result, gives an image of Anglicanism that corresponds as much as possible with reality and, at the same time, stands in the full light of the *Ecumene*.

To achieve that end it was not enough to start exclusively from the Church of England. On the contrary, the starting point had rather to be chosen in the entirety of the Anglican Communion. This Communion embraces seventeen independent Anglican Churches throughout the world. We can find the best expression of the general sentiment of these churches in the reports of the decennial general meetings of the bishops, the so-called Lambeth Conferences, of which already nine have taken place since 1867. That is why we shall choose those reports as the chief sources for our examination.[27] Every Lambeth report is divided into three parts: an encyclical, the resolutions accepted by the entire Conference, and the complete reports of the committees that were presented to the Conference.

In our explanation of the material gathered from that source we shall take the criterion for our appreciation from the three confessional documents which Anglican churches consider authoritative sources for the knowledge of Anglican teaching and practice, namely, the *Book of Common Prayer*, the *Thirty-Nine Articles of Religion* and the *Ordinale* or book of ordinations. Both the *Articles* and the *Ordinale* are incorporated in every copy of the *Book of Common Prayer* of the Church of England.

---

[27] The reports of the first six Lambeth Conferences (1867, 1878, 1888, 1897, 1908, and 1920) have been published in one volume, *The Six Lambeth Conferences*, London, 1920. Those of the conferences of 1930, 1948 and 1958 have been published separately in their respective years by the S.P.C.K.

Next we shall draw from the official and semi-official reports, concerning the relations between the Anglican and other churches, that were presented to the Archbishop of Canterbury in the course of years. Finally we shall take into consideration ecumenical publications of individuals so far as they are important for the appreciation of the material that was drawn from official sources.

5. THE CHURCH OF ENGLAND AND THE ANGLICAN COMMUNION

We wish to conclude this first chapter with a few general remarks and some information concerning the Church of England and the Anglican Communion in order to give the reader some provisional orientation.

The Anglican Communion is a communion of churches bound together in a complete intercommunion, in which all acknowledge the Church of England as the mother church and recognize the Archbishop of Canterbury as the "first among equals" of the Anglican bishops.

According to the statistics in the official Year-Book of the Church of England of 1962, seventeen independent churches belong to the Anglican Communion, embracing together 298 dioceses.[28]

Forty-three of these dioceses belong to the Church of England. To the latter must be added fourteen dioceses that are located outside of England and do not belong to one or other of the independent churches but are directly under the metropolitan jurisdiction of the Archbishop of Canterbury. Five of the latter constitute the Archdiocese of Jerusalem formed in 1957, which has not yet attained to the status of an independent Anglican

---

[28] *The Official Year-Book of the National Assembly of the Church of England 1962*, London, 1962, pp. 25 ff.

Church but "remains ultimately responsible" to the Archbishop of Canterbury.

The Church of England comprises two ecclesiastical provinces, namely, those of Canterbury and of York. The Archbishop of Canterbury has the title of Primate of All England, the Archbishop of York is called Primate of England.

The Church of England bases itself on the point of view that the sixteenth century Reformation did not produce a break in the continuity of the Church as an organism when it introduced all its reforms of doctrine and the liturgy, although these were made on the basis of an agreement with the fundamental principles of the continental reformers.

The great See of Canterbury, which St. Augustine founded in 597 by the authority of Pope Gregory the Great, has since remained the principal archiepiscopal see of the *Ecclesia Anglicana*. Dr. A. M. Ramsey, who was enthroned as Archbishop of Canterbury in 1961, is its hundredth archbishop. Dr. F. D. Coggan followed him as Archbishop of the See of York, founded in 627. London, Durham, Winchester and several others belong also to the ancient pre-Reformation dioceses. The dioceses of Birmingham, Blackburn, Bradford, Chelmsford, Guildford, Leicester, Portsmouth and some others date only from the twentieth century.

Only in England does the Anglican Church have the character of an established church. It is clear that this constitutes only an accidental and not an essential characteristic. For, after all, that characteristic also applied, and still applies in some countries, to the churches in communion with Rome. It is true of most Lutheran churches and of other reformed churches. In 1953 there even appeared in Germany a study which, on the basis of sixteenth century correspondence between Anglican bishops and leaders of the community of Zurich, tried to show that the established condition of the church, as attained in England toward the end of the sixteenth century under the influence of Archbishop Whitgift, was principally of Swiss origin.[29]

A close connection between the Church and the State has existed in all Protestant countries since the sixteenth century Reformation. Separation between Church and State is not a phenomenon that springs from the Reformation, but one that came about at a much later date and arose in the reformed churches principally under the influence of pietism and liberalism.

In England also the relations between Church and State have undergone important changes, especially by the foundation of the Church Assembly and the introduction of the Enabling Act of 1919. To the extent that the relations between Church and State still signify a guardianship of the Church by the State in some matters, the Church of England is presently making efforts to rid itself of the last remnants of such a servitude.

The title "Supreme Head of the Church of England," which Henry VIII arrogated to himself, was changed already under Queen Elizabeth I to that of "Supreme Sovereign." This title merely signifies that no single aspect of the condition of the people escapes from the sovereignty of the ruler, as is formulated in the *Canon Law Revision of 1959:*

We acknowledge that the Queen's Most Excellent Majesty, acting according to the laws of the realm, is the highest power under God in this kingdom, and has supreme authority over all persons in all causes, as well ecclesiastical as civil.[30]

A disestablishment and disendowment of the Church was already completely achieved in the Episcopal Church of Scotland in 1689 by King William III, in the Church of Ireland in 1871, and in the Church of Wales in 1920. These are the three independent Anglican Churches which exist alongside and totally

---

[29] Kressner, *Schweizer Ursprünge des anglikanischen Staatskirchentums,* Gütersloh, 1953.
[30] *Canon Law Revision 1959,* London, 1960, A I, p. 2.

free from the Church of England in Great Britain and Ireland.

The thirteen other churches which also form part of the Anglican Communion are: the Protestant Episcopal Church in the U.S.A. with about one hundred dioceses and three and a half million baptized members, of whom two million are regular "communicants"; the Church of India, Pakistan, Burma and Ceylon; the Anglican Church of Canada (the only one that calls itself officially "Anglican"); the Church of England in Australia and Tasmania; the Church of the Province of New Zealand; the Church of the Province of the West Indies; the Chung Hua Sheng Kung (the Holy Catholic Church in China); the Nippon Sei Ko Kai (the Japanese Catholic Church); the Church of the Province of West Africa; the Church of the Province of Central Africa; the Church of the Province of East Africa; and the Church of Uganda and Ruanda-Urundi.

All these churches form together the Anglican Communion. They issued from the Church of England through the emigration of Anglicans from England to non-European countries and through the activities of Anglican mission societies. Although they are entirely independent from the juridical standpoint, they remain united with the Church of England by the bonds of a perfect church communion.

It would be merely a source of confusion if, because of a strange continental self-consciousness, we were to lump the Anglicans together with the so-called free churches of England and America, such as Methodists, Baptists, and others, giving them the common name of Anglo-Saxon Christianity. Anglicanism is too deeply and firmly rooted in continental Christianity of almost twenty centuries' duration to be placed in the same category as the Anglo-Saxon free churches that have more or less broken away from the tradition of the Church.

As for the name, one Anglican church calls itself expressly Protestant as well as Episcopalian; two churches call themselves

33

expressly Catholic; two call themselves Episcopalian; and only one, the Church of Canada, since 1955 calls itself Anglican.

All Anglican Churches, however, are one in their conscious endeavor to preserve the apostolic faith and character of the Church's worship of the first centuries, though trying to incorporate in it the contributions of the Reformation and those of their own time so far as they have positive and permanent value.

This typical Anglican attitude in respect to tradition and enrichment is at the basis of the moderation and comprehensiveness of Anglicanism. It marks world-Anglicanism as being, as it were, a provisional prototype of the reunited *Ecumene,* the world-Christianity of the future. That Anglicanism comprises only a small number of Christians does not detract from that fact. The total number of baptized Anglicans is estimated at about forty million, the total communicants no more than about twenty-five million. A pastoral letter of the episcopate of the Protestant Episcopal Church of the U.S.A. of September, 1961, speaks at length about the vocation of the Anglican Church Communion:

> We are a small church. Our whole Anglican Communion is a small part of the total Christian community. But the calling and mission of a church cannot be measured by numbers only. With mingled pride and humility we can recognize that in our membership are found a disproportionate share of men and women who occupy positions of great responsibility and influence in our sorely troubled world.
>
> Securely enshrined in our inheritance is our vision of the Great Church, whose mission is to all sorts and conditions of men. That is preserved for us in our historic creeds rooted in scripture and in our common prayer. Our deepest allegiance is not to the Episcopal Church nor to the Anglican Communion, but to "the one Catholic and Apostolic Church."[31]

The churches that form part of the Anglican Communion have an episcopal church structure. This is based on the con-

---

[31] *The Christian Century,* Chicago, 1961, p. 1306, col. 1.

viction that "it is evident unto all men diligently reading holy Scripture and ancient Authors, that from the Apostles' time there have been these Orders of ministers in Christ's Church: Bishops, Priests and Deacons."[32]

The offices, services and the public worship are explicitly conceived by Anglicans as being those of the entire universal Church, although clothed in the customary form they have received in the Anglican churches. Hence, for example, the complete title of the *Book of Common Prayer* reads as follows: "The Book of Common Prayer and Administration of the Sacraments and other Rites and Ceremonies of the Church [that is, of the universal Church] according to the use of the Church of England."

According to Anglican conviction, the continuity of the whole Church of all centuries has its origin, guarantee and expression in the historical episcopate, that is, in the episcopal office so far as it rests on an uninterrupted episcopal succession. The episcopal concept of the Church includes the conviction that the power to establish (to ordain, to consecrate) particular persons and invest them with an office by the imposition of hands belongs exclusively to the bishops. According to Anglican belief a purely presbyterial ordination to office, though implying a certain succession in office, is a break and therefore a defect in the historical continuity with the whole Church of all centuries.

It is characteristic of official Anglicanism—leaving out the private opinions of Anglo-Catholic Anglicans—to refrain from expressing the consequences which that defect in historical continuity brings with it for the churches concerned. To express this in a more positive way: the churches of the Anglican Com-

---

[32] The Preface of "The Form and Manner of making, ordaining and consecrating of Bishops, Priests, and Deacons, according to the Order of The Church of England." This Preface is part of the *Ordinale* of 1549 and has been preserved without change in all later revisions. The present *Ordinale* dates from 1662 and can be found at the end of the *Book of Common Prayer*.

munion repeatedly express their conviction that the ministerial functions in non-episcopal churches are not less evidently blessed by God, in spite of the fact that they are not based on ordination or consecration. A defect of that sort, in the appointment of a minister for an ecclesiastical function, if it was done in agreement with the law and order of the church concerned, should not lead to the conclusion that the preaching, the sacramental actions and the public worship remain fruitless or do not contain any working of grace.

Besides the episcopal structure, all Anglican churches also agree in their common concept of the nature, form and content of public worship as the latter is expressed in the *Book of Common Prayer,* also simply called the *Prayer Book.* However, every independent Anglican church has its own *Prayer Book.* Although it has the same general structure as those of the other churches, it differs in many details in the texts and prayers it contains. The same is also true of the episcopal organization of the Church. Every independent church has incorporated the episcopal structure in its own way in one or the other form of synodal church administration in which both laymen and laywomen are represented.

In spite of the unity that exists among Anglican churches, it is a fact that their differences have become increasingly greater. As a consequence of their historical formation, some Anglican churches show an evident Protestant-Evangelical character; others are more or less Anglo-Catholic in their orientation. However, the increasing diversity is due principally to the fact that almost all churches are busy, each in its own way, with the revision of the liturgy, doctrine and church law. If in this respect there is still a certain common line of conduct, this is due principally to the conversations of the bishops in their Lambeth conferences.

On rare occasions there is a manifestation of tension in the relations between an individual Anglican church and the whole Anglican Communion. Thus there arose among many evangelical Anglicans a feeling of dissatisfaction, discontentedness and disappointment because the project for a reunited Church of Ceylon (Lanka) had, on the one hand, received the backing of the Lambeth Conference of the entire Anglican Communion in 1958. But on the other hand, the plan to give full communion with the Church of England to the Church of Lanka, which was proposed at one of the Anglican Communion's Convocations, did not meet with full approval. We shall deal again with that question in the chapter "Reunion in India."[33]

The comprehensiveness of Anglicanism makes it necessary for it to take into account all existing modalities when it has to make decisions. That is why internal problems and tensions of an ecumenical nature occur not only in its relations with other churches, but also within the Anglican Communion itself. Hence, the Anglican Communion presents us, in this respect also, with a microcosm of the *Ecumene.*

---

[33] Cf. pp. 170 ff.

CHAPTER TWO

The Attitude Toward Rome

1. INTRODUCTION

WE begin our study of contemporary Anglicanism with an examination of the Anglican Communion's attitude toward the Church of Rome, as it is expressed in the Lambeth reports.

Our choice of such a beginning is related to the fact that Anglicanism developed a distinct form of Christianity having its own character and identity, only after the conflict and final break of Canterbury with Rome.[1]

It is difficult for an impartial onlooker to decide whether Canterbury severed relations with Rome or Rome severed relations with Canterbury. He will probably be inclined to believe that they both broke away from each other. The same is true also of the rupture between Rome and Constantinople, between Rome and the Reformers, and between Rome and the Old Catholics. In all these cases it is the opinion of the separated churches that Rome caused the break by excommunication, whereas Rome believes that the excommunication was provoked and was justified in each case.

In regard to the Church of England, it is undeniable that the rupture between Canterbury and Rome has resulted in profound changes and that it has actually meant a new beginning in many

---

[1] Cf. above, pp. 25 f.

38

important respects. Before that break the *Ecclesia Anglicana,* the Church of England, was in complete agreement and communion with the See of Rome in the matter of teaching, liturgy, church practice, spirituality, church organization, church law and church language.

Although the Church of England emphasizes the continuity of the Church of England with the pre-Reformation Church, its rupture with Rome has led to the development of a new form of Christianity which is called Anglicanism. In this development the Reformation has played a much greater role and has left incomparably deeper traces in Anglicanism than is realized and acknowledged by some groups within and without the Anglican churches.

When we begin our investigation of the Anglican attitude toward Rome, as it is expressed in the Lambeth reports, we notice first of all that the Church of Rome is never called the Catholic Church. And this is not to be wondered at. The Church of England and the other churches of the Anglican Communion would repudiate themselves if they considered the Church of Rome to be the Catholic Church and placed themselves outside this Church. The Anglican churches, moreover, agree in this with all other churches of East and West that are not in communion with the Apostolic See, since they believe that they do not have to recognize the special claims of the latter.

In the Lambeth reports the church in communion with Rome is usually designated as "The Roman Church" or "The Church of Rome." The reports of 1897, 1908, and 1920 prefer the name "Latin Communion" as their title for the discussion of the attitude toward Rome; those of 1930, 1948, and 1959 use the name "Roman Catholic Church."

This uncertainty about what name to give to the Church of Rome indicates a searching, a groping for the place the Anglican Communion can conveniently accord to her amidst the other churches.

39

If we wish to understand Anglicanism properly, it is important to keep in mind that this question of name is not the same as that between Constantinople and Rome, which is a question about which church is the true Church, that is, which one of the two is the one and only Catholic Church. According to the Anglican concept of the Church, it is impossible for such a question to be raised by Anglicanism.

According to Anglican belief, no single church on earth can consider itself the only true Church, because all communions of baptized Christians in which the Word of God is announced and the sacraments of baptism and the Lord's Supper are administered are true churches. Moreover, no single church on earth is a "true" church in the sense of one infallible Church, that is, without errors, and is a complete church without spot or wrinkle. A "true church" according to Anglican terminology means a "real," "authentic" church.

Properly speaking there is but one "true" Church, namely the Church that is built on the foundation that was laid by the apostles. It is enough to know that one's own church, namely here the Church of England, belongs to the true, authentic and real apostolic Church of Christ.

Hence, Article I of the revised Canon Law of the Church of England of 1959 states that "The Church of England ... belongs to the true and apostolic Church of Christ, and, as our duty to the said Church of England requires, we do constitute and ordain that no member thereof shall be at liberty to maintain or hold the contrary."[2] The latter words are most probably intended as a warning to some Romanizing Anglo-Catholics who sometimes give the impression that the Church of England can hardly be looked upon as a pure expression or as an actual branch of the "Catholic" Church.

In Anglican usage, the "Catholic" or "Universal" Church

---

[2] *Canon Law Revision 1959*, p. 2.

means the entire communion of all the believing and baptized Christians. Built on Christ as her only foundation, the Church, as is said in a hymn, is "by schisms rent asunder, by heresies distrest" on account of the sins and the erring spirit of men. That is why she needs constant reformation and renewal, according to the Reformation dictum: *ecclesia reformata semper reformanda,* that is, even a reformed church must always be reformed anew.

2. THE FIRST TWO LAMBETH CONFERENCES: NEGATIVE ATTITUDE TOWARD ROME

In a few years it will be a century since the first Lambeth Conference, which took place in 1867, brought together about one hundred Anglican bishops. From that very first beginning there appeared already to the assembled bishops the vision of a final completely restored unity of all Christians. The unitive forces that had created the unity of the Anglican Communion among the Anglican churches would, in the course of time, spread their influence until the whole of Christianity would once more receive from God the blessed gift of Unity in Truth, as was said in the first pastoral encyclical. This encyclical of the united episcopate of the Anglican Communion was addressed, after the Conference of 1867, to "the Faithful in Christ Jesus, the Priests and Deacons and the Lay Members of the Church of Christ in Communion with the Anglican Branch of the Church Catholic."

In this first encyclical there was already mention of the attitude to be assumed toward Rome and it was worded in a way which expressed only rejection:

Furthermore, we entreat you to guard yourselves and yours against the growing superstitions and additions with which in these latter days the truth of God hath been overlaid; as otherwise, so especially by the pretension to universal sovereignty over God's heritage asserted for the See of Rome, and by the practical exaltation of the Blessed Virgin Mary as mediator in the place of her Divine Son, and by the addressing

41

of prayers to her as intercessor between God and man. Of such beware, we beseech you, knowing that the jealous God giveth not His honour to another.[3]

The encyclical of the second Lambeth Conference of 1878 spoke in similar terms about the See of Rome:

The fact that a solemn protest is raised in so many Churches and Christian communities throughout the world against the usurpations of the See of Rome, and against the novel doctrines promulgated by its authority, is a subject for thankfulness to Almighty God. All sympathy is due from the Anglican Church to the Churches and individuals protesting against these errors, and labouring, it may be, under special difficulties from the assaults of unbelief as well as from the pretensions of Rome.

We acknowledge but one Mediator between God and man—the Man Christ Jesus, Who is over all, God blessed for ever. We reject, as contrary to the Scriptures and to Catholic truth, any doctrine which would set up other mediators in His place, or which would take away from the Divine Majesty of the fulness of the Godhead which dwelleth in Him, and which gave an infinite value to the spotless Sacrifice which He offered, once for all on the Cross for the sins of the whole world.

It is therefore our duty to warn the faithful that the act done by the Bishop of Rome, in the Vatican Council, in the year 1870—whereby he asserted a supremacy over all men in matters both of faith and morals, on the ground of an assumed infallibiilty—was an invasion of the attributes of the Lord Jesus Christ.[4]

Although during the second Lambeth Conference the question of the reunion with non-Anglican churches was not yet discussed, the suggestion was already offered that a day be appointed every year for prayer for unity of the Christian world. At the same time, the encyclical of 1878 ended with an expression of hope that all the Christians of the whole world should take note of its contents and make known their ideas about it:

We do not claim to be lords over God's heritage, but we commend the results of this our Conference to the reason and conscience of our

---

[3] *The Six Lambeth Conferences*, p. 50.
[4] *Ibid.*, p. 94.

brethren as enlightened by the Holy Spirit of God, praying that all throughout the world who call upon the name of our Lord Jesus Christ may be of one mind, may be united in one fellowship, may hold fast the Faith once delivered to the saints, and worship their one Lord in the spirit of purity and love.[5]

3. THE LAMBETH CONFERENCE OF 1888: INFALLIBILITY VERSUS OPENNESS

The attitude of the Anglican Communion toward the Church of Rome in connection with ecumenism was first discussed during the third Lambeth Conference of 1888 in the report concerning Home Reunion, that is, reunion within the territory of English-speaking peoples. It is the report of the first of the three committees, named at the beginning of the Conference, that had to report concerning existing or to-be-established relations with the various Christian churches throughout the world. It was the first real ecumenical attempt, on the broadest possible scale, that was ever undertaken since the division of the churches.[6]

The Committee with deep regret felt that, under present circumstances it was useless to consider the question of Reunion with our brethren of the Roman Church, being painfully aware that any proposal for reunion would be entertained by the authorities of that Church only on condition of a complete submission on our part to these claims of absolute authority, and the acceptance of those other errors, both in doctrine and in discipline, against which in faithfulness to God's Holy Word, and to the true principles of His Church, we have been for three centuries bound to protest.[7]

This quotation is very important as a starting-point. Every word of it is purposively and carefully chosen. It tells clearly

---

[5] *Ibid.*, p. 98.

[6] The title of the report reads: "Report of the Committee appointed to consider what steps (if any) can be rightly taken on Behalf of the Anglican Communion towards the Reunion of the Various Bodies into which the Christianity of the English-speaking races is divided." Cf. *ibid.*, pp. 156 ff.

[7] *Ibid.*, p. 159.

and frankly what constitutes essentially the basis and the standard that determines the attitude toward Rome. When the Lambeth reports show that the bishops of the Anglican Communion are gradually giving more attention to the problem of an eventual rapprochement between Canterbury and Rome, it is not right to conclude that the Anglican churches are at work on an essential change of standpoint on their part.

Both within and outside the Anglican churches, one sometimes hears the view expressed that the rupture between Canterbury and Rome, on the one hand, and that between the Reformers and the Church of Rome, on the other, have little relation with one another and that, being of a totally different nature, their simultaneous occurrence must be considered a pure coincidence. This view is not only in conflict with the historical facts, but it also makes it impossible to understand the more profound and actual intentions of Anglican declarations and suggestions.

It is true, of course, that the Anglican churches, on account of their greater respect for historical developments, are outwardly more like the Church of Rome than the other reformed churches. But this does not mean at all that they, as we shall show in a subsequent chapter, belong fundamentally to the "catholic" type.

External points of agreement between the Anglican churches and the Church of Rome, that are absent from the other reformed churches, must be submitted to a closer theological examination. Such an examination shows in every instance that those apparent agreements are interpreted, on the basis of Sacred Scripture, the Gospel and Christian Faith, in such a way that, consciously or unconsciously but in any case really, they agree with the fundamental principles of the Reformation. It stands to reason that this can be understood only by those who have a sufficient knowledge of the nature, the mentality, the attitude and the spirituality of the Reformation. Because of a certain lack of familiarity with continental Protestantism, the Anglicans do not always seem to realize how "Protestant" they actually are.

Leaving aside private opinions, and basing ourselves on official expressions and decisions, we are led to believe that the points upon which the Anglican churches are outwardly in agreement with the "catholic" churches are conceived in an evangelical and reformational sense.

It is incorrect for Roman Catholic observers to conclude from this that the Anglicans are unprincipled, illogical and even insincere. Such a judgment rests on a misunderstanding, which is fostered by extreme Anglo-Catholics within Anglicanism and extreme Protestants outside of it, who both deny the close relationship between Anglicanism and the Reformation.

When we now examine more closely the passage in the Lambeth report of 1888 concerning the Church of Rome, there appears to be a twofold rejection.

In the first place there is the rejection of Rome's "claims of absolute authority." In this the Anglican attitude is completely in accord with that of all other non-Roman churches. But perhaps it is not immediately evident that that rejection implicitly applies also to every other church that claims an exclusive and absolute authority for its own confession.

It is necessary for us to study the Anglican rejection in the light of a tradition that is four centuries old. It begins with the two classical vindications of the Anglican standpoint, namely, the apologetics of Jewel in 1562 and that of Hooker in 1594.[8] Then there are the numerous works of the seventeenth century which saw the flowering of Anglican theology in the Caroline Divines. Finally, in our own times there are many works in which the authentic Anglican view is safeguarded against the danger

---

[8] Jewel, *An Apology of the Church of England*, 1562; see *The Works of John Jewel* ed. by the Parker Society, Cambridge, 1848, vol. 1, pp. 81–552 (a new edition was published in 1963 by Cornell University Press); Hooker, *Treatise on the Laws of Ecclesiastical Polity*, bks. I–IV, 1594, bk. V, 1957, bks. VI to/and VIII, published posthumously in 1648, 1662 and 1648. (Modern ed. in Everyman's Library, London, 1907, 2 vols.) Concerning Jewel see also J. E. Booty, *John Jewel as Apologist of the Church of England*, London, 1903.

of sliding to one or another Protestant side or toward the Roman Catholic side.

When we take all these things into consideration, the principal reason for the rejection of all claims to absolute authority appears to lie in the firm conviction that absolute authority belongs exclusively to "God's holy Word," as that Word speaks through Holy Scripture.

Anglicanism does not deny that the Church, helped by the light of the Holy Spirit, has in a certain sense announced "infallibly" the Word of God and the witness of the Scriptures concerning Christ. But it denies that this *per se* always happens or that there exist ecclesiastical bodies or authorities that can lay claim to infallibility. Infallibility always resides in the Word of God itself and it is to this Word that reference must be made over and over again.

The view which the Reformers held concerning the place and function of the living, creative and universally decisive Word of God was shared by the classical Anglican theologians.[9] In this respect Anglican theology too starts from the principle of "the Bible alone" conceived in its original and positive sense.

In Anglicanism there are no official church authorities nor official church pronouncements that as such can claim infallible and absolute authority. In this most important respect Anglicanism clearly does not stand on the side of the churches of the "catholic" type, whether that of Constantinople or of Rome.

The Anglican position then results from the acceptance of the fundamental principles of the Reformation. However, these principles are explicitly combined with a typical Anglican openness toward both old and new acquisitions made by a humanistic and scientific reflection upon the sources. To these sources belong first of all Sacred Scripture, but also the writings of the Fathers of the Church, the decrees of the Councils of the

---

9 See the author's *Zeugnis der Reformation,* Essen, 1963.

46

undivided Church, liturgical books and all other sources by which it is possible to learn "the true principles of God's Church."

In consequence Anglicanism has never tried to determine once and for all the fine points of its confession. It has always made a sharp distinction between the core and essential content of the apostolic Faith and the detailed theological elaboration, between unchangeable fixed facts and defective and variable theological interpretations that are related to particular times. It has always shown repugnance toward abstract speculations that are made outside the field of positively established facts.

Anglicanism has always maintained an openness for correction and new insights. It lives by an accumulation of inheritances: the inheritance from the undivided Church, the inheritance from humanism, the inheritance from the sixteenth century Reformation and the inheritance of the new experiences and new insights that have been acquired during the centuries since the Reformation.

When Anglicanism appeals to tradition it does not mean that the latter is a separate source placed alongside and even above Holy Scripture. However, when there is question of the well-considered judgment regarding the intention of Scripture in respect to the forms which church life gradually accepted, especially during the first centuries, then tradition alone can make plain how God's Word has functioned from the beginning in the practice of the Church.

We meet with the same respect for antiquity and appreciation of "the true principles of God's Church" in the writings of the sixteenth century Reformers, namely in Melanchton, Bucer and Calvin, and, in later centuries, in men like Hugo Grotius and all the theologians who possessed a vast humanistic erudition and a knowledge of ancient Christian sources.

The Reformation from the very start had to combat a tension between the leaders and the people. Fanatical currents and other extremist movements sprang from the people who were animated chiefly by their dislike for everything that still reminded them of the loathed popish church. Such popular instincts worked underground, and in England they were uttered in season and out of season in the cry "No Popery." Not only the Anglican but also the continental Reformers have always met that kind of extremism with an appeal to the tradition of the ancient Church and the general opinion of the Church Fathers.

Hence the appeal to the normative authority of antiquity for the explanation and application of Scripture to problems concerning church structure, offices and liturgy does not create so great a difference between Anglicanism and Reformed Christianity as is often maintained today. In no case can it be claimed that this appeal is a characteristic which would justify the banning of the Anglican churches from the paternal home of the Reformation. Nor could Anglicanism on its account be ranked with the churches that have a concept of authority and an attitude toward Scripture and tradition that is completely foreign to official and authentic Anglicanism.

The passage which we have quoted above contains a second rejection, namely, of "other errors [besides the claim of absolute authority] both in doctrine and in discipline." The report does not name those errors. But it is important for us to get a clear picture of the nature and extent of the errors that are meant by the report.

No doubt the bishops must have thought principally of the Roman errors that were condemned in the *Thirty-nine Articles of Religion* of the Church of England. These *Articles* have sometimes been called, both ironically and irenically, "Articles of Division." Some Anglicans look upon them as antiquated documents of a bygone age. However, they must be held as an authoritative source of the doctrine of the Church of England, for Article 5 of the *Canon Law Revision 1959* states:

The doctrine of the Church of England is grounded in the Holy Scriptures and in such teachings of the ancient Fathers and Councils of the Church as are agreeable to the said Scriptures. In particular such doctrine is to be found in the Thirty-nine Articles of Religion, the Book of Common Prayer and the Ordinal.[10]

Which doctrines and practices of the Church of Rome do the *Thirty-nine Articles* reject as being erroneous?

In Articles 9–21, there is an indirect condemnation of several doctrines concerning original sin, free will, justification, superfluous good works, sin after baptism, election and predestination, the attaining of eternal salvation, the Church and church authority, all these being considered as Roman errors. Anglicanism, with full conviction and perfect awareness, has taken position on the side of the Reformation against the Church of Rome regarding all those points.

If it could be shown, as some have attempted to do, that those thirteen articles can be understood in a way that makes them agree with the teaching of the Council of Trent, it would follow that the doctrine of the Reformation likewise agrees in all those important points with the Church of Rome. But it would not follow in any way that the Anglican churches stand not on the side of the Reformation but on the side of Rome, for the doctrine of Articles 9–21 is purely reformational. We shall say more about this in the following chapter.

In Article 22 we meet with the first expression by name of the Roman errors:

The Romish Doctrine concerning Purgatory, Pardons, Worshipping and Adoration, as well of Images as of Reliques, and also invocation of Saints, is a fond thing vainly invented, and grounded upon no warranty of Scripture, but rather repugnant to the Word of God.

After that, in Article 25, there is the rejection of the devotion to the Blessed Sacrament which arose in the Middle Ages:

---

[10] *Canon Law Revision 1959*, p. 10.

The Sacraments were not ordained of Christ to be gazed upon, or to be carried about, but that we should duly use them.

Article 28 rejects the doctrine of transubstantiation:

Transubstantiation (or the change of the substance of Bread and Wine) in the Supper of the Lord, cannot be proved by holy Writ; but it is repugnant to the plain words of Scripture, overthroweth the nature of a Sacrament, and hath given occasion to many superstitions.

The same article ends by declaring explicitly that:

The Sacrament of the Lord's Supper was not by Christ's ordinance reserved, carried about, lifted up, or worshipped.

Finally Article 31, in sharp words that closely follow the position of the continental Reformation, attacks the Roman concept of the Sacrifice of the Mass:

The Offering of Christ once made is that perfect redemption, propitiation, and satisfaction, for all the sins of the whole world, both original and actual; and there is none other satisfaction for sin, but that alone. Wherefore the sacrifices of Masses, in the which it was commonly said, that the Priest did offer Christ for the quick and the dead, to have remission of pain or guilt, were blasphemous fables, and dangerous deceits.

In imitation of the continental Reformers, Anglicanism conceives the celebration of the Lord's Supper as the Holy Communion. It is the celebration of the memorial of the death of God's only begotten Son Jesus Christ on the Cross, who, as is said in the Anglican prayer of consecration, "there [on his Cross] by his one oblation of himself, once offered a full, perfect and sufficient sacrifice, oblation and satisfaction, for the sins of the whole world; and did institute, and in his holy Gospel command us to continue a perpetual memory of that his precious death until his coming again."

Whenever a reference is made to this liturgical text to indicate the sacrificial character of the Anglican Communion

Service, it is important to keep in mind that we have here a reformational concept of sacrifice which is thought of, first of all, as an offering of praise and thanksgiving and, secondly, as an offering in the sense of a general consecration of oneself to God. In the Anglican prayer of thanksgiving after communion God is asked "mercifully to accept this our sacrifice of praise and thanksgiving," and the prayer goes on: "And here we offer and present unto thee, O Lord, ourselves, our souls and bodies, to be a reasonable, holy and lively sacrifice unto Thee."

Against Roman Catholic doctrine and practice Anglicanism placed a new idea of the sacrificial character of the Lord's Supper which is in agreement with the witness of the Reformation. It puts every emphasis on the all-sufficient character of the sacrifice of Christ, namely, in the sense that the Mass in no way has the character of a propitiatory sacrifice and must not in the least be considered as a sacrifice in the true and authentic sense of that term.[11]

Bicknell's excellent commentary on the *Thirty-nine Articles*, reedited and revised by Dr. Carpenter, the present Bishop of Oxford, is of the opinion that Article 31 "has its eye throughout on mediaeval abuses and on the attempt of the Council of Trent to shelter them as far as possible."[12] It would not be a denial of the Eucharistic Sacrifice. The same would also apply in part to the other condemnations contained in the articles just quoted.

In its explanation of each article the commentary strives nobly to exonerate the Roman Church from the doctrines that

---

[11] Session XXII of the Council of Trent (Sept. 17, 1562), Denziger, nos. 937a–956, deals with the Holy Sacrifice of Mass. Cap. 2 says: "It is a visible sacrifice that is propitatory for the living and the dead." Canon 1 states: "If anyone says that in the Mass there is not offered to God a true and proper sacrifice, or that 'to offer' is nothing more than that Christ is given to us as our food, let him be anathema."

[12] Bicknell-Carpenter, *The Thirty-nine Articles of the Church of England,* London, 3rd ed., 1953, p. 417.

51

are unjustly attributed to her. It also tries to show that the *Thirty-nine Articles* should be understood in their original Catholic sense. Thus, the sixth paragraph of the chapter that deals with the articles concerning Holy Communion bears the title "The Eucharistic Sacrifice." The sacrificial character of the Holy Eucharist is explicitly defended and is conceived in a more "catholic" way than was intended by the writers of the *Thirty-nine Articles*. If this is regarded as a proof that there is a gradual development of Anglican theology in a catholic direction and, on the other hand, one considers the contemporary development of Roman Catholic sacramental theology, one is certainly justified in seeing here a real rapprochement.

However, the commentary remains opposed to the pronouncements of the Council of Trent regarding the Mass, although it does not appear to be ignorant of the differences that exist in that matter among Roman Catholic theologians. The commentator has no objection against calling the Sacrifice of the Mass a representation of the Sacrifice of the Cross until the return of Christ. But he rejects explicitly the Sacrifice of the Mass as being "truly propitiatory" and a "true and proper sacrifice." The writer is also aware of the fact that the papal declaration of nullity of Anglican orders in 1896 is largely based on the different view taken of the sacrificial character of the Mass:

> The latest Roman denial of our orders is based on our rejection of any such view which makes the sacrifice of the Eucharist additional to that of Calvary. As long as it is taught, in however refined a form, the protest of our Article will not be out of date.[13]

We would be going beyond the scope of this chapter if we here investigated more deeply the differences between Rome and Canterbury revealed by those articles, for the purpose of this chapter is merely to find out what is the official attitude of the Anglican Communion toward the Church of Rome.

---

[13] *Ibid.*, p. 418.

In regard to the report of 1888, we must still mention that the encyclical with which the report begins points out a contrast between the Eastern churches and the Latin church:

> We reflect with thankfulness that there exist no bars, such as are presented to communion with the Latins by the formulated sanction of the Infallibility of the Church residing in the person of the supreme pontiff, by the Doctrine of the Immaculate Conception, and other dogmas imposed by the decrees of the Papal Councils. The Church of Rome has always treated her Eastern sister wrongfully. She intrudes her Bishops into the ancient Dioceses, and keeps up a system of active proselytism.[14]

4. The Lambeth Conference of 1897: The Anglican Ordinations

The Lambeth Conference of 1897 did not commit the study of the problem of church unity to three separate committees, as had been done before, but entrusted it to one committee. This has been the practice of all subsequent Lambeth Conferences, although it appeared desirable most of the time to divide the Ecumenical Committee, as we shall call it henceforth, into a number of subcommittees.

The Ecumenical Committee of 1897 had the task "to consider and report upon the subject of Church Unity in its relation (a) to the Churches of the East; (b) to the Latin Communion; (c) to other Christian bodies."[15] Here for the first time, as is now customary, a separate paragraph was devoted to the Roman Catholic Church.

In 1897 that paragraph was concerned exclusively with the question of Anglican ordinations. As is generally known, in the preceding year, Pope Leo XIII in the bull *Apostolicae Curae* of September 13, 1896, had declared that these "ordinations were and are totally null and void" (*irritas prorsus fuisse et esse*

---

[14] *The Six Lambeth Conferences*, p. 115.
[15] *Ibid.*, pp. 243 ff.

omninoque nullas). He had confirmed and as it were renewed what had been decreed regarding those ordinations by the popes who had preceded him.[16]

This surely was not a fortunate and hopeful beginning when one is contemplating the possibility of eventual rapprochement and reunion between Canterbury and Rome. From the ecumenical standpoint we are thus faced with a most thorny question, and this for several reasons.

First of all, it is perfectly plain that the matter in question is not a purely canonical one, as if the Pope wished to recall that the ministers who have received the ordination for their office according to the Anglican rite are thereby not yet empowered to exercise their office in the Church of Rome. The Church of England, as appears in her *Ordinale* of 1549, also knows such a purely juridical exclusion. For we read in the preface:

> And therefore to the extent these orders should bee continued, and reuerentlye used, and estemed in this Church of England, it is requysite, that no man (not beynge at thus presente Bisschop, Priest, nor Deacon) shall execute anye of them, excepte he be called, tryed, examined, and admitted, accordynge to the forme here after folowinge.[17]

That regulation, as can be shown in the practice of the Church of England, applies only within the English Church and has no intention of saying anything to the detriment of the offices and the manner of investiture or ordinations in other churches.[18]

---

[16] "And so, agreeing with all that has been decreed in this matter by Our Predecessors, and fully confirming and as it were renewing those decrees *motu proprio* by Our own Authority, we declare with certain knowledge and proclaim that the ordinations that were made in the Anglican Rite were and are totally null and void." Denziger, no. 1966.

[17] *The First and Second Prayer-Books of King Edward the Sixth,* ed. in Everyman's Library, London, 2nd impr., 1927, p. 292.

[18] See, e.g., Sykes, *Old Priest and New Presbyter,* Cambridge, 1956, Chap. II: "A parity of ministers asserted," pp. 30 ff.; Chap. III: "An imparity of ministers defended," pp. 58 ff. Cf. Meyer, *Elizabeth I and the Religious Settlement of 1559,* St. Louis, 1960, pp. 75 ff.

The words of Pope Leo XIII, "were and are totally null and void," express the fact that there is here no question of illiceity but of nullity. The word *irritas* used in the Latin text means invalid in the sense of being without effect or purpose and useless, just as *omninoque nullas* seems to repeat in another way that the ordinations in question are in themselves *totally null and void*. Here then is a declaration which is not simply historical or juridical but has an ontological nature. It wants to indicate that those ordinations in no way produce in the order of supernatural reality what they claim and intend to confer.

This is no small matter. Now that we no longer meet one another in a purely polemical and apologetic manner but in an ecumenical spirit, we begin to realize what that means. It means that there is a church which has existed for several centuries with millions of Christian members, a church in which day after day a host of devoted ministers believe they are doing what, as they really think, Christ has committed to them; and there is another church which has pronounced the judgment that the first not only is not a true church, but that it also wrongly imagines that its ministers really speak and act on the authority of Christ and wrongly imagines that their administration of the sacraments has the meaning and effect they attribute to it and, in good faith and confidence, expect from it.

The sacrament of baptism administered by Anglican clergymen makes only a seeming exception to that. Baptism is not recognized by the Church of Rome because the minister of a particular church has been validly ordained and has administered the sacrament as a minister of a true Church, but the Church of Rome considers a baptism valid solely on the basis of her doctrine that every baptism is valid, whoever might administer it, provided he has the intention of "doing what the Church does." Hence the recognition of a so-called "non-Catholic" baptism says nothing in favor of the particular church, nor in favor of the ministry and the sacraments of that particular church.

What can a church do after being struck by such an annihilating blow as the declaration of nullity of her ordinations undoubtedly is, except take note of it and disregard it? If a church accepted such a pronouncement she would by that very fact acknowledge that she is not a church in the true sense of the term and would lower her sacramental ministry to the level of empty ceremonies. She would simply commit suicide. The declaration of nullity of the Anglican ordinations, as was said in the extensive answer of the Archbishops of Canterbury and York of March 29, 1897, was "aimed at overthrowing our whole position as a Church."[19]

On the other hand it appears, from the bull *Apostolicae Curae* and the reply of both archbishops, that the question has diverse sides and can be approached in very different ways. The Pope dealt with the question according to ecclesiastical custom and the teachings of moral theology concerning the form and intention that are required for a valid ordination. The archbishops, on their part, started in a typically reformational way, from Holy Scripture and the tradition of the ancient church. Moreover, they pointed out that the Pope did not take into account the preface of the *Ordinale* of 1549 in which the general intention is expressed, namely, that the purpose in view is that of continuing the offices of bishop, presbyter and deacon that have existed from apostolic times. The Pope, in opposition to that, stresses the personal intention of those who composed the *Ordinale* and of the bishops who under Edward VI and under Elizabeth I acted as consecrators.

The Pope took into consideration the fact that particular passages of the Roman rite were intentionally discarded by the Anglican *Ordinale* of 1549 and, together with that, the fact

---

[19] *Anglican Orders*, 1957 (reprint), p. 23. In the Latin ed.: "Quae totum nostrum statum eccelsiasticum subvertere conarentur" (p. 21).

that the Eucharistic Service, in the *Book of Common Prayer,* no longer has the character of a Sacrifice of the Mass but is conceived as a Communion Service. From this he concluded that the intention of the authors was not the one that was required for validity. On that account the words "Receive the Holy Ghost" were given a new content, which, the Pope claimed, influenced the form of the ordination and made it invalid.

Father Francis Clark, S.J., in a recent work has made a careful analysis of the concept of intention and the arguments that were based on it in the papal bull, for the sake of bringing more light to the debate that has gone on since 1896 between Roman Catholic and Anglican writers about the question of ordinations.[20] He gives, besides, a complete survey of the literature on this subject by writers of both sides.[21]

We shall go more deeply into the problem of the validity of Anglican ordinations in our final chapter, with an eye on the present ecumenical situation. We are now concerned only with the attitude which the Lambeth Conference of 1897 took in respect to the declaration of nullity.

The reply of the Archbishops of Canterbury and York was more historical than dogmatic in nature. Their views of the consequences of the Reformation as these affected the Church of England were totally different from those of Rome, and on that account they believed that the papal bull had given a wrong presentation of things. For that matter, the archbishops argued, if the objection raised in said bull against the form and intention of the *Ordinale* of 1549 were to be accepted as valid, it would follow, on the basis of similar historical facts, that the Church of Rome had also passed through periods when its ordinations failed to fulfill the requirements regarding the form ("Receive the Holy Ghost") and the matter (the laying on of hands) and were therefore invalid:

---

[20] Clark, *Anglican Orders and Defect of Intention,* London, 1956.
[21] *Ibid.,* pp. 203 ff.

Thus in overthrowing our orders, he [the Pope] overthrows all his own, and pronounces sentence on his own Church. Eugenius IVth indeed brought his Church into great peril of nullity when he taught a new matter and a new form of Order and left the real without a word. For no one knows how many ordinations may have been made, according to his teaching, without any laying on of hands or appropriate form. Pope Leo demands a form unknown to previous Bishops of Rome and an intention which is defective in the catechisms of the Oriental Church.[22]

Looked at from the Anglican standpoint, it is precisely the Church of Rome which has fallen from one novelty into another in the course of the Middle Ages, whereas the Church of England has restored the old in accord with God's Word and the true principles of God's Church.

All this goes to show that Rome and Canterbury started from totally different standards and concepts of authority. Hence the arguments used by the opponents in the controversy did not really attain their goal in regard to their opponents. Clark's book points this out also:

Those who are unprepared to admit that the official *magisterium* of the Roman Catholic Church and the approved teaching of her theologians provide sure guidance in these matters of sacramental theology, will not accept the validity of my premises, that is of the Roman Catholic premises.[23]

The debate about the validity of Anglican ordinations will then come to nothing as long as it confines itself strictly to the theme of the ordination itself. It should, on the contrary, be conducted on as wide an ecclesiological plane as possible. It is useless and senseless to renew the discussion concerning the validity of Anglican ordinations as long as there exists no agreement concerning the nature, structure, function and authority of the Church and regarding the nature and practice of the sacraments, in particular of the Holy Eucharist.

---

[22] *Anglican Orders*, p. 60. [23] Clark, *op. cit.*, p. 202.

For that matter, in reality no discussion has taken place regarding that subject. In the pre-ecumenical period the churches merely talked against one another. Both the bull *Apostolicae Curae* and the Anglican reply were in the nature of a monologue. The conclusion was already established before an exchange of views between the parties had taken place.

Regarding the possibility of holding an ecumenical discussion, the question arises whether Pope Leo XIII has not excluded that possibility in advance by the concluding remarks of his Letter:

> We decree that the present letters and whatever they contain may never be impugned or refuted as if they rested on any fault or defect that had crept in or because of any wrong intention on our part; but they are and will remain always valid and in force, and every one, whatever his rank or position, must live according to them both as regards his interior conviction and his external conduct. We also decree that anything that is undertaken against them whether knowingly or in ignorance by any one and whatever may be his reasons or authority or pretext, we, in advance, declare null and void; all things to the contrary notwithstanding.[24]

Here every imaginable possibility is mentioned by name and is excluded in advance and forever. The only consolation lies in the fact that these words are an example of a fixed curial style which perhaps is not taken so strictly and severely in Rome as it is usually taken outside Rome. The concluding paragraph is worded in a pretentiously authoritative way that in our own day fails to attain its purpose.

In any case this is not an infallible proclamation of a dogma, but a disciplinary regulation or ordinance which of itself is not infallible. All who are under the jurisdiction of the Pope are therefore obliged to obey it so long as it remains in force.

But the possibility is not excluded that conditions might

---

[24] Latin text in *Anglican Orders*, p. 15.

change, that the relations between the churches might become quite different; new facts and views might come to light so that it might become desirable and even perhaps imperative that the case of the ordinations be re-opened. The decision, on the Roman side, rests naturally with the Pope. And it is wholly probable, in view of the present growth of a new ecumenical attitude, that the Pope will consider that he is not bound by the ordinances of his predecessors regarding what is permissible in the ecumenical field.

This, however, does not at all mean that the question of Anglican ordinations is not one of the thorniest of ecumenical problems. It seems to me that the Pope's declaration of nullity of Anglican orders rests on a few damaging historical facts. There is principally the fact that those who composed the *Ordinale* of 1549, and almost all Anglican bishops under Edward VI and Elizabeth I, conceived the nature of the priesthood and the ordination to office practically in the sense given to them by the Reformers, although they accepted the scriptural and apostolic foundation and origin of the threefold function of bishops, presbyter and deacon. Some recent studies based on an examination of the sources have merely confirmed that view. Thus the American Lutheran church historian Carl Meyer comes to the following conclusion:

> On the 17th of December, Matthew Parker was consecrated in Lambeth Chapel. William Barlow, John Scory, who also preached the installation sermon, Myles Coverdale, and John Hodgkins participated in the solemn rite. Neither Matthew Parker nor the queen nor others were concerned that he be consecrated in Apostolic Succession. He was consecrated by bishops because of the dignity of the office, not because of the necessity of keeping a direct continuity. Apostolic succession became the concern of churchmen of a later generation.[25]

An overwhelming amount of material could be adduced to show that, although at the beginning of the reign of Elizabeth

---

[25] Meyer, *op. cit.*, p. 82.

I, there were still a few Romanists among the bishops, the majority by far were Zwinglians, Calvinists, Puritans or even Lutherans in their ideas about Church and church offices. I believe that we must exclude the supposition that these bishops, when acting as consecrators, personally interpreted their own intention in a "catholic sense," that is according to the intention for the consecration or ordinations of bishops, priests and deacons which the Church of Rome considers absolutely necessary for their validity. Hence the problem here is to what extent the personal interpretation of the intention established by the Church has an influence on the validity of an ordination.

Dr. Norman Sykes, former church historian at Cambridge who died in 1961 as Dean of Winchester, has supplied most important material concerning the question of the Anglican concept of church offices in his book *Old Priest and New Presbyter*.[26] He is in perfect agreement with what we have just said. According to Sykes, the Anglican concept of such offices in the sixteenth century was not that of a *"sacerdos"* (priest) but of a *presbyter* conceived in the sense attributed to it by the Reformers, although the word "priest" continued to be used.

Let us now ask what was the reaction of the Lambeth Conference of 1897 to the papal bull *Apostolicae Curae*.

The paragraph in the report of the ecumenical commission that deals with that matter begins with the remark that Pope Leo XIII had published a series of documents in which he made known his desire of attaining unity in Christianity, "but unfortunately asserting as its only basis the recognition of the papal supremacy as of divine right."[27] With respect to the bull concerning Anglican ordinations and the subsequent reply of the archbishops of Canterbury and York, the ecumenical committee made the following remark:

---

26 Sykes, *op. cit.*
27 *The Six Lambeth Conferences*, p. 246.

Though controversy is rarely a method of promoting unity, there are grounds for thankfulness in the courteous tone in which much of this controversy has been conducted; in the abandonment by the Pope of much irrelevant and spurious matter which previously rendered discussion hopeless; in the limitation of the sphere of controversy to definite points; in a large amount of subsidiary literature embodying the results of much research; and in the desire shown on both sides to understand and not consciously to misrepresent one another. If this spirit increases, even controversy will not have been in vain; and we await the issue of such controversy with entire confidence.[28]

This passage gives a clear picture of the ecumenical mentality that has characterized Anglicanism until now. Anglican ecumenism is more an attitude than a system, more a vision than a pre-established project. It proceeds on its way searching and putting out feelers. It expects little or nothing from polemics and controversial theology. The Anglican churches are concerned with finding new possibilities and creating friendly relations; and they expect from them positive and practical results without getting entangled over and over again in speculative considerations. To the extent that insuperable difficulties seem to present themselves, the Anglican churches try to draw as much good as possible from a bad situation. They do not close the door but wait patiently for better opportunities and look hopefully to the future.

This ecumenic attitude toward the Church of Rome did not keep the Lambeth Conference of 1897 from expressing her sympathy to Protestant minorities who were fighting for full freedom of religion in Roman Catholic countries, and even toward groups within the Church of Rome itself: We recognize with warm sympathy the endeavours that are being made to escape from the usurped authority of the See of Rome as ourselves regained our freedom centuries ago.[29]

In particular the Lambeth Conference expressed its sympathy

---

28 *Ibid.*, p. 246.   29 *Ibid.*, p. 194.

with the attempts made by some at that time in Mexico and elsewhere to establish their own national hierarchy that would be independent from Rome and, further, "with the brave and earnest men of France, Italy, Spain, and Portugal, who have been driven to free themselves from the burden of unlawful terms of Communion imposed by the Church of Rome"[30] for the reception of the sacraments. These words which appear in the encyclical of 1897 are taken from one of the resolutions of the Lambeth Conference of that year which ends with the words: "We continue to watch these movements with deep and anxious interest, praying that they may be blessed and guided by Almighty God."[31]

In respect to the fundamental attitude toward the Church of Rome, the paragraph concerning the Latin Communion is satisfied with repeating literally the passage of the Report of 1888 which we have sufficiently dealt with above.[32]

As we now study how the attitude of the Anglican Communion toward Rome has developed in the course of later Lambeth Conferences, we see that there has been a slow but constant improvement. At the same time, however, we must note that the Anglican bishops attribute that betterment principally to the hopeful changes which they joyfully discover in the Church of Rome. They do not look for the cause of the conflict in themselves.

The Anglican churches agree with all other churches in looking upon the Church of Rome as the only one to which serious objection must be taken, from the general Christian standpoint. All the churches attribute the principal cause of the schisms to Rome. Their hope for a future restoration of unity is based principally on the expectation that the Church of Rome will finally realize that it must be ready to revise itself in many

---

[30] *Ibid.*, p. 194.   [31] *Ibid.*, p. 205.
[32] Cf. p. 42.

points. It must renew itself in order that it may, on its part, render possible the reconciliation, rapprochement and reunion that have been desired for a long time by the other churches.

The Anglican Communion like the other reformed churches considers that reunion with Rome depends on the decision of the Church of Rome to submit to the unadulterated Word of God. Whenever Anglican bishops study the situation, they look for signs in the ecumenical firmament that point in that respect to a new dawn. They look forward to them "more than sentinels wait for the dawn" (Ps. 129:6).

5. THE LAMBETH CONFERENCE OF 1908: HOPEFUL SIGNS AND VEXING PROBLEMS

In 1908 the ecumenical commission of the Lambeth Conference began its report with a general consideration. In this introduction it recalls the thirty-fourth resolution of the preceding conference of 1897 which said that "every opportunity be taken to emphasize the Divine purpose of visible unity among Christians, as a fact of revelation."[33]

Starting from the data of revelation, the commission was of the opinion that a practical conclusion should be drawn in regard to one important condition that must be fulfilled by any project for future reunion. There lies a hidden danger in all attempts to bring about the reunion of the separate churches, if these churches are interested only in the ecumenical problem as it presents itself in their own concrete situation and do not take into account the entire communion of Christians. That is why the commission proposed to the Lambeth Conference a resolution which contained the following:

This Conference reaffirms the resolution of the Conference of 1897 [follows Res. 34, 1897]. It desires further to affirm that in all partial

---

[33] *The Six Lambeth Conferences*, p. 205.

projects of reunion and intercommunion the final attainment of the divine purpose should be kept in view as our object; and that care should be taken to do what will advance the reunion of the whole of Christendom and to abstain from doing anything that will retard or prevent it.[34]

This is not an abstract theoretical resolution but a concretely practical one that can be put into execution. It can properly be considered as the most important directive and the true fundamental principle that guides the Anglican churches in their ecumenical thought and conduct. The bishops of the Anglican Communion already had a clear and precise view of the most important fundamental principle for any truly efficient ecumenical endeavor at the time when the modern ecumenical movement had scarcely begun.

To that fundamental principle the Anglicans have remained faithful. Unless one has a proper grasp of that principle he will often be unable to understand the role and influence of the Anglican ecumenical problematics and attitude with respect to other churches. Hence it is in that light that we should try to understand what the report of the Commission says about "the Latin Communion." The Commission of 1908 thought to have noticed three important changes in the attitude between the Latin Church and the Christian world in general, namely:

1. They notice the freer entrance of Roman Catholic theologians into the general field of modern scholarship. . . .

2. They notice the tendency of many who are not of the Roman Catholic Communion, or, indeed, in many cases, members of any episcopal Church, to look with sympathetic hope towards that great Communion as embodying ideals which they find to be largely lacking in much of the sectional Christianity of to-day, and this all the more when they see a new spirit of intellectual liberty and ecclesiastical and social reform stirring within its borders.

3. At the same time they perceive in the current literature of the

---

[34] Resolution 58, 1908, *ibid.*, p. 331.

Roman Catholic Church a growing interest in the practical concerns of other Churches and not least of our own, which is sometimes accompanied with a sense of deficiencies in the Latin Church itself for which a remedy will have to be sought outside.[35]

These and similar changes, which are still going on and which are evident today to any impartial and well-disposed onlooker, were pointed out by the Anglican bishops as long ago as 1908. And they already concluded that "these indications brighten the outlook for the future."[36] But, at the same time, they thought it their duty to maintain their stand, in adherence to the previous Lambeth Conferences, "that under present circumstances it is useless to consider the question of possible intercommunion with our brethren of that Communion in view of the fact that no such proposal would be entertained but on conditions which it would be impossible for us to accept."[37]

However, this does not detract from the fact that the Anglican bishops make it clear that:

They desire to place upon record their conviction that no projects of union can ever be regarded as satisfactory which deliberately leave out the Churches of the Latin Communion; and nowhere more than here would they urge the importance of the cultivation of relations of friendly courtesy on the part of our representatives abroad towards the ecclesiastical authorities in the countries where they live, and the desirability that all chaplains chosen for service on the continent of Europe and elsewhere would be instructed to show this courtesy.[38]

Finally the bishops of the ecumenical commission devoted an extensive exposition to the thorny question of mixed marriages insofar as Anglicans meet with the problem outside their own country. The bishops warned against the consequences of a marriage with a Roman Catholic party, since the Roman Catholic Church demands that the children born of such a wedlock

---

35 *Ibid.,* p. 426. 36 *Ibid.,* p. 426.
37 *Ibid.,* p. 426. 38 *Ibid.,* p. 426.

must be raised "in a religious system which the Anglican parent cannot conscientiously accept."[39]

The encyclical of 1908 does not mention the Church of Rome by name. There is no doubt, however, that the bishops had her constantly in mind, as is evident from the expressions that were clearly addressed to her. For example, the bishops thought it necessary to emphasize that "we belong to a Church which, in the words of one of our number who has entered into rest, is the 'Church of free men, educating them into a knowledge of the liberty wherewith Christ hath made us free.' "[40] Or also, "We dare not, in the name of peace, barter away those precious things of which we have been made stewards."[41]

The opinion of the Lambeth Conference of 1908 regarding marriages with Roman Catholics inspired the draft of a separate resolution concerning that matter:

We desire earnestly to warn members of our Communion against contracting marriages with Roman Catholics under the conditions imposed by modern Roman canon law, especially as these conditions involve the performance of the marriage ceremony without any prayer or invocation of the divine blessing, and also a promise to have their children brought up in a religious system which they cannot themselves accept.[41a]

There are on the part of the Anglicans principally two serious grievances against the Church of Rome. One is concerned with the restrictions suffered by Protestant minorities in some Roman Catholic countries. The second concerns the practice regarding mixed marriages. According to Anglican opinion, the fact that the Church of Rome believes that she possesses the whole truth in all its purity and that the other churces are in error, is not a valid reason for demanding the fulfillment of a condition that a conscientious person is unable to accept.

The Church of Rome should even be the first to disapprove

---

[39] *Ibid.,* p. 427.
[41] *Ibid.,* p. 333.
[40] *Ibid.,* p. 295.
[41a] *Ibid.,* p. 333.

such a condition, since a person is asked to make a promise that is in fundamental opposition to his personal religious conviction. Such a promise can lead only to insincerity. According to Anglican opinion, the fact that the Church of Rome demands such a promise from a non-Catholic party shows that she thinks that she needs not take account of the religious conviction of such a party because the latter conviction is devoid of all positive and actual value.

6. THE LAMBETH CONFERENCE OF 1920: THE OPEN DOOR

World War I made it necessary to postpone the convocation of the next Lambeth Conference for several years. The conference was held in 1920 amidst really new religious and social circumstances. In both the Christian churches and the lives of nations a wind began to blow in a direction differing from that of the time before the war.

Immediately after World War I a powerful effort was made toward fellowship between nations and toward the establishment of a lasting peace on the basis of international law. This effort was backed up by the Christian churches through the practical work for peace of the World Federation for the Promotion of International Friendship Through the Churches. In 1948 this World Federation was absorbed into the World Council of Churches founded in Amsterdam in 1948. The same happened in 1961 to the International Mission Council.

The year 1920 witnessed the definitive beginning of the ecumenical movement in the preparations which led to the convocation of a world conference *On Life and Work* in Stockholm (1925) and *On Faith and Order* in Lausanne (1927). The ecumenical movement was now really a going concern.

Today when we look back at the period between the two world wars, it would seem that at that time there was only a very first beginning, a first attempt to bring about a reorientation, a provisional prelude for the profound changes which we are presently undergoing in every field and not least in that of religious and church life. The year 1920 marked only a beginning in the history of the ecumenical movement; and yet it was a beginning that was pregnant with far-reaching consequences.

World War II appeared necessary to disorganize the churches and nations to such an extent that a return to pre-war conditions was out of the question and to make people realize that they had to build a new world that was in many respects radically different from the old.

The third assembly of the World Council of Churches at New Delhi has given clear proof of the definitive victory that was won by ecumenical consciousness in practically all Christian churches. In the light of this ecumenical development we cannot but gratefully admire the initiative that was taken in 1920 by the Anglican Communion by means of her ecumenical Lambeth Appeal, addressed to all Christians without distinction. We shall return to that appeal in a separate chapter.

The encyclical and the eighty resolutions of the Lambeth Conference of 1920 do not mention the Church of Rome by name even once. The third part of the report of the ecumenical committee, which deals with the attitude toward reunion with episcopal churches, begins nevertheless with a consideration of the Latin Communion:

> Your Committee feels that it is impossible to make any Report on Reunion with Episcopal Churches without some references to the Church of Rome, even though it has no resolution to propose upon the subject. We cannot do better than make our own the words of the Report of 1908, which reminds us of "the fact that there can be no fulfilment of the Divine purpose in any scheme of reunion which does not ultimately include the great Latin Church of the West, with which our history has been so closely associated in the past, and to which we are still bound by many ties of common faith and tradition." But we realize that—to continue the quotation—"any advance in this direction

69

is at present barred by difficulties which we have not ourselves created, and which we cannot of ourselves remove."

Should, however the Church of Rome at any time desire to discuss conditions of reunion we shall be ready to indicate that there are movements going on in the Church of Rome which may be fruitful in the future. . . . It is obvious that no forward step can be taken yet; but the facts thus referred to may help to create in the future a very different position.[42]

The report then mentions a number of facts and events on the plane of human attitudes which show that in many Roman Catholics personally a happy change is taking place in respect to their attitude, judgment and appreciation concerning non-Roman Catholic fellow-Christians. Here also, encounters dating from World War I seem to have contributed greatly toward "better knowledge and understanding of one another's position." The conclusion drawn by the report is: "It is obvious that no forward step can be taken yet; but the facts thus referred to may help to create in the future a very different position."[43]

This quotation speaks for itself. The Anglican Communion expressly involves the Church of Rome in her ecumenical thought and effort. She purposively holds the door open toward Rome. She follows with close attention what is taking place in the Church of Rome. She hopes that signs will soon appear which will make it possible to entertain informal or even official relations with that church. She is constantly on the watch in the direction of Rome to discover any favorable sign which the Anglican Church would be able to greet with joy.

7. THE LAMBETH CONFERENCE OF 1930: THE MALINES CONVERSATIONS

The ecumenical committee of the seventh Lambeth Conference of 1930 repeated and stressed once again the declarations

---

[42] *Lambeth Conference 1920,* p. 144.
[43] *Ibid.,* p. 144.

of 1908 and 1920 to the effect that no single plan for Church reunion can finally fulfill God's will and purpose in respect to unity, if it consciously or unconsciously leaves out of consideration the great Latin Communion. The Anglican Communion has been convinced from the very beginning of the ecumenical movement that no reunion including the whole *Ecumene* is possible so long as the Church of Rome is not involved in it or does not let herself be involved.

Hence in 1930 the committee added a more explicit explanation of its intentions to the declaration of 1908 and 1920 as follows:

> However little prospect there may be at present of the attainment of any such ideal, the Committee feels that in any attempt at Reunion the unity of the whole Church must be in their minds, and they are not without hope that the attitude of the Church of Rome may in some parts of the world at any rate change in the not very distant future.[44]

Moreover, the paragraph of 1930 devoted to the Church of Rome—which for the first time was entitled Roman Catholic Church instead of Latin Communion—was entirely in the atmosphere of the Malines Conversations. These conversations had been conducted from 1921 to 1925 between Roman Catholics and Anglicans.[45] In a certain sense we can consider these conversations as the fruit of the Lambeth Appeal, although they had a strictly private character. It appears from the words with which the paragraph concerning the Roman Catholic Church begins that a copy of the Lambeth Appeal was sent to the Pope in 1920, "and that a polite reply was received." After this short remark the report immediately deals with the Malines Conversations: "However, the most important item we have to

---

[44] *Lambeth Conference 1930*, p. 131.

[45] Cf. *The Conversations at Malines 1921–1925* (Report presented to the Archbishop of Canterbury by the Anglican Members), London, 1926; Frere, *Recollections of Malines*, London, 1930; Bivort de la Saudée, *Anglicans et Catholiques*, 2 vols., Paris, 1948.

communicate to the Conference is the series of Conversations which took place at Mechlin under the chairmanship of Cardinal Mercier."

The report emphasizes the fact that both the Archbishop of Canterbury and Cardinal Mercier had expressly declared that those who took part in the conversations had not received any official commission from their churches; hence they could not be considered official representatives of their respective churches. The aim of the conversations was merely a *rapprochement des coeurs,* a closer union of hearts.

The true friendship that existed between Cardinal Mercier and Lord Halifax is well known. And it is certainly not Cardinal Mercier nor Lord Halifax who are responsible for the failure of the Malines Conversations, and for the fact that they had to be stopped. Nor is it due to them, as is clear from the reports, that some of the Anglican participants felt profoundly disappointed, as was the case with Walter Frere, the famous Anglo-Catholic liturgiologist who was Bishop of Truro from 1923 to 1938. After the death of Cardinal Mercier in 1926, Rome prohibited the continuation of the conversations.

Soon after that came the encyclical *Mortalium Animos* of January 6, 1928, of which it cannot be said that it greeted the development of the ecumenical movement with joy nor that it showed a genuine interest in its future progress. In this respect it is manifest that since then there has taken place an increasing understanding and a growing positive interest in the movement on the part of Rome.

On the other hand the ecumenical committee of 1930 did not let itself be discouraged by that set-back. It remained convinced that ecumenical discussions and conferences possess real value, if they are conducted in a spirit of loyalty, and "it much regrets that by the action of the Pope all such meetings have been forbidden, and Roman Catholics have been prohibited from taking part in conferences on Reunion. This regret, they have reason to believe, is shared by many members of the Church of Rome."[46]

8. THE LAMBETH CONFERENCE OF 1948: DISAPPOINTMENT

This was the situation at the outbreak of World War II. It was only in 1948, the same year that the World Council of Churches was definitively formed, that the Lambeth Conference could assemble once more. For the first time one can notice a somewhat bitter tone in the paragraph concerning the Roman Catholic Church. The paragraph opens as usual with the declaration that the realization of God's will and purpose of unity is unthinkable without the participation of the Church of Rome. The Committee adds however:

> But the Encyclical Letter on fostering union (*Mortalium Animos*) issued by Pope Pius XI in 1928 made it at once again abundantly plain that the only method of reunion which Rome will accept is that of submission to the Papacy. There are no signs whatever of any abatement of this demand in the last twenty years. Nor is there any possibility of its acceptance by the Churches of the Anglican Communion. It should be remembered that in addition to the question of the position of the Papacy, there are still most serious divergences in faith and practice between ourselves and the Roman Catholic Church, which make the prospect of hopeful approaches towards intercommunion unpromising for the present.[47]

The committee then recalled the failure of the Malines Conversations and the *Monitum* of June 5, 1948, which expressly forbade Roman Catholics to take part in ecumenical conferences. It mentioned also the successful cooperation between Roman Catholics and other Christians during World War II in Germany, the Netherlands, France and England, and the repeated appeals

---

[46] *Lambeth Conference 1930*, p. 131.
[47] *Lambeth Conference 1948*, II, p. 66.

of the Pope for the cooperation of all Christians in the social and international field. Yet it added:

We are frankly puzzled by the apparent contradiction between these repeated general invitations to co-operation which the Pope himself has issued and the attitude of many Roman Catholics in particular countries when it comes to definite programmes.

It has also been a disappointment that certain co-operative relationships which seemed to promise well in some countries during the war have not been maintained. The fact of their not being maintained in particular countries may be purely accidental, but we are genuinely perplexed. Difficulties occur over the meaning and application of religious freedom; and there are other difficulties of various kinds.[48]

The committee ended its indictment of Rome's unbending attitude pointing out that in the personal sphere there were to be found notable exceptions to the unwillingness to cooperate; many friendly contacts of a personal nature had been established; and in some countries Roman Catholics had been permitted to pray the Our Father together with others during their meetings for social cooperation. Its conclusion reads as follows:

We are conscious of the urgent need of co-operation between Roman Catholics and other Christians on a common ground where ultimate questions of Church-order and doctrine which divide us are raised. We believe that the area, outside the field of faith and order, is very large. We would therefore greatly value further lucidation from the Roman Catholic side on the manner of such co-operation, and would be thankful if the way could be found to make it fully effective. We feel that no effort will be wanting on the side of members of the Anglican Communion.[49]

It is principally the Anglican churches who for a quarter of a century have unremittingly stressed the priority of *Faith and Order* over *Life and Work,* for they are convinced that the ecumenical problem is in the long run one of complete restoration of Christian unity in faith and church communion. It is therefore

---

[48] *Ibid.,* p. 67. [49] *Ibid.,* p. 68.

74

to be regretted that it is precisely in their relation with the Church of Rome that they have seen themselves obliged, against their will, to withdraw completely to the field of a merely practical cooperation.

Although the door remained open in that direction, we are still justified in saying that in the Lambeth Conference of 1948 the nadir was reached with respect to the mutual understanding between Canterbury and Rome.

9. THE PRESENT: HOPES

A first improvement in the situation occurred on the part of Rome in December, 1949, by the enactment of an Instruction addressed to all bishops in which they were asked "not only to watch zealously and practically over that whole activity [namely, for a rapprochement, co-operation and dialogue between Roman Catholics and other Christians] but to foster and direct that activity with prudence."[50]

We are justified in seeing in that Instruction a definitive turning point in the attitude of the Vatican toward the ecumenical movement. It marks the beginning of a slow but steady improvement in the relations between the Church of Rome and the other Christian churches. This improvement has developed particularly during the pontificate of Pope John XXIII.

We note that that improvement was recorded and greeted with joy in the report of the ecumenical commission of the Lambeth Conference of 1958:

Although the Roman Catholic Church retains its conviction that the only goal of re-union must be submission to the Papacy, there are some welcome signs of an increasing recognition by the Roman authorities of the importance of the Ecumenical Movement.[51]

[50] *Acta Apostolicae Sedis,* 1950 (vol. 42) pp. 142 ff.
[51] *Lambeth Conference 1958,* II, p. 48.

The report then devoted a brief consideration to the Instruction of the Holy Office to the bishops concerning the fostering of an ecumenical dialogue and noted the steady growth in the participation of the faithful of diverse churches in the International Week of Prayer for Christian Unity from January 18 to 25, that has met "with much official Roman Catholic approval."[52]

The commission expressed its agreement with Father Couturier's formulation of the intention for which to pray during the Church Unity Octave. It excludes all *a priori* opinion regarding the method of reunion, for it reads: "that the unity of the Christians may be attained as was desired by Our Lord and in a way that is in accord with His will." The commission believed that "the simultaneous observances of this Week by Roman Catholics and by members of other Churches are a valuable contribution to the efforts towards unity."[53]

This then was the mutual attitude of the Anglican Communion and the Church of Rome in 1958 after more than half a century of ecumenical prayer, watchfulness, reflection and labor.

During the few years that have elapsed since then, the ecumenical situation has undergone profound changes thanks to the interest, the understanding, and the love of Pope John XXIII with respect to the efforts of the modern ecumenical movement. Although the Second Vatican Council, that opened on October 11, 1962, had as its first purpose internal renewal within the Church of Rome, it was then and remains evident that Pope John and his successor desire that the Council should make a positive contribution toward the fostering of Christian unity.

It was soon realized that the tasks of the Council were truly enormous, that it was necessary to establish permanent conciliary commissions that would prepare regular small conciliary assemblies. In particular the ecumenical secretariate, established

---

[52] *Ibid.*, 6, 49.   [53] *Ibid.*, 6, 49.

under the chairmanship of Cardinal Bea, is destined to remain permanently for the sake of maintaining ecumenical relations with representatives of other churches. Similar secretariates were soon formed in England and in France. All this is a reason for hope; but perhaps it is also a last chance. The later development of affairs on the part of Rome will be definitively decisive —who knows for how long—for the Anglican churches in regard to the Church of Rome. It is therefore with feelings of great interest and hopeful expectations that we are waiting for the results of the Second Vatican Council begun in 1962 and the Lambeth Conference that will be held in 1968.

The present ecumenical openness of the Holy See, which manifested itself dramatically in the meeting of Pope Paul VI and the Ecumenical Patriarch of Constantinople Athenagoras in Jerusalem on January 5, 1964, induced Archbishop Ramsey of Canterbury to set up an Anglican Commission on Roman Catholic relations. The aim of this commission is to provide a general basis for the efforts to reach Christianity unity.

CHAPTER THREE

The Anglican Attitude Toward The Reformation

1. INTRODUCTION

THE evangelical movement and ecclesiastical renewal, which in the sixteenth century led to a break with the Pope and the Roman Catholic Church and the formation of new and local or national independent churches, is usually designated simply as "The Reformation." Hence all churches which owe their origin to that movement and whose teaching and church practice agree with the most profound and real principles of the Reformation are reckoned among the reformed churches. The Church of England, also, which considers itself the reformed prolongation of the medieval *Ecclesia Anglicana,* has belonged to those reformed churches—apart from a short interruption between 1553 and 1558—since 1533.

When we base ourselves on and start from the fundamental concerns of all the sixteenth century reformers, their standpoint toward the Gospel and the nature of the Church, and their unanimous rejection of nearly all the medieval practices of the Church, we have to admit that all the reformed churches are in mutual agreement concerning those principal fundamentals. One can rightly speak of an original and authentic primitive witness of the Reformation which was unanimously accepted by all the reformers and reformed churches, including the reformers of the Church of England and its bishops.[1]

However, we note also that some important differences of opinion regarding theology, church structure and the liturgy manifested themselves among the reformers from the very beginning. As a result, the same kind of differences exist between the various reformed churches and even between theologians belonging to one same church.

During the epigenetic period that followed the Reformation, those differences became more and more pronounced; they brought about an increasing estrangement between the reformational churches and led to the formation of diverse types of churches, such as the Lutheran, the "Reformed" and the Anglican. The churches of Geneva, Bern, Basle and Zurich in Switzerland, and the national state churches of Lutheran, "Reformed," and Anglican countries ultimately went more or less their own individual ways, although they remained in correspondence with one another for some time. In this respect the regular correspondence that was maintained between the Church of England and the churches of Zurich and Bern is of great importance for obtaining a correct knowledge of the ecumenical situation of that time.[2]

It would be contrary to historical facts and the content of official church documents if someone thought the differences between the reformational churches themselves were more important than their fundamental agreement and that, for instance, the sixteenth century Church of England should not be reckoned as belonging fundamentally to the reformational churches.

The differences between the Lutheran, "Reformed" and Anglican churches regarding the way the fundamental principles were

[1] Cf. the author's *Das Zeugnis der Reformation*, pp. 20 ff.
[2] *Original Letters relative to the English Reformation*, ed. for the Parker Society, Cambridge, 1846. Robinson, ed., *The Zürich Letters*, Cambridge, 1842.

developed and applied in theology, church structure and liturgy, though in themselves not unimportant, are nevertheless of a minor nature when they are compared with the common acceptance of the most profound principles of the Reformation. These differences took nothing away from the witness of the Reformation regarding the Gospel. They did not affect the *esse* but only the *bene esse* (not the being itself but only the well-being) of the Church, to use an expression dear to the Anglicans. That is why the classical interpreters of the Anglican opinion looked upon the difference between an episcopal and a presbyterial church structure as an important and yet not essential difference.

This distinction is of great moment for a proper understanding of the ecumenical situation. It is important to know whether the Anglican churches differ only in accidentals or also on essential points from the reformational churches and what is the right view of the connection between Reformation, on the one hand, and the ecclesial continuity, on the other. One thing is certain: a church will be more important for the attainment of the ecumenical goal in proportion to the degree in which it has preserved that continuity intact.

2. CONTINUITY WITH THE CATHOLIC AND APOSTOLIC CHURCH

When the reformational churches are said to be "new" churches and to "date" from the sixteenth century, it means that the Reformation was actually a new beginning for all those churches in respect to the preaching of the faith, public worship, the care of souls and the entire church practice, as well as in the fields of exegesis, theology and eventually even of philosophical and scientific thought. This applies as much to the Church of England and Anglicanism as to the other reformational churches and to World Protestantism in general.

This admission of "being-new," however, does not mean that the churches that arose from the Reformation wished in any way to deviate from or to break with "the holy and unquestionable Christian Faith," as this was expressed in the universally accepted Creeds of the ancient Church of the first centuries. All heresies—and there have been many—which were rejected by the undivided Church, were also resolutely rejected and combated by the Reformation.

It is even more important for the proper understanding of the present ecumenical situation to recognize the fact that not only the Church of England, but all the reformational churches without exception, have resolutely and consciously claimed continuity with the One, Catholic and Apostolic Church whose existence began on the first Pentecost. In particular the churches of the "Reformed" type have, precisely for that purpose, preferred to call themselves "Reformed," "Réformée," "Reformiert," "Gereformeerd," because they want to point out that they consider themselves to be the "Catholic" or "Universal Christian" Church, a "Church" that has preserved its continuity with the pre-Reformation Church but at the same time has renewed and reformed itself "in accord with the demand of God's Word."

The fact that the churches of the "Reformed" type have always emphasized the spiritual aspect of the Church as the people of God to which all the saints of the Old Covenant belonged just as much as the "true Christian believers" of the New Covenant, does not mean that they did not want a visible Church but only an invisible Communion. In general the "Reformed" churches have attached more importance to church structure and church functions and offices that are based on Holy Scripture than the Lutheran churches.

If in post-Reformation centuries there came about a weakening of the notion and realization of the Church and its functions, this must be attributed principally to pietistic and liberal currents. But in the course of the present century the "Reformed"

81

churches have found again in a great measure a balance between the personal and the ecclesiastical elements in their life of faith, and between the spiritual and the external aspects of the church.

Hence the new church order of the Dutch Reformed Church no less emphatically professes its continuity with the One, Holy, Catholic and Apostolic Church of the *Credo* than the Canon Law Revision of the Church of England:

The Dutch Reformed Church, in accord with her confession, [is a] manifestation of the One, Holy, Catholic or Universal Christian Church. . .[3]

The Church of England, established according to the laws of this realm under the Queen's Majesty, belongs to the true and apostolic Church of Christ.[4]

Both churches want to maintain the continuity of the national church with the Catholic, Universal, Universal-Christian Church of Christ, which is world-wide and dates from the first Pentecost.

It cannot be denied that that continuity is more clearly expressed in the Church of England and the other Anglican churches, namely, in the structure of their church and liturgy, than in most other reformational churches. Yet there is in this respect little difference from some churches of the Lutheran type.

As regards the "Reformed" churches we have only to read the fourth book of Calvin's *Institutio* concerning the functions of *episcopos, presbyteros* and *diakonos* in the Church of the first centuries. He speaks of the need for continuing the functions of those offices according to their original intention and practice. It appears clearly that, at least, it was not the intention of Calvin and of the "Reformed" churches to break the bond and continuity with the old Church but rather precisely to renew and

---

[3] *Kerkorde der Nederlandse Hervormde Kerk,* 's Gravenhage, 1951, p. 1, art. 1.

[4] *Canon Law Revision 1959,* p. 2, art. 1.

restore that continuity. However, Calvin looked upon those ancient Christian offices as having rather a local than a diocesan character.[5]

One sometimes hears the opinion that the Church of England has essentially and consciously preserved her continuity with the pre-Reformation Church that was established in England in 597 by St. Augustine of Canterbury, whereas the "Protestant" churches of the continent broke their continuity with the pre-Reformation Church. In reality, however, there is here merely a variation in emphasis which later became so pronounced that it seemed to constitute an essential difference.

It is principally due to the Anglo-Catholics in the Anglican churches—while in perfect good faith—that many Anglicans have formed a too one-sided idea of the Reformation and of continental Protestantism. Hence also, many non-Anglicans have formed a one-sided concept of the Church of England and Anglicanism that is not in accord with historical facts nor with official documents.[6]

3. THE REFORMATIONAL CHARACTER
OF THE ANGLICAN CHURCH

A significant example of the one-sided ideas about the Reformation that dominate Anglo-Catholic circles is the famous report, *Catholicity*, which fourteen prominent Anglo-Catholic theologians, among whom was the current Archbishop of Canterbury, presented to the then presiding Archbishop of that See.

---

[5] *Institutio christianae religionis*, ed. by Barth-Niesel, München, 1936, lib. IV, cap. 3–5, p. 42.
[6] Cf. *The Fulness of Christ*, London, 1950, a report produced by evangelical Anglicans, and *The Catholicity of Protestantism*, London, 1950, a report produced by a group of theologians of the Free Churches. Both were presented to the Archbishop of Canterbury in reply to the Anglo-Catholic report entitled *Catholicity*, Westminster, 1947. Concerning the intercommunion between Anglicans and Old Catholics, see Chap. 5, pp. 145 f. and 167.

On the part of both the so-called Free churches and of about seventy Evangelical-Anglican theologians, among whom was the present Archbishop of York, a second report was composed which rightly and very firmly combated the one-sided view about the Reformation expressed by the Anglo-Catholics and rejected it as being out of harmony with reality.[7]

It is a well-known fact that the Anglicans impress visitors from the continent as being but little aware of their connection with the Reformation and disliking to be reckoned among Protestants. It is therefore not surprising that ecumenically-minded Catholics and Protestants ask themselves what is the real attitude of the Church of England and the other Anglican churches toward the Reformation.

In reply, let us recall first of all that the king must, according to the Constitution, belong to the Church of England and on the occasion of his crowning must swear loyalty in accord with the question asked him: "Will you to the utmost of your power maintain in the United Kingdom the Protestant Reformed Religion established by Law?"[8] Secondly, the Anglican Church in the United States calls itself the "Protestant Episcopal Church." Those things show that there was a time when the Anglican churches took it for granted and accepted without difficulty that they were looked upon as Protestant.

Moreover, from the purely historical standpoint, it is certain for many reasons that the Church of England and the churches that have sprung from her must be reckoned as belonging to the family of Reformation churches. Cranmer, the first "Protestant Reformed" Archbishop of Canterbury, had been trained in the principles of the Reformation, at Wittenberg, by no less a man than Luther himself.

---

[7] Cf. the preceding footnote. The report *The Catholicity of Protestantism* contains a very illuminating explanation in Chapter Two, "The Concept of Catholicity and the Faith of Protestants," pp. 21 ff.

[8] Cf. *The Form and Order of the Coronation Service.*

The first phase in the history of the English Reformation was clearly marked with a Lutheran character. Traces of Lutheranism as well as Calvinism can be found in *The Thirty-nine Articles*. The Anglican *Book of Common Prayer* arose from a consistent application of Reformation principles.[9] Some of the authors were Calvinistically inclined, others were more under the influence of Zurich. Bucer, who in 1552 played a role in the revision of the original *Prayer Book* of 1549, was the expatriate reformer of Strassburg.

During the final stabilization of the Church of England under Elizabeth I, Lutheran-Melanchtonian and moderate-Calvinistic influences asserted themselves; and at the same time there were, in particular, close relations between Anglican bishops and the Swiss-reformed communities of Zurich and Bern.

Both *The Thirty-nine Articles* and the *Book of Common Prayer* have since remained fundamentally unchanged, with the exception of a few secondary changes introduced after the Restoration in 1662. Hence it would be difficult to deny that the Reformation exercised a profound and decisive influence upon official Anglican doctrine and liturgy, as these were given their definitive form and content in the sixteenth century.

Again, the preaching and the theological writings of the Anglican bishops and theologians of the sixteenth century were in no respect less reformational than those of the Reformation theologians of the mainland, in regard to religious climate and doctrinal content. When we carefully analyze the data taken from authentic sources, we are forced to conclude that the official teaching, the theology, the liturgy and church order of sixteenth century Anglicanism possess an interior unity and a harmonious wholeness that bear evident marks of the Reformation.

In regard to the official *Thirty-nine Articles*, we have pointed

---

[9] Cf. the author's *Der Weltprotestantismus*, Essen, 1960, pp. 174 ff.

out in a previous chapter that they are in perfect agreement with the Reformation in rejecting certain Roman doctrines and practices. But it is at least equally important to note that they also agree with the Reformation in their affirmation of the most essential doctrines and practices of the Reformation. This is evident especially in articles 9–21.

We find in these articles the theological and confessional expression of the sum total of what constitutes the true heart of the original and positive witness of faith of the Reformation. This witness of faith wished to be neither more nor less than a pure and faithful reproduction and explanation of the living Word of God and the Gospel of Jesus Christ, as it speaks directly to man from Holy Scripture.

If we wish to have a correct understanding of *The Thirty-nine Articles,* we must begin by making a clear distinction between the theological forms of expression that were tied to the particular time and the real, lasting content of faith. We do not mean that these two should be opposed to each other but only that they should be distinguished. We must not dwell on the theological form, for it is but a means, but should penetrate beyond it to the real content and core of the matter with which the Reformation and the authors of the *Thirty-nine Articles* were concerned.

According to its positive witness, the Reformation was concerned with the most profound problems regarding Christian faith and life. When Jesus sent His apostles into the world to announce the Gospel to all men until the end of time, it meant that mankind, in its sinful situation and existential want, could not and cannot be saved by anything except the Word, the Message that comes from God. Only through this Word does man learn to know God and himself; only by God's Word does he obtain a right view of the relation between God and man. This relation, in fact, rests entirely on the work of salvation accomplished once and for all by Christ.

86

It is always a question of announcing this Gospel in a living and life-giving manner. Both theology and the functions of the Church are at the service of the Gospel. When the means are raised to the rank of an end and thus are no longer capable of fulfilling their purpose, they lose their meaning and significance. Instead of being a guide to the Fountain of Life, they become an obstacle. What is most important in the life of every man is that he understand the Gospel, as the latter is intended, and that the Gospel be operative in his personal life as "the power of God unto salvation" (Rom. 1, 16).

The first and most important purpose of the Reformation was not to war against existing evils or to abolish abuses or discard a theology that was no longer of any use. In that case it would have had a purely negative character. The chief purpose of the Reformation was expressly positive in nature. It was designed primarily to restore to Holy Scripture the place in the preaching, the piety and practice of Church life which belongs to it as the Word of God.[10]

On the basis of Holy Scripture, the Reformation wished to give a new and positive witness regarding the most profound intention and the most essential content of the Gospel of Jesus Christ as the absolutely unique message that is capable of saving, redeeming and freeing man.

The Reformation secondarily protested against theological opinions and pious practices. These, it thought, were obstacles to the pure understanding of the Gospel and a life that was truly in accord with it. It was not interested, however, in protestation as such nor did it intend to produce a division in the Church. There is no doubt about it: the Reformation was not born from an individualistic, subjectivistic and separatist sectarian mentality. The Reformation was by nature eminently positive; it wanted to restore, to be constructive and generative. The degenerative

---

[10] Cf. Hendrikx, O.S.E.A., *De Heilige Schrift als Bron van Vroomheid in de Loop der Eeuwen,* Nijmegen, 1962.

forces which manifested themselves later in most Reformation churches had an essentially different origin.

All the Reformation churches, including also the Church of England, were the result of a purposeful and carefully thought-out attempt to give a new ecclesiastical form to the full riches of the Gospel in the structure, liturgy and confession of the Church. The Reformation was convinced that it was able to learn and understand this Gospel directly from Sacred Scripture as the only source of God's Word.

If the Reformation put full emphasis on the famous *"sola's"* (*sola Scriptura, sola fide,* and *sola gratia*—Scripture alone, faith alone and grace alone), this does not mean that its exclusivism was purely negative. On the contrary, it was intentionally positive. The Reformation most firmly warned all those who were in immediate danger of going astray in the labyrinth of self-chosen ways that there was only one way out. It pointed to the absolutely unique road to salvation, a way that passes solely through Jesus Christ and leads man back to God, an absolutely unique way of salvation created and indicated by God Himself that leads man from the state of sin, wretchedness and perdition to complete salvation and redemption.

The strong accent thus placed on the seriousness of sin does not allow us to call that view pessimistic, no more than we can accuse a surgeon of pessimism when he declares that the sickness of the patient is most serious and that it is only by a major operation that his life can be saved.

When we truly understand the profound meaning and purpose of the Reformation, there can be no doubt in our minds that the authors of the *Thirty-nine Articles* of the Church of England were likewise in full earnest on the side of the positive as well as exclusive witness that must be considered as constituting the original and fundamental object and intention of the Reformation.

If it is true that the authors of the *Thirty-nine Articles*—and of the *Book of Common Prayer* and the *Ordinale*—consciously and positively thought and lived on the basis of the most fundamental principles of the Reformation, it must also be admitted without any hesitation that the original, authentic and official sources of Anglicanism must be understood in a reformational sense.

This is not a matter of accidental and passing phenomena peculiar to some period of time; it is a question of the heart, the most essential content of the Gospel according to the witness of the Reformation. We are therefore forced to conclude that those official sources express the true nature of Anglicanism and that it is identical with the nature of the sixteenth century Reformation and of today's World Protestantism, insofar as the latter has truly remained authentically reformational.

It stands to reason that in the present chapter it is not possible to give a detailed description of the various positive facets and essential elements that characterize "The Witness of the Reformation." We refer for this matter to our work that has appeared under that title.[11] Neither can we indicate in detail which elements of the *Book of Common Prayer* and the *Thirty-nine Articles* originated in the Reformation. In regard to the *Thirty-nine Articles,* let us merely observe that they agree with the true intentions and positive content of the testimony of the Reformation in the following points:

1. The Gospel of Jesus Christ loses its deepest meaning and significance as long as sin is not taken with perfect earnestness; and if man lives under the illusion that he is able by his own powers to perform good works that are pleasing to God, in spite of the corruption of human nature; hence that he can by their means dispose himself for the work of salvation or can accomplish his own justification. Man, even as believer and as re-born, remains by nature inclined to every kind of evil; hence he must

---

[11] Cf. footnote one.

89

expect his salvation and redemption exclusively from what God in and through Christ has done for him.[12]

2. The *articulus stantis et cadentis ecclesiae,* the "article by which the church and its preaching stands or falls," as Luther says, is the article about justification by faith alone (*sola fide*):

> We are accounted righteous before God, only for the merit of our Lord and Saviour Jesus Christ by Faith, and not for our own works or deservings; Wherefore, that we are justified by Faith only is a most wholesome doctrine, and very full of justified comfort, as more largely is expressed in the Homily of Justification.[13]

3. The next article agrees with Luther's repeated declaration that he not only did not wish to disapprove or abolish good works, but that a man rather begins, of necessity, to produce good works from the moment that he believes truly and sincerely. It states:

> Albeit that Good Works, which are the fruits of Faith, and follow after Justification, cannot put away our sins, and endure the severity of God's Judgement; yet are they pleasing and acceptable to God in Christ, and do spring out necessarily of a true and lively faith; insomuch that by them a lively Faith may be as evidently known as a tree discerned by the fruit.[14]

4. Article Nineteen gives a typical reformational definition of the Church:

> The visible Church of Christ is a congregation of faithful men, in the which the pure Word of God is preached, and the Sacraments be duly ministered according to Christ's ordinance in all those things that of necessity are requisite to the same.[15]

No single church is free from error: "As the Church of Jerusalem, Alexandria, and Antioch have erred; so also the Church of Rome hath erred, not only in their living and manners of

---

[12] *The Thirty-nine Articles,* Art. 9, 10, 13.
[13] *Ibid.,* Art. 11.   [14] *Ibid.,* Art. 12.
[15] *Ibid.,* Art. 19a.

Ceremonies, but also in matters of Faith." Likewise the General Councils of the undivided Church "may err, and sometimes have erred, even in things pertaining unto God. Wherefore things ordained by them as necessary to salvation have neither strength nor authority, unless it may be declared that they be taken out of Holy Scripture."[16]

5. Article Twenty declares that Holy Scripture is the absolutely unique norm regarding what must of necessity be believed for salvation:

> Wherefore, although the Church be a witness and keeper of Holy Writ, yet, as it ought not to decree any thing against the same, so besides the same ought it not to enforce any thing to be believed for necessity of Salvation.[17]

The articles just quoted must therefore be interpreted, even on the mere basis of their content and theological wording, as having a positive and explicit reformational intention. And any doubt that might arise about that will be immediately dispelled if we reflect that the authors of those articles, as appears from their writings, sermons and letters, had with full conviction chosen the side of the continental reformers. There are innumerable facts that prove that the sixteenth century Church of England's religious thought and conduct, as well as its way of acting and the whole mentality that lay at its foundation, had a specifically Protestant character.

The sometimes fierce battle that was fought between Anglicanism and Puritanism was not a battle between Catholicism and Protestantism; it was fought with "Reformation weapons" on the soil of the Reformation. Even the so-called *Caroline Divines* of the seventeenth century, who are more or less unjustly regarded as precursors of modern Anglo-Catholicism, were fundamentally reformational in their thinking. For example, Chillingworth, who had as godfather no less a man than William Laud

---

[16] *Ibid.*, Art. 19b and 21. [17] *Ibid.*, Art. 20b.

the Archbishop of Canterbury who was beheaded in 1645, wrote a book called *The Religion of Protestants, a Safe Way of Salvation.*[18]

Thorough and extensive studies of the sources have been made in recent years, such as those of Horton Davies, the church historian of Princeton University, of Charles and Catherine George, and that of Carl Meyer. They have confirmed again the reformational and Protestant character of the Church of England and of the Anglican position. Moreover, recent publications in England likewise point to the same conclusion.[19]

Therefore, it seems hard to understand, in view of the clear evidence, how any one could doubt the reformational character of Anglicanism or even interpret the *Thirty-nine Articles* in a Catholic sense. However, we are now in the midst of an ecumenical dialogue concerning the relations between Rome and the Reformation. Great emphasis is now put on the things that unite, whereas the things that separate are reduced in part to misunderstandings and one-sidedness or else they are seen in the totally new light that is cast on the situation by modern exegetical and theological discoveries. Hence we understand more easily that irenic persons have tried to bridge the gap. They have tried, among other things, to prove that the *Thirty-nine Articles* can be interpreted in a Catholic sense and even that they are in

---

[18] First published in 1637. New editions London, 1719, and Oxford University Press, 1839. An excellent anthology of passages taken from a hundred seventeenth century Anglican theologians may be found in More and Cross, *Anglicanism, The Thought and Practice of the Church of England illustrated from the religious literature of the seventeenth Century,* London, 1935, 811 pages. This book contains important data concerning the disputations between the Anglican and Roman Catholic theologians of the time. In connection with the forthcoming ecumenical dialogue it would be very useful if someone were to publish a work evaluating this Roman Catholic-Anglican controversy.

[19] Horton Davies, *Worship and Theology in England,* 3 vols., Princeton, 1961; Charles and Catherine George, *The Protestant Mind of the English Reformation,* Princeton, 1961; Carl Meyer, *Elizabeth I and the Religious Settlement of 1559,* St. Louis, 1960. For other works see the Bibliography at the end of this book.

complete agreement with the declarations of the Council of Trent.

As early as the first half of the seventeenth century there were men like the Benedictine Dom Léandre, the Oratorian Panzani and the Franciscan Davenport who tried to interpret the *Thirty-nine Articles* in a Catholic sense in view of a *rapprochement* between Canterbury and Rome.[20] The discussions about an eventual Roman-Anglican *rapprochement* reached their end for a long time in the reply of William Wake, Archbishop of Canterbury, to Bossuet's *Exposition of the Doctrine of the Catholic Church.*[21]

As is well known, John Henry Newman in the famous *Tract 90* made a new attempt in 1841 to interpret the *Thirty-nine Articles* in a Catholic way; he was thus brought into conflict with the then Anglican Bishop of Oxford. It is even more remarkable that Newman after his entrance into the Roman Catholic Church continued to maintain that his Catholic interpretation, with the exception of Article Thirty-one, had been fully justified.[22]

It is possible that this should be explained by the fact that he was unacquainted with the sources of the continental Reformation and looked upon Protestantism as the religion of free inquiry and private judgment, in which there is no room for authority and tradition, for objectivity and catholicity.

In the long run, the attempt to make the official confessions and declarations say something other than what they originally

---

[20] Rouse-Neill, *A History of the Ecumenical Movement,* London, 1954, pp. 138 ff.; Nédoncelle, *Trois aspects du problème anglo-catholique au XVIIième siècle,* Paris, 1951, p. 95; Tabaraud, *Histoire critique des Projets formés depuis trois cents ans pour la Réunion des communions chrétiennes,* Paris, 1824, pp. 261 ff.

[21] Sykes, *William Wake, Archbishop of Canterbury,* Cambridge, 1957, Vol. I, Chap. 1, "Withstanding Peter to the Face," pp. 17 ff.

[22] In his work *Via Media,* Vol. 2, p. 351 (in Longmans ed.) Newman said in 1883: "The Tract as a whole I have been able to defend." Cf. the author's *Die Kirche im Leben und Denken Newmans,* Salzburg, 1937, pp. 252 ff.

intended, for the sake of helping the cause of reunion between the churches, will do more harm than good. That is why there is a danger in every pre-conceived attempt to interpret the *Thirty-nine Articles* in a Catholic sense; or even, contrary to the official sources and historical facts of the reformational milieu to which it belongs, to exile Anglicanism and give it shelter in a family of churches among which it will, at most, be an adopted child or rather will be looked upon as a stranger.

Such a method, instead of shedding light upon the ecumenical situation, can merely serve to obscure the view of it. It renders no service to the ecumenical movement nor to Anglicanism. The principal task and vocation of Anglicanism with respect to the restoration of Christian unity can, as we shall try to show in the final chapter, only be seen and understood when we get a true and precise view of the proper character of Anglicanism, and positively not if we give a wrong interpretation of it or try to reason it away.

4. The Anglican Dislike of Being Called "Protestant"

In today's ecumenical life we have to deal with contemporary Anglicanism. If what we have said until now about the origin and character of Anglicanism and the place of the Anglican churches among the churches that have sprung from the sixteenth century Reformation is correct, how can we explain that there are Anglicans who deny the reformational character of Anglicanism, who disguise it or—to the extent that there is evidence of it—at least regret it? And how is it possible that there are reformed Christians who do not recognize the reformational witness in Anglicanism and simply include the Anglican churches among the "catholic" churches?

To my mind there are many factors that have contributed to that false view. The reason must be found principally in the fact that it is in a struggle of almost a century against Puritanism that Anglicanism has acquired its typical features. Among these we may name the characteristically Anglican view of Holy Scripture, the undivided Church and her tradition, the positive value and meaning of the Reformation, the way the Reformation principles should be applied to church structure and liturgy and the character of a genuinely biblical piety and attitude of life.

This struggle was not a war between neighbors but between members of the same household who originally had accepted the Reformation principles with equal conviction and had the same meticulous grievances against Roman doctrine and practice. The struggle between Anglicanism and Puritanism was decidedly not about being for or against the Reformation. It was exclusively concerned with the manner in which the original and authentic principles of the Reformation should be applied to the practice of church life and the relations between church and state.

The Anglicans saw in Puritanism a one-sided, extremist, unbalanced and, in many respects, unscriptural application of the Reformation. They were convinced that Puritanism was farther removed from the actual intention and religious mentality of the Lutheran and Swiss reformers than the position and the methods of Anglicanism.

One striking difference between the Church of England from its first beginning and the other Reformation churches is the fact that it did not fasten itself to one distinct reformer. In the century from 1550 to 1650 there were among the Anglican bishops many convinced Calvinists, but also many who were either Lutheran or Melanchtonian, Zwinglian or more Biblical-humanistic in their opinions. The *Book of Common Prayer,* the *Thirty-nine Articles,* and also the *Ordinale,* show traces of the most varied Reformation origins.

Within this broad perspective Anglicanism also preserved a living interest in what was good in the pre-Reformation church.

In this respect the criterion was principally Holy Scripture; and next to it was the tradition of the undivided Apostolic Church, but explicitly only to the extent that that tradition did not diverge from the evident intention of Holy Scripture but merely clarified the latter.

From the very beginning until our own day a "Protestant underworld" has existed in England. Now and then, in season or out of season, this underground raises cries of "no popery" that bear no relation to any danger of Papism. Then there is the fact that in 1640 Puritanism got the upperhand in the Church of England and that it even won a complete victory from 1645 to 1660. The *Book of Common Prayer* was discarded, the Westminster Confession replaced the *Thirty-nine Articles,* William Laud the Archbishop of Canterbury and King Charles I were both beheaded and the episcopal church structure was replaced by a presbyterial order. We may add in passing that there was immediately a dispute about whether a presbyterian-synodal organization or a congregational-independent church structure was in conformity with the requirements of God's Word.

If that situation had continued, Anglicanism would be remembered only as a special form of reformational Christianity belonging to the dead past. However, the restoration of royalty and of the episcopal hierarchy in 1660, and the reintroduction of the almost unchanged *Book of Common Prayer* in 1662, re-established Anglicanism completely. At the same time, the Puritans left the Church of England for good and formed two "free" churches: the Presbyterian and the Congregational churches. It is clear that, from the Anglican standpoint, this was an advantage in the sense that the Church of England only then had the opportunity of realizing her specifically Anglican ideals.

It would be going beyond the scope of the present chapter to investigate what use she has actually made of that opportunity. In no way did the Restoration Settlement of 1662 signify a rapprochement toward Rome. It is more proper to say that after

1660 a certain latitudinarianism got the upperhand and that the doors of the Church of England were opened wide for a Platonic, liberal and rationalistic humanism.

The two great Revivals which the Church of England has known since that time were those of the Methodist Movement of the two Wesleys, which led to the formation of their own church around 1750, and the Oxford Movement that aroused a Catholic consciousness in the Church of England and resulted in a few conversions to the Roman Catholic Church around 1850.

Moreover, there are no trends, currents or movements that have appeared within the Church of England since the Reformation that have not left evident traces in the Anglicanism of today. This is the principal reason why foreigners and outsiders often find it so difficult to form a correct idea of the character of Anglicanism and to understand and justly appraise the positive value of the actions and omissions of the Anglican churches.

In any case, it is incorrect to hold that the Anglican Church is a conglomeration of the most diverse and contradictory dogmatic, liturgical and ecclesiological ideas. It is true that most Anglican churches have a number of parties, such as the evangelical and Anglo-Catholic, and in each again are found various nuances from the extremely orthodox to the most liberal. These are organized in various associations and an outsider might sometimes get the impression that the Anglican churches are on the point of breaking up into opposite camps. But to his astonishment the long foretold and, by some, even hoped for breakup and collapse does not come about.

The explanation for that puzzling phenomenon must be sought in the fact that an Anglican church is not a conglomeration of loosely connected and mutually contradictory sub-churches, low, high and broad, but rather a microcosm of the whole of Christianity. Outside Anglicanism we find separate types of Christianity but in an Anglican church all those types are found together.

97

Although they are not always combined in a harmonious unity, they are in a dynamic tension, attuned to one another in such a way that there is a possibility that someday a new synthetic unity will arise from those opposites.

This process is now in full swing within Anglicanism. The vast majority of the bishops, theologians, "low church" clergy and practicing faithful belong to the moderate Anglicans. These have succeeded in attaining a certain harmony in their thought, their belief, their worship and piety. This harmony is typically Anglican and has been able to integrate elements of diverse Christian origin into a new unity.

Especially since World War II, this so-called "central churchmanship" has enjoyed a very great development. It is more and more gaining the leadership in Anglican churches at the expense of the evangelical, Anglo-Catholic or modernistic-extreme groups which have isolated themselves from one another. Such an isolation of parties has in fact endangered Anglicanism during the first half of the present century. But this danger seems to have been overcome thanks to the still continuing growth of the ecumenical spirit. The more the moderate type of Anglicanism of "central churchmanship" develops, the more the Anglican Communion will grow in the direction of a prototype of reunited Christianity, and be recognized as such by other churches.[23]

The ultimate object to which the development of Anglicanism is directed is not a unity in which one specific type of church wins a victory over all other existing forms of Christian belief and life. The ultimate end is a unity of faith and church order, of liturgy and piety, of witness and service, which lacks no essential and valuable element that is contained in the full riches of God's Revelation and in the full meaning and functioning of Christ's work of salvation. The restoration of Christian unity cannot be achieved in any other way than by leading dispersed

---

[23] Ramsey, *An Era in Anglican Theology,* New York, 1960, pp. 168 ff.

Christianity back from a particular interpretation to the full truth, from a subjective insight to objective reality and from individual schemes to the project and intention of Christ.

This is the typical Anglican view, attitude and mentality, and it explains why Anglicans do not like to be called "Protestant." That is also why they prefer not to look upon the sixteenth century Reformation as a more or less absolute norm; they rather see it as a transitory episode in the history of their churches. For this reason also they look upon themselves primarily as members of the Universal or Catholic Church.

In this connection, one should keep in mind that the Anglican use of the terms "Protestant," "Catholic" and "Reformed" differs from the meaning these terms usually receive in other European countries. The reason is that things developed differently in England and on the continent, so that the history of Protestantism in England has a special character. In the Anglican mind those terms sound differently, they evoke other connotations and associations than in Protestants and Catholics of the European continent and the United States.

An Anglican is generally very sensitive to remarks that suggest that he is not Catholic. He wishes to be considered a Catholic. But this does not mean that his concept of Catholicism is identical with that which is usually met with elsewhere. His defensive gesture in the presence of such remarks that suggest that he is a Protestant must in no way be interpreted as meaning that even today his idea of Holy Scripture and the Gospel is not determined, and his spirituality is not influenced, by the Reformation.

We can safely say that the original Reformation principles still form the fibers of the many-colored Anglican canvas. They still continue to constitute the firm foundation and the hidden substratum of the Anglican's searching and groping in the ecclesiastical and religious field, even when he himself fails to notice it because of the centuries of estrangement from continental thought and life. Moreover, how could one explain the many relations which Anglican churches have maintained since the Reformation with the most diverse types of reformational churches, if they were not aware of any relation with them?

The defensive attitude toward Protestantism is principally connected with the fact that the Anglican churches have always had to fight against both Puritanical and sectarian tendencies. "Protestantism" makes Anglicans think of rigid dogmatism, liturgical vandalism, theological antagonism, sectarian individualism and subjectivism, and anti-churchism. It reminds him of excesses and one-sidedness of every sort, of a certain lack of erudition and gentlemanship, in short, of a whole complex of unpleasant memories and associations. That is why an Anglican dislikes to be regarded as a Protestant.

The term "Protestantism" has, at least for many Anglicans, gradually acquired an unpleasant sound in the ecclesiastical and religious history of England. It is affected by many unpleasant hereditary undertones. This may be one of the reasons for the great and patient tolerance which Anglicans have shown toward the extreme forms of Anglo-Catholicism that developed from the Oxford Movement of the last century, in spite of the fact that these forms are more foreign to the spirit of Anglicanism than are Puritanism and Methodism or any other movement which has not denied its connection with the Reformation.

It must now be evident that one should not try to force Anglicanism into a Catholic or Protestant corner, as has been done sometimes from both the Roman Catholic and the reformational sides. It is even more unjust to complain, as is also done, that Anglicanism itself does not know what it believes and aims at, that it vacillates between two ideas and wishes to make friends with everyone by compromising the truth. It is also a proof of little understanding when what Anglicans do or fail to do is attributed to a lack of logic and sincerity. All such ideas about Anglicanism show that many have been unable to

100

penetrate to the heart of the matter and have failed to understand Anglicanism as it actually is and wishes to be in the eyes of others.

5. THE LAMBETH CONFERENCES AND THE REFORMATION

After this phenomenological survey of the world of Anglicanism, let us return to the Lambeth Conferences. Their delegates travel in the most diverse directions to engage in conversations with any kind of church that is ready for such dialogues. We want to investigate now how the Lambeth reports illustrate the Anglican attitude toward the Reformation.

There is a sriking difference between the Anglican and the Lutheran or "Reformed" churches. The latter still continue repeatedly and insistently to appeal to the sixteenth century Reformation and its principles, whereas the Anglican churches seemingly forget them. We say "seemingly," for there are all kinds of indirect manifestations which show that the Reformation principles underlying the birth and development of Anglicanism are still at work in the words and deeds of the Anglican Communion of the present time.

The word "Reformation" appears only once in the Lambeth reports but, strange to say, it refers mostly to a few generally not extensive movements which are aimed at practices of the "Roman" Church in some "Catholic" countries, and not to the sixteenth century Reformation and its principles.

We saw in the preceding chapter that some Lambeth Conferences explicitly accepted a resolution in which sympathy was manifested toward such "Reformation movements." They had in mind countries like Germany, Switzerland, Austria and France, which had witnessed the birth of "Old Catholic" or "Christian-Catholic" churches or communities in full ecclesiastical communion with the "Old Catholics" of Holland and some small episcopal communities in Mexico, Spain, Portugal, Italy and Brazil, which broke away from the Church of Rome in the second half of the previous century.

A special commission, appointed for the purpose during the Lambeth Conference of 1897, gave a rather detailed report about the origin, the views and the size of those so-called "Reformation churches."[24] It is clear that none of those churches consider themselves "reformed" in the usual sense of the word.

We shall deal more fully in our chapter on "Ecumenical Relations" with the Old Catholic churches, with which the Anglican Communion, in the course of this century, reached an agreement of "full communion." The other "Reformation movements" no longer come under consideration in the Lambeth Conferences of the present century. However, resolutions were accepted in 1920 which reject an eventual intercommunion with the so-called "Old Catholic Church in Great Britain" and with the "Reformed Episcopal Church" in England. The reason was that the validity of the episcopal consecrations performed in those churches could not be accepted.[25] The Lambeth Conference of 1948, at the request of the churches involved, examined also the status of the "Spanish Reformed Episcopal Church" and the "Lusitanian Church of Portugal."[26] According to the Report of 1958 their status is exactly the same as that of the Old Catholic churches; and the Lambeth Conference of 1958 expressed the hope that it will reach the same relations with those new episcopal churches as exist with the Old Catholic churches.[27]

When we base ourselves exclusively on the resolutions of the Lambeth Conferences concerning the Old Catholic Church and related churches, we might be led to the conclusion that the Anglican churches evidently range themselves among the Catho-

---

[24] *The Six Lambeth Conferences*, p. 240.
[25] *The Lambeth Conference 1920*, p. 34.
[26] *The Lambeth Conference 1948*, II, p. 77 (Resolution 73).
[27] *The Lambeth Conference 1958*, II, p. 56 (Resolutions 51 and 52).

lic churches and not in the family of the Reformation churches. But such a conclusion would rest upon a one-sided view.

The Anglican churches have in fact formed relations with churches that, like the Church of England, have a reformational origin and which, moreover, have maintained their reformational character to the present day. But such relations by themselves do not prove that there exists a close relationship with the doctrine and the principles of the Reformation, as they find expression in the official denominational writings of the reformational churches.

However, such a relationship manifests itself at once in the statement of the ecumenical commission in 1888 concerning the Church of Sweden:

> As its standards of doctrine are to a great extent in accord with our own and its continuity as a national Church has never been broken, any approaches on its part should be most gladly welcomed with a view to mutual explanation of differences, and the ultimate establishment, if possible, of permanent intercommunion on sound principles of Ecclesiastical polity.[28]

This statement appears to be based on the supposition that the differences discussed therein are not fundamental ones, since both churches accept the same doctrinal norms. These then are clearly Reformation norms, for it could not be expected that the Church of Sweden would have replaced her Lutheran norms by "Catholic" norms.

The same follows also from a resolution of 1930 regarding the so-called "free churches":

> The Conference notes with satisfaction and gratitude the great measure of agreement on matters of faith reached at the Conferences held from 1921 till 1925 between representatives of the Church of England and representatives of the Federal Council of Evangelical Free Churches.[29]

---

[28] *The Six Lambeth Conferences,* p. 161.
[29] *The Lambeth Conference 1930,* p. 53 (Resolution 44).

Those Conferences had taken place at the same time as the unsuccessful Malines Conversations.

During the Lambeth Conference of 1948 the term "Reformation" appears for the first time in the sense of the sixteenth century movement. Yet the Anglican bishops seemed to hesitate about acknowledging a relationship, and still less an agreement, of what they call the "English Reformation" with the "Protestant Reformation." For, on the occasion of the merger of the Anglican, Presbyterian, Congregationalist and Methodist churches into the United Church of South India in September 1947, the ecumenical commission of the Lambeth Conference of 1948 remarked:

> For the first time since the great division of Christendom into Catholic and Protestant Churches an act of reunion between these two traditions has happened. . . . The Church of South India exists. . . . They have what they wanted. . . . In Madras on that September day a union was brought into being between heirs of the Protestant Reformation and a Church which retained the Catholic tradition as it is known in the Church of England.[30]

This text shows clearly that the churches of the Anglican Communion do not consider themselves to be heirs of the "Protestant Reformation" but, as appears in the report of the commission for affairs that concern the Anglican Communion, they look upon themselves as heirs of the "English Reformation": "We commence our report by emphasizing again the fact that the Churches of the Anglican Communion are Catholic in the sense of the English Reformation."[31]

What is meant here by "in the sense of the English Reformation"? If these words are understood as expressing a contrast with the Protestant Reformation, there would seem to be a danger of giving a false impression, when we compare them with the true content of the text and the rubrics of the *Book*

---

[30] *The Lambeth Conference 1948,* II, pp. 41 and 42.
[31] *Ibid.,* II, p. 83.

of Common Prayer and of the *Thirty-nine Articles,* as well as the principal works of Anglican theology that were written during the period of the Reformation.

One or more members of the ecumenical commission seems to have been aware of that danger. For, immediately after the passage quoted above concerning the reunion in South India, there follows a sentence which, in connection with the whole text, looks like a subsequent insertion into the original ecumenical report:

> We may rightly observe that the Church [the Anglican], which brings into its union the Catholic tradition, had already, in combination with it, the Evangelical tradition which had been rekindled by the Reformation.[32]

It would be very useful, in view of Christian unity, if all churches entering into relationship with the Anglican Communion insisted on an exact, explicit and detailed declaration not merely in regard to the formal intention, but above all regarding the material content of the expression "in the sense of the English Reformation." What precisely are those who belong to other churches to think regarding the nature, content and intention of Anglicanism, when the report of the commission on the Anglican Communion emphatically wishes to assure them that "they [the churches of the Anglican Communion] are Catholic but reformed; they are reformed but Catholics"?[33]

At bottom, is this really different from what all Reformation churches have always emphatically declared before they, to some extent, lost their church consciousness under the influence of pietism and liberalism? Can it not be said equally of all other Reformation churches, that they have wished to continue the pre-Reformation Church in their own countries, in a reformed and national form? Would they not, making the required adjustments, agree with the further remarks of the report: "The

---

[32] *Ibid.,* II, p. 42.   [33] *Ibid.,* II, p. 83.

105

English Reformers were not trying to make a new Church. It continued to be the Church of England, the *Ecclesia Anglicana*, as Magna Carta described it in 1215."[34] The Anglican Communion is not a sect. She is truly a part of the Catholic Church.

Are not all Lutheran and Reformed churches convinced of the fact that they really form a part of the universal Christian Church? Did not the Lambeth Conferences accept that the Swedish Church had preserved her national continuity? Why then is this not true also of other Reformation state or national churches, some of which have from the beginning preserved an episcopal structure?

Moreover, why choose the historical continuity of the Church structure as the sole standard for judging? Are the place and explanation of Holy Scripture, the concept of the authority of the Church and its confession, its teaching regarding the many matters that are at issue between Rome and the Reformation, the form and content of the liturgy, the practice of the sacraments, the devotion to the Blessed Virgin and the other saints, the spirituality and outlook on life of so little importance that they can add nothing to the case when there is question of determining whether a church is Catholic or reformational?

When the Anglican churches call themselves "Catholic," they positively do not mean it in a pre-Reformation and Roman Catholic sense, but fundamentally in the Reformation sense regarding all the points we have just mentioned. Is it then possible to maintain that the Church of England, as it has gradually reformed and stabilized itself after 1533, has in mind the same *Ecclesia Anglicana* as that of Magna Charta of 1215, when we consider her view of Holy Scripture, the Gospel, the Christian Faith and the nature of the Church? Is it possible to cling to such a view when the continuity is purely national, historical and canonical in regard to the Church's outward structure,

---

[34] *Ibid.*, II, p. 83.

whereas the Church of England was completely on the side of the Reformation in regard to all essential points of faith, liturgy and life, that led to the break between Rome and the Reformation? Is there no danger that the extremely important discussion concerning the place of the Church of England amidst the Christian churches will thus degenerate into a debate about the purely formal question of what meaning should preferably be attached to the words "reformed" and "Catholic"?

It stands to reason that the more extreme groups among Anglo-Catholics justly point out that they, in contrast with the other Anglicans and with "Protestants," try as much as possible to preserve conformity with the post-Tridentine Roman Catholic Church in doctrine, liturgy and church practice. They no doubt conceive the "English Reformation" in a Catholic sense. But the question is whether this is in accord with the real intention of the "English Reformation" and with the actual content of the text and the rubrics of the *Book of Common Prayer.* Is it not an occasion for great confusion when one tries to give the impression to other churches that Anglicanism must be interpreted in an Anglo Catholic sense?

The actual situation regarding the attitude and relation of Anglicanism to the Reformation seems, until now, to have been blurred in ecumenical discussions instead of being clarified. It is important for the success of the projects of reunion in which the Anglican churches are involved, and it is in the interest of the whole of Christianity in an ecumenical perspective, that the Anglican declarations should not confine themselves to more or less vague statements which can be interpreted in very diverse ways. What is needed is a complete and detailed clarification regarding the standpoint of doctrine and the real nature of the churches of the Anglican Communion.

As long as this important point is not cleared up, it is not surprising that both Protestants and Roman Catholics ask them-

107

selves whether the Anglican Church is sufficiently principled and straight forward when there is question of ecumenical conversations. This is so much more regrettable because we seem to be close to a confrontation between East and West and between Rome and the Reformation. It is becoming increasingly evident in the progress of the ecumenical movement that an unfalsified Anglicanism can prepare the way for other churches, precisely because its proper nature has prevented it from letting itself be seduced either by "pre-Reformation" or "Protestant" excesses.

At the same time, we must not remain blind to the fact that striking changes have taken place lately in the life of the Anglican churches. The Church of England is girding itself to loosen its centuries-old bond with the state and, in any case, to get rid of every kind of state interference which handicaps the interior life of the church.

The catholicizing tidal wave that has struck the Anglican churches since the Oxford Movement is now on the ebb. Anglo-Catholicism, as Ramsey puts it, impresses modern man as too romantic and unbiblical. The church feels called to stand in the midst of everyday life. She has discovered that many questions that have long occupied her are of minor importance in comparison with the question how modern man must be brought back to the Bible and how the Gospel must be preached if he is to understand the Glad Tidings.

Dr. Ramsey assures us in his latest book that Karl Barth has profoundly moved the Anglican churches and re-orientated them toward the Reformation: "Very few indeed were led to an interest in Barth's dogmatic theology: rather more were led to an interest in classical Reformation." As a result of the biblical and liturgical movements, he adds, "a new *milieu* of converse was appearing for Anglicans with Free Churchmen in this country, and with Lutherans and Reformed in other countries, as a result of theological development, within which Roman Catholics also had had their part."[35]

The "rediscovery of the Church in the Bible and of the Bible in the Church" is taking place everywhere in the Christian world. This on the one hand leads to a better general understanding of the meaning of the Reformation, and on the other hand opens very promising perspectives for an ecumenical rapprochement in the near future. The ultimate "mission of the Church cannot mean less than the whole Church bringing the whole Gospel to the whole world."[36]

---

[35] Ramsey, *An Era in Anglican Theology,* pp. 142 and 144.
[36] *The Lambeth Conference 1958,* II, p. 66.

CHAPTER FOUR

Appeal to All Christian People

1. ECUMENICAL REALISM

WHEN we survey the whole Christian *Ecumene*, it appears to be in a situation in which diverse Christian churches, all of which consider themselves to be true churches, bring the Gospel, each in its own way, to a world that is divided into many mission fields.

The germ of this situation, which was neither intended nor desired by Christ, was already present in the first Christian communities. On the occasion of division and threatening schism the Apostle Paul was obliged to ask the question: "Has Christ been divided up?"[1]

There is only one Christ, one Body, one Gospel, one Faith, one Baptism, one Bread and Chalice, one Kingdom, one World, one Mankind, one *Ecumene*. What, however, is the actual situation regarding the unity of Christians? To the questions of His disciples: "Sir, didst thou not sow good seed in thy field? How then does it have weeds?" Christ answered: "An enemy has done this."[2] This answer can also be applied to the ecumenical situation.

Not only the World but the Church also has, in the course of centuries and with respect to her human side, been the scene of destructive and disruptive forces of demonic origin. It is by

---

[1] Cor. 1:13.   [2] Matt. 13:27–28.

110

way of the heart of man, as Jesus explicitly said to His disciples, that the power of the evil one manifests itself in every society of men and also in the Church. We are all guilty. There is not a single church, great or small, old or young, degenerated or restored, which in some way or other has no guilt in respect to the existing ecumenical situation.

It is from this situation that we must start. Although we cannot resign ourselves to this situation, we must look at it with the utmost objectivity and realism. In this respect we cannot be too sober and realistic. We must not seek to absolve ourselves or our church and still less put all the blame on others. The rule which generally holds in all human situations applies in particular here: "All have sinned," all need God's forgiveness and mutual forgiveness, and all "are justified freely by his grace through the redemption which is in Christ Jesus."[3]

The complete restoration of the unity of all Christians is before all a matter of forgiveness, reconciliation and redemption. This means, among other things, that the unity will be restored only when all churches, in their human side, allow themselves to be shorn of their proud, self-satisfied and selfish ecclesiastical "Ego."

This applies also to the churches of the Anglican Communion. They know and realize it. The Lambeth reports have increasingly given expression of that realization. It is in the realization of their own guilt and shortcomings that the Anglicans' Lambeth Conference of 1920 sent out an urgent appeal to all Christians without distinction to strive practically and not merely theoretically for the restoration of Christian unity.

Hence the first thing we must note regarding the Lambeth Appeal of 1920 is that it was born from a pure and profound realism. It starts from the ecumenical situation as it actually exists. It asks itself what the situation in reality ought to be and

---

[3] Rom. 3:23–24.

tries to make practical suggestions concerning the way the situation intended by Christ can be restored and realized.

One who thinks that the Anglican churches are too "vague," that they do not know what they want and that they fall from one absurdity into another, looks at the ecumenical problem in a way that is too abstract, too one-sidedly intellectualistic and therefore too simplistic. We are dealing here with an extremely complicated reality which has come to us from the past and of which we ourselves form a part. We are dealing with a historically developed reality and with living human beings, not with abstract theses or positions and logical conclusions. We shall need, of course, much intelligence and common sense when we work together to heal the ecumenical situation, but intelligence and common sense alone will certainly be inadequate for the task.

The actual ecumenical situation is an inheritance from the past. To this inheritance belong treasures of truth, riches of wisdom and fruits of piety, which possess an imperishable value. It would be foolish, superficial and ungrateful to rashly repudiate the past and sacrifice it to the present and the future.

With this reservation we must also keep in mind that Christians are human beings who, as Newman used to say, are constantly on the lookout, because they look forward to the coming of the Kingdom and the Coming of Christ. A Christian is a man of the future. His life is directed to an ultimate goal. On that account he has to be saved daily from all past things, from "every encumbrance and the sin entangling us, and run with patience to the fight set before us."[4] That is why a Christian cannot be resigned to a situation transmitted from the past which is a burden and an encumbrance for the expansion of the Kingdom of Christ.

The ultimate goal, which has been kept in mind by the Angli-

---

4 Heb. 12:1.

can Communion from its first ecumenical efforts in the last century until now, is the proclamation and preaching of the one true Gospel by the one and entire Church to the one and entire world.

We have become conscious in our own century of the fact that the whole of mankind all over the world constitutes a united whole. All questions have acquired world-wide dimensions. Mankind in our time is in a very special way "in the pangs of travail." Straight through all calamities of war and revolutions there is a tendency to unification of mankind, to the unity of the entire world. The one and whole Gospel cannot be announced in this one and entire world with fruit and power of persuasion by a Christianity that is divided into many large or small churches. This positive conviction constitutes the background of the Lambeth Appeal of 1920, as well as that of the Declaration of Unity at New Delhi in 1961.

All ecumenical deliberations, inquiries and undertakings must be directed to that ultimate goal of the one and entire Church which truly functions in the world as an organic whole. That Church would signify the end of all isolated and sectarian attempts to lead one's own life and go one's own way, separated and independent from the total communion of the Christians who believe in Christ and have been baptized in Him. The offices and sacraments must function as offices and sacraments of the One Church, in which all ministers and all believers recognize one another as such and live with one another in practical and complete communion.

In this connection we must, it seems to me, be on our guard against two capital misconceptions. In the first place, it would be a serious misunderstanding if one were to confuse unity and "wholeness" with uniformity. The more pure, authentic and complete the sacramental unity, the more room there will be for differences in the forms of expression that are in accord with the revealed truth and the fullness of the Church.

113

Secondly, it would be an even more serious misconception if someone, on the basis of his personal view of faith, the Church, offices and sacraments, and disregarding the deepest convictions of large groups of Christians, were to think that he can and must insist on a sacramental intercommunion which offends the consciences of the many for whom essential truths of faith are involved in that matter.

It is true, indeed, that there are many churches which could accept "full communion" without any serious difficulty. I even believe that practically all churches that belong to the "Catholic" type can have full communion, just as all churches that belong to the "Reformation" type can have such a mutual communion. It is my earnest conviction that, in regard to "intercommunion," too many churches are too attentive to the past and too hesitant in taking the step toward intercommunion.

However, it would show lack of understanding and experience if someone thought that the ultimate end of the one and whole Church can be attained without any agreement about faith and solely by means of the common celebration of the Holy Eucharist. A complete and entire sacramental communion of all Christians and churches without distinction can result only from an agreement in faith. It must be attained by means of much prayer, patience and reflection.[5]

2. THE ECUMENICAL PRINCIPLES OF THE ANGLICAN COMMUNION

The Lambeth Appeal of 1920 did not drop out of a blue sky, but was the ripe fruit of a quarter of a century of systematic and purposeful explorations and discussions aimed in every direction and covering the widest possible ecumenical field.

The content, intention and aim of the appeal to all Christians without exception, that was made by the Anglican Communion

---

[5] *The Six Lambeth Conferences,* p. 114.

in 1920, can be correctly evaluated only when Anglicanism is seen in its true nature and interpreted on the basis of the ecumenical principles which guide the Anglican churches. Only misunderstanding and confusion will result if, in this respect, we start from Anglican ideas expressed by one or another extreme group instead of following the official formulations that enjoy the approval of the vast majority of the bishops of the Anglican Communion.

Moreover, it is safe to assume that this "common opinion" of the episcopate of the Anglican Communion is practically in accord with that of the majority of the clergy and laity in all Anglican churches. That is why it seems useful to give once more a brief summary of that "common opinion" concerning the nature and the ecumenical principles of Anglicanism.

The Lambeth Conferences from 1867 to 1920 occupied themselves more with organizational problems of the Anglican Communion than with the question of what specifically constitutes Anglicanism. However, the relations that were subsequently formed with churches of the Catholic type and of the Protestant type, raised all sorts of questions in those churches regarding the true nature and meaning of Anglicanism. This in turn made it necessary for the bishops to reflect together upon those questions in order to reply to those who were uncertain about Anglicanism.

That is why each of the Lambeth Conferences of 1930, 1948 and 1958 produced a detailed report about the Anglican Communion. This report contained a paragraph intended to explain and clarify the character of Anglicanism.

As we have mentioned in the preceding chapter, the Anglican self-examination has frequently raised new questions. The image the bishops gave of contemporary Anglicanism is evidently influenced by the wish—which after all is reasonable and commendable—of creating more order and harmony within the Anglican churches; on the other hand, it aims also at giving a

115

satisfactory answer to those whose questions reveal a feeling of discomfort.

It is important to note that the Lambeth Conferences understand Anglicanism primarily in a positive manner. They emphasize the fact that Anglicanism stands for both Catholic and Reformation; the Anglican churches consider themselves as being both Catholic and reformational. They want to preserve everything that was essential in the faith and practice of the undivided Church of the first ten centuries, and wish to restore anything of that kind that has been obscured during the crisis of the sixteenth century Reformation. At the same time, however, they desire to do full justice to the positive witness of the Reformation, and to make the gains produced by a renewed evangelical and reformational understanding of Holy Scripture permeate the preaching, the liturgy, the life of faith and practice of the Church.

The estrangement of continental Protestantism, on the one hand, and the growing influence of the Anglo-Catholicism born of the Oxford Movement, on the other, did disturb the characteristic equilibrium of Anglicanism to a certain extent. Anglicans in general, it seemed, found it easier to form a concrete image of the Catholic element than of the Reformation element in their religious life. As we remarked in the preceding chapter, the Anglican churches have, since World War II, shown a new interest in the true aim and concern of the Reformation. We can even speak of a new evangelical-Biblical enthusiasm. This interest will positively foster the contact with reformational and "free" churches, especially because these churches on their part are beginning to become more conscious of the positive value and meaning of the Catholic past.

The report of the commission of the Lambeth Conference of 1930 on matters concerning the Anglican Communion devoted a long consideration, divided into eleven sections, to the ideals

116

and the future of the Anglican Communion. From it we borrow the following quotations:

Our ideal is nothing less than the Catholic Church in its entirety. . . . The Anglican Communion includes not merely those who are racially connected with England, but many others whose faith has been grounded in the doctrines and ideals for which the Church of England has always stood.

What are these doctrines? We hold the Catholic Faith in its entirety; that is to say, the truth of Christ, contained in Holy Scripture; stated in the Apostles' and Nicene Creeds; expressed in the Sacraments of the Gospel and the rites of the Primitive Church as set forth in the Book of Common Prayer with its various local adaptations; and safeguarded by the historic threefold Order of the Ministry.

And what are these ideals? They are the ideals of the Church of Christ. Prominent among them are an open Bible, a pastoral Priesthood, a common worship, a standard of conduct consistent with that worship, and a fearless love of truth. Without comparing ourselves with others, we acknowledge thankfully as the fruits of these ideals within our Communion, the sanctity of mystics, the learning of scholars, the courage of missionaries, the uprightness of civil administrators, and the devotion of many servants of God in Church and State.

While, however, we hold the Catholic Faith, we hold it in freedom. Every Church in our Communion is free to build up its life and development upon the provisions of its own constitution. Local Churches (to quote the words of Bishop Creighton) have no power to change the Creeds of the Universal Church or its early organisation. But they have the right to determine the best methods of setting forth to their people the contents of the Christian faith. They may regulate rites, ceremonies, usages, observances and discipline for that purpose, according to their own wisdom and experience and the needs of the people.[6]

The ideals mentioned in this passage are not thought of as goals that are more or less unattainable and which one hopes at most to see realized in the distant future. They are ideals in the sense of being indispensable elements capable of serving as norms for a situation that may be considered "ideal," that is, satisfactory.

---

[6] *The Lambeth Conference 1930*, pp. 153 ff.

According to the Anglican view, such a religious situation must be characterized at least by an open Bible, a pastoral priesthood, a common worship and respect for the spiritual freedom of individual believers, local communities and national churches.

An open Bible is a Bible which can be read with an open mind by the faithful and whose interpretation is not in advance ecclesiastically determined in every detail. All pronouncements of the church remain at all times subject to the norm of God's Word as contained in Holy Scripture. There must always remain a free exchange between the individual and the common understanding of the Bible. God's Word must in no way be fettered; it must be unimpeded by ecclesiastical interpretations and prescriptions, and it must have the freedom to speak to every believer.

A pastoral priesthood is a priesthood in which the proclamation of God's Word, the administration of the sacraments and the entire public worship has a pastoral character and is in no way legalistic or moralistic. It is the exercise of a truly biblical and evangelical care of souls.

A common worship is a worship in which the priest, minister or preacher and the faithful appear together before God and engage in scriptural reading, prayer and song in such a way that there is no question of separation or even of opposition between the priest who exercises an active role and the "community" that is merely passive, or at most receptive. Common worship is a religious service that is conducted in the vernacular and not in an unintelligible ritual language. The service is also so simple and clear in structure and content that all the faithful are able to follow, understand and participate in it.

Individual freedom does not mean that the traditional and common element in the religious and ecclesiastical life can be dispensed with and that it cannot serve as a norm, having moral authority in certain respects. Individual freedom means that in the long run every believer must decide personally and according to his own conscience whether and to what extent he feels bound by pronouncements and prescriptions whatever their ecclesiastical origin. There exists no infallible authority outside or alongside the direct voice of God's Word in Holy Scripture.

The ministers are servants of God's Word, servants of Christ, servants of the whole Church; and neither the Church nor the servants of the Church may exercise tyranny over the consciences of the faithful. The freedom that is here spoken of is not the humanistic freedom of liberalism, but, according to Anglican ideas, it is the freedom of the children of God, the freedom by which Christ has liberated all who believe in Him and which St. Paul, particularly in his epistle to the Galatians, defends as an inalienable privilege and precious possession of the believer.[7]

The four "ideals" of the open Bible, the pastoral priesthood, the common worship and Christian freedom must without any doubt be considered characteristic fruits of the Reformation. In this respect there is no difference between a Protestant and an English Reformation, and the Anglican churches continue to live together with all reformational churches on the patrimony of the Reformation.

Starting from the report of the commission for the matters that concern the Anglican Communion, the Lambeth Conference of 1930 took the following resolutions:

The Conference approves the following statement of the nature and status of the Anglican Communion, as that term is used in its Resolutions: The Anglican Communion is a fellowship, within the One Holy Catholic and Apostolic Church, of those duly constituted Dioceses, Provinces or Regional Churches in Communion with the See of Canterbury, which have the following characteristics in common:

a. They uphold and propagate the Catholic and Apostolic faith and order as they are generally set forth in the Book of Common Prayer as authorized in their several churches;

b. They are particular or national Churches, and, as such, promote

---

[7] Gal. 4:5 ff.

within each of their territories a national expression of Christian faith, life and worship; and

c. They are bound together not by a central legislative and executive authority, but by mutual loyalty sustained through the common counsel of the Bishops in conference.

The Conference makes this Statement praying for and eagerly awaiting the time when the Churches of the present Anglican Communion will enter into communion with other parts of the Catholic Church not definable as Anglican in the above sense, as a step towards the ultimate reunion of all Christendom in one visibly united fellowship.[8]

The last paragraph contains a clear formulation of the ecumenical point of view and aim of the Anglican churches. They look upon the unity and fellowship already attained and fully practiced within the Anglican Communion as a provisional first step which works in the direction of a unity and fellowship that will gradually extend to non-Anglican churches. The ultimate goal will be attained only when all churches are incorporated into the unity and full communion of one only, visible, "fellowship." That is why the ecumenical endeavor of the Anglican churches aims at attaining what is presently called "full communion" with a gradually increasing number of non-Anglican churches.

Three fundamental principles lie at the foundation of the ecumenical thought and action of the Anglican churches, and practically every Lambeth Conference expresses them in one or another form. They are the following:

1. It is a datum of revelation that Christ willed and intended that His Church on earth should be a single fellowship, that in it the unity and fellowship of all Christians without distinction should be a clearly visible reality, and that this unity and fellowship should be evident to the whole world. This visible unity and fellowship has been lost to a great extent through church divisions. It still exists in the communion of affiliated churches.

---

[8] *The Lambeth Conference 1930*, Resolution 49, p. 55.

The purpose of the ecumenical movement is nothing less than the complete restoration of the visible unity and full communion of all Christians.

2. Although it stands to reason that the restoration of visible unity and full communion will be more easily achieved between churches that have the same confession and structure, it is nonetheless necessary that, when plans are made for reunion or put into execution, the ultimate goal should receive first consideration, namely, the ultimate restoration of the unity of all churches and the full communion of the whole of Christianity. That is why it is necessary to take account of the positive contributions of all churches toward the realization of that ultimate end. Churches that are closely related with one another should avoid fostering their own unity and making commitments for the future which would jeopardize the unification of all Christians.

3. The ecumenical outlook should therefore be as wide as possible. This means that no project of reunion can be satisfactory if it does not take into consideration the greatest church, the church in communion with the See of Rome, the Latin Communion, or the Roman Catholic Church. Every ecumenical step taken in the direction of the complete restoration of the visible unity must begin with the wish and endeavor of involving that church in the full communion of all Christians.

It is my experience that many Roman Catholics in England tend primarily to assume a negative and critical attitude toward those principles and toward the Anglican proposals and projects that are based on them. They start from the conviction that the visible unity and fellowship of the true believers is already fully realized in the one true church that is in communion with the See of Rome; and it seems to them that, on that account, there is no room for any other response on their part than that of refusal or rejection in respect to Anglican ecumenism.

The reaction of Roman Catholics to the Anglican appeals

would be quite different if they started from the consideration of the actual state of division of Christians, whatever might have been the cause, and from the fact that Anglicans are baptized Christians who believe in Christ and are convinced that they belong to the Church of Christ. If the Roman Catholic keeps this in mind, then precisely because he is a Roman Catholic Christian, he will realize that the existing division is contrary to Christ's will and intention, and he will rejoice with all his heart whenever he witnesses an earnest endeavor to restore the unity that has been lost for such a length of time.

The Anglican Communion is as firmly convinced as the Church of Rome that she is a "church" in the full and true sense of the word. Hence if one of the two churches constantly refuses to recognize the other as a true "church," this will merely lead to a greater estrangement instead of a rapprochement.

It stands to reason that each church starts her ecumenical thinking and striving from her own principles and convictions. These should in no way remain unexpressed. However, their acceptance should not be *a priori* presented to other churches as a prerequisite for rapprochement and reunion; but they should be discussed together in an open and free dialogue.

The churches will not be able to work together advantageously for the restoration of the lost unity and fellowship if they do not have a sincere interest in one another's religious convictions and intentions, if they are not ready to listen with attentive openness to one another's arguments and eventual grievances in a true and existential encounter.

The ecumenical method is essentially different from the polemical and apologetic method that has been used for centuries. All the churches that follow the ecumenical method, however firmly convinced they may be of the truth of their own views, wish to find the other churches where they actually are and not where, according to their own opinion, those other churches ought to be. When the churches establish this kind of encounter, they then seek together for the answer to the question what Christ's will and intention are in regard to the visible unity and fellowship of all Christians.

As early as 1908 the encyclical of the Lambeth Conference pointed out that "there is no subject of more general or more vivid interest than that of Reunion or intercommunion."[9] It emphasized that a period of preparation will be necessary before its realization:

> This preparation must be made by individuals in many ways, by co-operation in moral and social endeavour and in promoting the spiritual interests of mankind, by brotherly intercourse, by becoming familiar with one another's characteristic beliefs and practices, by the increase of mutual understanding and appreciation. All this will be fruitful in proportion as it is dominated by a right ideal of reunion.[10]

The encyclical then uses a sentence which can serve as a suitable introduction to our study of the Lambeth Appeal of 1920:

> We must set before us the Church of Christ as He would have it, one spirit and one body, enriched with all those elements of divine truth which the separated communities of Christians now emphasize severally, strengthened by the interaction of all the gifts and graces which our divisions now hold asunder, filled with all the fulness of God.[11]

In my opinion it will certainly be a gain for the whole of Christianity if various churches, in obedience to God's Word and the guidance of God's Spirit and in a united effort, try to discover anew in its inviolate totality the fullness of the Church and the riches of all that lies enclosed in God's Revelation. No church in this endeavor has to give up anything that God has granted her. But also, no church may in advance refuse to "learn" from other churches or to let them enrich her by what she has missed on account of her separation. For we are here

---

[9] *The Six Lambeth Conferences,* p. 313.
[10] *Ibid.,* pp. 314 ff.   [11] *Ibid.,* pp. 314 ff.

concerned with no less a matter than the complete restoration of the visible unity and communion of all Christians in the one Church of Christ "which indeed is his body, the completion of him who fills all with all."[12]

This ecumenical vision prompted the Lambeth Conference of 1920 to make the Lambeth Appeal, an urgent call to all churches without any distinction to engage in mutual cooperation for the eventual attainment of the restoration of Christian unity. No ecumenical cooperation will have lasting value and significance unless it is helpful for the restoration of the unity in both the biblical and the catholic sense. When this is not the case, so-called ecumenical undertakings will risk drawing attention away from what constitutes the essential aim and, thus, slowing up the process of reunion instead of fostering it. The realistic sense that is proper to the Anglicans has always preserved them from a sham-ecumenism that tries to evade giving a concrete answer to the question concerning the restoration of visible unity.

3. THE LAMBETH APPEAL OF 1920

The bishops gathered in the Lambeth Conference of 1920 prefaced their "Appeal to all Christian people," by calling themselves "Bishops of the Holy Catholic Church in full communion with the Church of England." In this way they put themselves on a level with "Bishops of the Holy Catholic Church" who belong to another Church Communion and live in full communion, for example, with the Church of Rome or with the Church of Constantinople. However, they do not address themselves to these churches as such nor do they exclude any particular churches. They address themselves to *all Christian people,* irrespective of the church they belong to. It will be the task of individual Christians, both ministers and all other faith-

---

[12] Eph. 1:23.

ful, to stir up the church to which they belong and prompt her to march on the road that will lead to complete Church reunion.[13]

In the second paragraph of the Introduction, the bishops formulate the starting-point from which, in their opinion, an endeavor for reunion must begin. This starting-point consists in the acknowledgment of "all those who believe in our Lord Jesus Christ, and have been baptized into the name of the Holy Trinity, as sharing with us membership in the universal Church of Christ which is His Body." On this basis all baptized Christians are able to discover and encounter one another.

The fact of being baptized means that the division among Christians does not penetrate to the foundation, but is in a certain sense only superficial. Essentially and fundamentally all Christians, whatever particular church they may have been baptized in, are already, according to official Anglican conviction, really and sacramentally united with one another in the Body of Christ, in the One Holy Catholic and Apostolic Church which is professed in the *Credo*.

If all Christian churches could agree with one another on that fundamental point, it could serve as a true starting-point for an ecumenical rapprochement, dialogue and ultimately complete visible unity in church structure and Christian confession. The foundation, motive and meaning of the ecumenical endeavor lies in the fact that Christians are already "one" by their faith and baptism. Every form of disunion and division is in conflict with that unity. The Christians of all churches, on the basis of that unity which fundamentally is already a fact, must deliberate together regarding the causes of disunion and the means of overcoming the obstacles and attaining re-union. In particular, the question should be discussed why Christians can in their personal relations consider one another true Christians when at

---

[13] For the full text of the Lambeth Appeal, see below pp. 277 ff. In the quotations from the Appeal made in the subsequent pages we will not explicitly refer each time in a footnote to this Appeal.

the same time the churches are unable to consider one another as churches in the true sense of the word. What changes must be introduced in the structure and functioning of the churches in order that all churches may recognize and accept one another as representatives and parts of the One Church of Christ?

The Introduction ends with the words:

> We believe that the Holy Spirit has called us in a very solemn and special manner to associate ourselves in penitence and prayer with all those who deplore the divisions of Christian people, and are inspired by the vision and hope of a visible unity of the whole Church.

The vision and hope is then explained and developed in nine paragraphs.

1. The bishops start from the conviction that "God wills fellowship." He does not want men to live in isolation alongside or in opposition to one another. What is meant by "fellowship" is perhaps best expressed by saying that God wills that men should constitute one family, one people and act toward one another as such. We could also translate that idea by saying that God wills unity, concord and communion.

This unity and communion is already a reality:

> By God's own act this fellowship was made in and through Jesus Christ, and its life is in His Spirit. We believe that it is God's purpose to manifest this fellowship, so far as this world is concerned, in an outward, visible, and united society, holding one faith, having its own recognized officers, using God-given means of grace and inspiring all its members to the world-wide service of the Kingdom of God.

This is the ideal of the Catholic Church. This is the way the Church in the midst of the world should clearly manifest itself to everyone. In this sense, however, the Catholic Church is as yet only a project and an ultimate goal. As long as divisions continue to exist among Christians, the Church cannot manifest itself in the world in the way God wills it and in the way He has revealed His will and purpose in and through Christ.

126

2. In the second paragraph the bishops give a brief description of the existing division. They distinguish two large groups of churches—here called "communions" because the bishops wish to leave out of consideration the question whether these communities can consider themselves to be churches or not— namely, episcopal and non-episcopal communions. It stands to reason that the bishops of the Anglican churches reckon themselves as belonging to the first group. "There are other ancient episcopal Communions in East and West, to whom ours is bound by many ties of common faith and tradition." But the bishops declare with no less emphasis that they are in close relationship with the great non-episcopal communions.

There are the great non-episcopal Communions, standing for rich elements of truth, liberty and life which might otherwise have been obscured or neglected. With them we are closely linked by many affinities, racial, historical and spiritual. We cherish the earnest hope that all these Communions, and our own, may be led by the Spirit into the unity of the Faith and of the knowledge of the Son of God. But in fact we are all organized in different groups, each one keeping to itself gifts that rightly belong to the whole fellowship, and tending to live its own life apart from the rest.

Typically Anglican is the great attention paid to the external church structure, as well as to national, historical and spiritual characteristics. Dogmatic and theological causes of division are much less stressed in Anglicanism than in other churches, be they "Catholic" or "reformational."

3. In the third paragraph the bishops candidly express their opinion regarding the causes of disunity:

The causes of division lie deep in the past, and are by no means simple or wholly blameworthy. Yet none can doubt that self-will, ambition, and lack of charity among Christians have been principal factors in the mingled process, and that these, together with blindness to the sin of disunion, are still mainly responsible for the breaches of Christendom. We acknowledge this condition of broken fellowship to be contrary to God's will, and we desire frankly to confess our share

127

in the guilt of thus crippling the Body of Christ and hindering the activity of His Spirit.

Thus far the actual situation. It would be a great gain if the Christians of all churches were willing to look at the situation honestly and with an open mind to see it as it really is; if they realized that they share in the common guilt; and, in spite of their different views about the proper remedy, if they could agree about the diagnosis of the deadly illness of a divided Christianity. Only a clear diagnosis will offer a chance of finding the suitable remedy. Any sort of ostrich-like policy in ecumenical matters acts as an impediment and will sooner or later lead to disappointment. It is impossible to take too serious a view of the situation, provided the earnest concern gives rise to the firm resolution not to remain resigned but to make every effort to obtain a cure. The important point is not to be full of ecumenical enthusiasm but to do concrete ecumenical deeds.

4. The fourth paragraph puts the ecumenical endeavor in the frame of our own times. The present generation is witnessing profound changes in every field. That is why people presently ask for a new vision and new measures. As long as the Body is divided, it is unfit for the task of awakening Faith in our contemporaries, of spreading the Kingdom of Christ:

> The times call us to a new outlook and new measures. The Faith cannot be adequately apprehended and the battle of the Kingdom cannot be worthily fought while the body is divided, and is thus unable to grow up into the fullness of the life of Christ. The time has come, we believe, for all the separated groups of Christians to agree in forgetting the things which are behind and reaching out towards the goal of a reunited Catholic Church. The removal of the barriers which have arisen between them will only be brought about by a new comradeship of those whose faces are definitely set this way.

> The vision which rises before us is that of a Church, genuinely Catholic, loyal to all Truth, and gathering into its fellowship all "who profess and call themselves Christians," within whose visible unity all the treasures of faith and order, bequeathed as a heritage by the past

to the present, shall be possessed in common, and made serviceable to the whole Body of Christ.

There is need for a radical change and reversal in the way of judging the faith, the worship, the practice, in short the existence and the life of other churches. During the polemical era, any church that differed from one's "own" church was rejected in advance and often without being understood. On the contrary, one of the chief characteristics of the new ecumenical period is the fact that the churches are growing in respect for one another and question each other. This is done not for the sake of getting means to attack the other but for the sake of completing and enriching one's "own" church. The churches must be willing to learn from one another what is essential for the reunited Church and, in regard to accidental points, to leave room for as much variety as possible.

5. As is true of all great and worthwhile things, here also with respect to the realization of that vision we are engaged in, is a venture, "an adventure of goodwill and still more of faith, for nothing less is required than a new discovery of the creative resources of God. To this adventure we are convinced that God is now calling all the members of His Church."

6. The bishops are not satisfied with a general appeal for rapprochement, dialogue and reunion. They have also asked themselves which elements ought to be incorporated in the re-united Church on the basis of tradition and the experience of twenty centuries of Church and Christianity. Those elements are not presented as conditions, but merely as objectively established facts. The bishops did not ask themselves which conditions Anglicans consider essential and are, therefore, to be fulfilled by other churches before the latter can receive recognition. They went to work not in a dogmatic but a historical way. They were of the opinion that every unprejudiced Christian of good will is able to realize that there are four universal-Christian elements that have a lasting significance and without which a reunited

129

Church is unthinkable and impossible. These four elements, which sometimes are called the "Lambeth Quadrilateral," are enumerated in the Lambeth Appeal. What interests us most here, however, is not their mere mention but the way in which they are described:

> We believe that the visible unity of the Church will be found to involve the whole-hearted acceptance of:
>
> The Holy Scriptures, as the record of God's revelation of Himself to man, and as being the rule and ultimate standard of faith; and the Creed commonly called Nicene, as the sufficient statement of the Christian faith, and either it or the Apostles' Creed as the Baptismal confession of belief:
>
> The divinely instituted sacraments of Baptism and Holy Communion, as expressing for all the corporate life of the whole fellowship in and with Christ:
>
> A ministry acknowledged by every part of the Church as possessing not only the inward call of the Spirit, but also the commission of Christ and the authority of the whole body.

Some have interpreted the Lambeth Quadrilateral as a result of a process of subtraction, in which the characteristics of a Church and a Christian are reduced to a minimum, or also as an intentionally vague statement which neither binds nor obliges anyone. Such critics fail to understand and wrongly interpret what the bishops of the Anglican Communion wanted to say and the line of thought they had in mind.

The bishops were thinking, not of their own church, but of the whole of the Church. They asked themselves what elements were considered necessary, characteristic and sufficient for the fullness and genuineness of being-a-church and being-a-Christian during the first centuries and before divisions of the Church had begun. These church divisions, including the one between Rome and the Reformation, differed essentially from the heresies of the first centuries that led to the formation of individual churches. The latter meant a break with the Catholic Faith, whereas the later divisions were precisely the result of endeavors

130

to purify the Church and to restore her according to the original standards of Catholic faith and Catholic practice.

By the fact that the Anglican churches, as well as the other Reformation churches, recognize the ancient Christian *Credo's,* and in particular the so-called Confession of Nicea, they have placed themselves on the side of the Catholic Church and against all errors with which the latter had to fight for her existence during the first centuries. That is why the Anglican Communion believes that the starting-point, the basis and standard must be sought in the ancient and undivided Church.

As is evident from the following paragraph, the bishops when dealing with the offices in the reunited Church, in the fourth point, had in mind the threefold office of bishops, priests (presbyters) and deacons. However, they did not wish to foreclose the discussion between episcopal and non-episcopal churches, but merely wished to stress the fact that reunion will have to pay attention also to the question of what conditions must be fulfilled by the offices, the ministers and their functions in order to win the recognition of the whole Church.

The first project of the Lambeth Quadrilateral came from the Protestant Episcopal Church of America. Already in 1888 it was adopted by the whole Lambeth Conference as the basis for an eventual reunion in English-speaking countries, the so-called "Home Reunion." The formulation of the four points was then somewhat different. Thus in the fourth point, there was a mention of the "historic episcopate":

1. The Holy Scriptures of the Old and New Testaments, as "containing all that is necessary for salvation," and as being the rule and ultimate standard of faith.

2. The Apostles' Creed, as the Baptismal Symbol; and the Nicene Creed, as the sufficient statement of the Christian faith.

3. The two Sacraments ordained by Christ Himself—Baptism and the Supper of the Lord—ministered with unfailing use of Christ's words of institution, and of the elements ordained by Him.

131

4. The Historic Episcopate, locally adapted in the methods of its administration to the varying needs of the nations and peoples called of God into the Unity of His Church.[14]

7. In our seventh and ninth chapters we shall examine in greater detail the questions regarding the offices and church structure and the reasons that prompted the Anglican bishops to give preference to the term "historical episcopate." In the seventh paragraph of the Lambeth Appeal, the bishops already give a provisional explanation of it, seemingly in order to forestall some objections that might be offered:

> May we not reasonably claim that the Episcopate is the one means of providing such a ministry [namely recognized by the whole Church]? It is not that we call in question for a moment the spiritual reality of the ministries of those Communions which do not possess the Episcopate. On the contrary, we thankfully acknowledge that these ministries have been manifestly blessed and owned by the Holy Spirit as effective means of grace.

Roman Catholic critics have often thought that there is here a certain amount of contradiction. On the one hand, they say, the Anglicans consider an episcopal church order as a necessary and essential condition for an eventual reunion with non-episcopal churches; on the other hand, in their desire to approach the latter, they say that an episcopal church order is really not necessary since the offices and services in non-episcopal churches are equally recognized, blessed and used by the Holy Spirit. Extreme groups of Anglo-Catholics agree with that criticism, but it is connected with a dogmatic point of view that is wholly foreign to official Anglicanism. The Anglican bishops do not reason from the standpoint of dogmatic positions; they start from historical facts. They do not doubt that the Holy Spirit is like a "wind [that] blows where it will"[15] and like a spirit who uses any means that the Christian believers in good faith

---

[14] *The Six Lambeth Conferences,* pp. 122, 158.
[15] John 3:8.

and with sincere prayer make use of because they are convinced that this is the way Christ willed it.

The Anglican bishops do not wish to pronounce a judgment on the efficacy of the offices of other churches, save insofar as it can be done in a favorable sense when that efficacy is clearly manifested. However, they also want to ask the non-episcopal churches whether they are not convinced, on the basis of historical considerations, that reunion of the churches will not be possible unless all cooperate and help fully to restore in the reunited Church the apostolic offices that originally existed in the undivided Church. One cannot expect the churches that have preserved the apostolic offices until now to take a step backward for the sake of reunion; nor can one demand that in a reunited Church they be satisfied with a church structure and offices which do not preserve the continuity with the Church of all centuries.

8. For the vast majority of Christians this is a matter of conscience. The Church is not a human organization but a mystical and supernatural Reality that, from the first beginnings, continues through the centuries to the Day of Christ's Final Coming, precisely by means of offices and sacramental ministrations. When the fullness of the offices and the ministrations suffered loss as a result of grievous crises, it stands to reason that all churches desiring reunion—even were it merely "by way of deference to one another's consciences"—should cooperate in a complete restoration of the offices and ministrations as these were known in the undivided Church and have been preserved by many church communions up to our own times.

That is why the bishops in the following paragraph propose some practical measures in order to prevent hurting the consciences of some at the moment of reunion, either because of their "Catholic" or their "Reformation" inheritance. In particular, the bishops say all should be on their guard against expecting or demanding that others should renounce their former ministries for the sake of reunion:

133

God forbid that any man should repudiate a past experience rich in spiritual blessings for himself and others. Nor would any of us be dishonouring the Holy Spirit of God, whose call led us all to our several ministries, and whose power enabled us to perform them.

The reunited Church will be a very wide communion in which also the offices and ministrations of the churches that, after living in isolation, have been incorporated in the total Church communion are now united in a wider bond. The reunion with the whole Church will in a certain sense signify for the ministers concerned a "new call to wider service in a reunited Church."

The Anglican bishops, however, did not want to impose their solutions upon other churches. The sole purpose of their appeal was to offer a few practical and concrete suggestions in order to prevent their appeal being considered a purely speculative, abstract and theoretical document.

9. Finally, the Anglican bishops also pointed out that an actual reunion of all concerned will necessarily require of them one form or another of adaptability and willingness to adjust themselves, as well as other sacrifices. Every church and Christian will have to pay a greater attention to the interests of the whole communion of the reunited Church than to the familiar and cherished practices inherited from their own church. Without a true spirit of sacrifice and self-renunciation, reunion will remain a mere pious wish which will never attain fulfillment:

The spiritual leadership of the Catholic Church in days to come, for which the world is manifestly waiting, depends upon the readiness with which each group is prepared to make sacrifices for the sake of a common fellowship, a common ministry, and a common service to the world.

We place this ideal first and foremost before ourselves and our own people. We call upon them to make the effort to meet the demands of a new age with a new outlook. To all other Christian people whom our words may reach we make the same appeal. We do not ask that any one Communion should consent to be absorbed in another. We do ask that all should unite in a new and great endeavour to recover

and to manifest to the world the unity of the Body of Christ for which
He prayed.

4. DISAPPOINTING RESULTS

Almost a half century has gone by since the bishops of the
Anglican Communion appealed to all Christians to labor with
zeal and speed for the realization of the Christian unity that is
so urgently necessary.

Except in England, the reaction to their appeal was not en-
couraging. After the failure of the unofficial Malines Conversations (1921–1925) under the leadership of Cardinal Mercier
and Lord Halifax, Pope Pius XI in his Encyclical *Mortalium
animos* expressed the Roman Catholic Church's rejection of the
non-Catholic endeavor for reunion, although he made no allu-
sion to the Anglican Lambeth Appeal. The Most Reverend
Randall Davidson, who resigned as Archbishop of Canterbury
in 1929, felt obliged to lament and say in his last discourse
before his death: "No helpful word or act comes from the City
of the Seven Hills." The Eastern Orthodox Churches assumed
a benevolent attitude of "wait and see."

The Anglicans met at first with the best understanding in the
Faith and Order Movement. However, as early as 1927, the
Anglican chairman of the World Conference of Lausanne, the
American Bishop Charles Brent, manifested his disappointment.
Dr. A. C. Headlam,[16] who was then Bishop of Gloucester, was
without doubt the most resolute and formidable defender of the
Anglican plan of reunion during the years that elapsed between
the Conference of Lausanne and the Conference of Edinburgh in
1937. It is due to him that the Faith and Order Movement was
granted a more or less independent place at the formation of
the World Council of Churches in 1948.

---

[16] Ronald Jasper, *Arthur Cayley Headlam, Life and Letters of a Bishop,*
London, 1960, pp. 267 ff.

The Anglican influence has slowly but surely decreased since that time. Although all great groups of churches have had a representative from the first beginnings in the presidium of the World Council, in the Central Committee and in the Staff at Geneva, we cannot maintain that the ecumenical purpose and method of the Anglicans have, up to the third assembly of New Delhi, met with much understanding, response and support. The kind of hearing that is accorded to the Anglican testimony depends not only on the question whether the Anglican churches are sufficiently represented, but even more on the particular persons that are chosen for that function.

It cannot be said that the spiritual climate of the World Council was at first favorable to the Anglican endeavor for re-union. Dr. Visser 't Hooft, who was Secretary-General of the World Council from the start, pointed out more or less clearly, that great dangers were lurking in an effort to bring about a visible unity of all Christians within one Church. Due to a variety of causes, a wind has been blowing in the Reformation churches and particularly in some "free" churches, since 1920, that is neither favorable to the original purpose of the Faith and Order Movement nor to the ultimate Anglican effort for unity. The term "Church" has been used more and more to signify the whole of Christianity in its dynamic effort to free itself from conventional bonds inherited from the past, to rediscover the Gospel and proclaim it in an entirely new way to the world of our own time.

Dr. Kraemer, in his well-known prophetic and energetic way, during the years of his directorship of the Ecumenical Institute of Bossey has tried to convince hundreds of hearers of the necessity of awakening the churches that have fallen asleep and to convert them from dead projects for reunion to the living proclamation of the Gospel. Names like those of Barth, Brunner, Bonhoeffer, but also names like those of Mott, Stanley Jones and other great missionaries belonging to "free" churches of

136

England and America, and, in regard to Scotland, a name like that of Torrance, show sufficiently how great and even stormy a wind the Anglican efforts for reunion have had to battle since 1920.

No criticism and especially no blame is meant by these remarks, but only an impartial description of the actual situation of things. We shall deal more fully with the problem that is involved in that situation in Chapter Eight. The future will show whether the formulation of the ultimate end of the ecumenical movement by the third assembly of the World Council at New Delhi signified a definitive turning point.

CHAPTER FIVE

Ecumenical Relations

1. RELATIONS WITH EASTERN CHURCHES

THE Lambeth Conference of 1888 was the first that in its encyclical expressed the readiness of the Anglican Communion to enter into relations with every church that wished to discuss the matter of establishing closer connections of "intercommunion" with her, in one form or another.[1] That encyclical expressed the wish that "the Spirit of Love move on the troubled waters of religious differences."[2] In particular it considered it desirable that a closer examination be made regarding the attitude toward the Lutheran churches of Scandinavia, the Old Catholic and related churches, and that the existing friendly relations with the Eastern churches be continued and strengthened.

In fact the Eastern and in particular the Greek and Russian churches were the first among non-Anglican churches with which Canterbury entered into official relations. As early as 1863, the bishops of the ecclesiastical province of Canterbury had accepted the proposal of the famous Bishop of Oxford, Samuel Wilberforce, to create a commission that, in cooperation with the existing commission of the Episcopal Church of

---

[1] *The Six Lambeth Conferences*, p. 114.
[2] *Ibid.*, p. 114.

America, would issue a report concerning an eventual intercommunion with the Greek-Russian Church.[3]

In the same year the Eastern Church Association was founded, which aimed at studying the Eastern churches. In 1893 this association was reanimated by A. C. Headlam, who later became Bishop of Gloucester. In addition, an Anglican and Eastern Orthodox Churches Union was formed in 1906, which was more directly aimed at entertaining ecumenical relations between Anglican and Eastern Orthodox Christians. The two merged, in 1914, into the Anglican and Eastern Association.

That is why the ecumenical commission of the Lambeth Conference of 1888 began its report regarding the attitude toward the Eastern churches by recalling the correspondence between Anglican and Eastern bishops. After that it mentioned the visit of the Greek Archbishop Lycurgus of Syra and Tenos to the Anglican Bishop of Ely: "When I return to Greece," this Eastern archbishop said at the time of his departure, "I will say that the Church of England is not like other Protestant bodies." This, as we have said, is the impression many receive who but for one moment stand on the doorstep of the Anglican Church but do not get acquainted with its life. The archbishop continued even: "I will say that it is a sound Catholic Church very like our own."[4]

This declaration must have made a peculiar impression upon the majority of the bishops of the Lambeth Conference who, especially in the previous century and in various sections of the Anglican Communion, were convinced Protestants, whether

---

[3] *Reports made to the Convocation of the Province of Canterbury by the Committee on Intercommunion with the Eastern Orthodox Churches, 1865–69,* ed. by Fraser. Roman Catholics also were interested at the time in the Anglo-Eastern relations, as appears from the books, published by Lee and others, *Sermons on the Reunion of Christendom by members of the Roman Catholic, Oriental and Anglican Communions,* London, 1864–65, and *Essays on the Reunion of Christendom by members of the Roman Catholic, Oriental and Anglican Communions,* London, 1867.

[4] See *The Six Lambeth Conferences,* p. 167, note 3.

evangelical or liberal. There must have been bishops who attached little faith to the hope expressed by Archbishop Lycurgus: "I trust that by friendly discussion union between the two churches may be brought about."[5] At any rate, some members of the commission saw to it that the report concluded with the words: "We think that Christians need to be cautioned against impatience in expecting quick results."[6]

It is almost a century since all these things happened. Correct as they are, the accounts given in today's press concerning friendly encounters between Rome, Eastern patriarchs and Anglican bishops seem to have given many the impression that they are witnessing something that is quite new in history. But this is not wholly correct. The ecumenical events of our time are not as new as many imagine. As soon as the first encounters have taken place, there are heard today precisely the same warnings that were sounded a century ago, and the advice to the faithful is to be on their guard against too great expectations.

In this chapter we intend to give the history of the ecumenical relations which the Anglican Communion has established since 1888 in the most diverse directions. This is a useful process, for in this way the facts will show us that it is easy to desire unity and to strive for it, but extremely difficult to achieve it. History alone is able to convince us that the "difficulties," as the former Archbishop of Canterbury expressed it, "are immense." In this way we also learn to appreciate the extent and seriousness of the difficulties. None of those difficulties can be avoided or circumnavigated in the process of unification. They will have to be overcome one by one in common discussion between the churches.

In the long run the unification will gain more from expert and responsible contributions based on a profound study of the many and diverse obstacles concretely encountered on the road to unity, than from vague and impatient professions and expectations of unity. The latter often manifest too superficial a

---

[5] *Ibid.*, p. 167. [6] *Ibid.*, p. 170.

vision of the nature and the seriousness of the ecumenical situation, as well as insufficient knowledge of the real problems for which practical solutions must be found, if the restoration of unity is to be achieved.

Impatience is often a sign of lack of faith instead of a sign of great faith and confidence. As the report of 1888 remarks in its conclusion: "Such impatience argues imperfect trust in the ultimate fulfilment of our Lord's prayer for His people that they 'all may be One.' "[7]

When we survey the encyclicals, resolutions and reports of the Lambeth Conferences from 1888 to that of 1920 inclusive, we cannot but admire the imperturbable patience with which every conference has repeatedly taken a close look at the ecumenical situation and has gone on with its ecumenical projects, preparations and examinations, although no important echo was heard nor any real result was recorded.

The relations with non-Anglican churches remained limited to letters of condolence on the occasion of the death of a patriarch; individual visits of some, especially Anglo-Catholic clergymen to Russia (before the Revolution of 1918); expressions of sympathy concerning the consequences of World War I and for the persecuted or expatriate members of the Russian Church; the gathering of information about offices and sacramental practice; and the naming of commissions of study for the enlightenment of the bishops regarding the doctrine and practices of other churches. But, with the exception of the English-speaking countries, all this was rather one-sided. The voice of the Anglican bishops was like that of one crying in the wilderness. It was as if their ecumenical activity, to which some bishops had consecrated years of study, time and energy, were taking place in a vacuum.

With respect to the Eastern churches, as a consequence of Resolution 61 of the Lambeth Conference of 1908, the Arch-

---

[7] *Ibid.,* p. 170.

bishop of Canterbury appointed a permanent Eastern Churches Committee. Its task was "to take cognisance of all that concerns our relations with the Churches of the Orthodox East."[8]

Resolution 62 of the same conference determined the line of conduct for the churches of the Anglican Communion in regard to admitting members of the Eastern churches to Anglican sacraments:

1. At all times to baptize the children of members of any Church of the Orthodox Eastern Communion in cases of emergency, provided that there is a clear understanding that baptism should not be again administered to those so baptized;

2. At all times to admit members of any Church of the Orthodox Eastern Communion to communicate in our churches, when they are deprived of the ministrations of a priest of their own Communion, provided that a. they are at that time admissible to Communion in their own Churches, and b. are not under any disqualification so far as our own rules of discipline are concerned.[9]

During the years that immediately followed the Lambeth Conference of 1908, it seemed that the Anglican Communion had not sued in vain for the hand of the Eastern Orthodox Communion, at least as regards the Russian Church. Mutual relations were established and these were even maintained during World War I. The Church of Russia in those years showed signs of an interior renewal and hoped to obtain a greater measure of independence from the state.

An abrupt end was put to that happy development by the Revolution of 1918. The report of the ecumenical commission of the Lambeth Conference of 1920 records that:

One of the last acts of the Great Sobor [Council] summoned by the Holy Synod was in September, 1918, to pass a resolution, welcoming "the sincere efforts of the Old Catholic and Anglicans towards union with the Orthodox Church," and calling on the sacred Synod "to organize a permanent commission with departments in Russia and abroad for the further study of Old Catholic and Anglican difficulties

---

[8] *Ibid.,* p. 332 .   [9] *Ibid.,* p. 332.

in the way of union, and for the furthering, as much as possible, of the speedy attainment of the final aim."[10]

Closer relations were also established with the Serbian and with the Greek Church during the war years. In 1920 a delegation appointed by the Ecumenical Patriarch of Constantinople came to London to discuss, with the bishops who were taking part in the Lambeth Conference, what relations could be established between the Orthodox and Anglican churches. The report of the ecumenical commission was optimistic in this regard:

> To this visit we have reason to attach the greatest importance. . . .
> We believe that we are steadily moving towards the goal of ultimate reunion. But there is much still to be done before this is reached, and our progress will be no less sure because it is slow. We still require to gain greater knowledge and understanding of each other's position. Explanations are needed on both sides, and it is clear that when the day comes for definite proposals of formal intercommunion to be made, they will have to be based on a large-hearted tolerance on both sides, and a readiness on the part of each Church to be content with holding its own uses and practices without attempting to ask for conformity to them on the part of the other.[11]

In view of the ecumenical outlook of the Anglican churches, it stands to reason that their relations with the Orthodox churches of the East did not prevent them from entertaining, at the same time, relations with Eastern churches which in the past had separated from the Orthodox Church and which "fall under the suspicion of heresy"· the Churches of Armenia, Assyria, West-Syria, Egypt and Abyssinia.

2. Relations with the Church of Sweden, the Moravian Brethren and the Old Catholic Churches

Finally, the Church of Sweden, the Communion of the Moravian Brethren and the Old Catholic churches regularly

---

[10] *The Lambeth Conference 1920*, p. 145.
[11] *Ibid.*, p. 147.

reappear in the reports of the Lambeth Conferences. However, the relations with these churches consisted, until 1920, mainly in expressions of friendship and in communications of information. In this same year negotiations had progressed farthest with the Church of Sweden. Prompted by the report of a commission that had been appointed in 1908 to deal with this church, the Lambeth Conference of 1920 accepted the following resolution.

The Conference welcomes the Report of the Commission appointed after the last Conference entitled "the Church of England and the Church of Sweden," and, accepting the conclusions there maintained on the succession of the Bishops of the Church of Sweden and the conception of the priesthood set forth in its standards, recommends that members of that Church, qualified to receive the Sacraments in their own Church, should be admitted to Holy Communion in ours. It also recommends that on suitable occasions permission should be given to Swedish ecclesiastics to give addresses in our churches.[12]

It is noteworthy that permission is granted to Swedish clergymen to speak in the Church of England but not to administer the sacraments. The emphasis which the subsequent resolution puts on the desirability of having Anglican bishops take part, as much as possible, in the consecration of Swedish bishops, gives the impression that not all the bishops of the Lambeth Conference were convinced of the validity of Swedish consecrations.

The fact that the Anglican bishops agreed with the Swedish-Lutheran concept of the priesthood needs closer examination. For this implies that the Anglican bishops found no contradiction between the Swedish-Lutheran and the Anglican concept of the office of the priesthood. Since they likewise agreed with the Eastern Orthodox and the Old Catholic concept of the priesthood, one would have to conclude that there is no fundamental contradiction between the Reformation (at least the Lutheran) concept and the Catholic concept. It would be worthwhile investigating whether the Anglican bishops believe that the East-

---

12 *Ibid.*, Resolution 24, p. 33.

ern Orthodox and the Old Catholic concept of the priesthood agrees with that of the Roman Catholic Church or rejects the Roman Catholic concept of the priesthood.

It should be noted that a considerable number of Anglican bishops are evangelical and admit no essential difference between the Anglican concept of offices and those of most "free" churches. Moreover, there are no fundamental differences of opinion between the Lutheran and the Reformed churches concerning the nature of the ministry. Taking all this, then, into consideration, we wonder whether the concepts of those diverse churches we have named, concerning ministry and priesthood, are indeed as little different as the above-quoted resolution presupposes.

In any case, in the problem of unification of the churches, it is not merely a question of the office of bishops and the apostolic succession but also of the nature of the priesthood. The questions that present themselves in that connection will have to be approached not merely in a theological but also in a historical way. A definite answer will have to be found to the question whether and to what extent the later development of the celebration of of the Holy Eucharist into daily Mass, and the practice of private masses is connected with a vision of the priesthood that is foreign to the primitive Church and perhaps even disagrees with the view of the Eastern and Old Catholic churches.

The Reformation was, among other things, a reaction against the late medieval practice of the priesthood. It has on that account led to a rather exclusive emphasis on the ministry as a service of God's Word, that is as, in reality, a prophetic office. Perhaps it would be helpful for a rapprochement of all the churches regarding this matter if all without distinction were willing to return to and start from the manner in which the Holy Eucharist was celebrated in the Church of the first centuries and the way the ministry functioned in the primitive Church.

Until 1920 the connections with the Old Catholic churches

of Holland, Germany, Switzerland and Austria were confined to "friendly relations." The episcopal consecration of the ex-Anglican clergyman A. H. Mathew by the Old Catholic Archbishop of Utrecht in 1908 had cast a shadow on these friendly relations and the Lambeth Conference of 1920 refused to recognize the so-called "Old Catholic Church of Great Britain" as a "properly constituted Church." On the other hand, the discord occasioned by that episcopal consecration was removed by a declaration on the part of the Old Catholic bishops in 1920, stating that:

> The episcopal consecration of the Rev. A. H. Mathew was surreptitiously secured by the production of false testimony, and would never have taken place had the consecrators known that the conditions stated in the questionable documents and required by our Episcopate were non-existent.[13]

The many years of discussions with the Moravian Brethren concerning the possibility of a mutual recognition of each other's offices and sacraments ended in a negative result because of the custom of the Moravian Brethren to allow deacons to confer confirmation and to permit them to celebrate Holy Communion.[14]

3. The Main Questions Considered in Dealing with Non-Anglican Churches

Two questions were predominantly considered in all relations with non-Anglican churches, namely:

1. What view do the churches of the Anglican Communion entertain about the offices of those churches?

2. What rules and conditions are operative in the churches of the Anglican Communion in regard to admitting members of other churches to Holy Communion?

---

[13] *Ibid.*, p. 155.   [14] *Ibid.*, Resolution 29, p. 34.

With respect to the first question, the Anglican churches officially hold that the office, in the full sense of that word, presupposes that the officers (bishops, priests or presbyters, and deacons) are consecrated (ordained) by a bishop who is historically in a line of apostolic succession. The whole emphasis is here placed on the word "historical." The condition that the transmission of office by the imposition of hands must be traceable without interruption to the ancient, undivided Church, must be understood in a purely historical sense. Anglican churches in this matter leave out of consideration all dogmatic and theological considerations. They also consider it of minor importance whether and in what manner the office of bishop is incorporated in a synodal church structure and how it functions in the church.

It is understandable that the Anglican churches allow their own members, for serious reasons, to take part in the communion administered in episcopal churches (the Roman, Eastern, Old Catholic and Swedish-Lutheran Churches), but not in reformational or "free" churches which have lost the historical episcopate. However, we must remember that this official attitude is not shared by a number of Anglican bishops and clergymen and by many Anglican believers. The evangelical Anglicans look upon the offices of non-episcopal churches as authentic offices. They are even disposed to take part in communion in those churches rather than in churches of the "Catholic" type. Finally, it is very important to note that the Anglican churches have never made a negative declaration concerning the value and the "efficacy" of the official ministrations in non-episcopal churches.

As to the second question, the official stand of the Anglican churches is that all baptized Christians, whatever the church or Communion to which they belong, can and are permitted to receive communion in an Anglican service, if they believe that the "Sacrament of the Lord's Supper" was instituted by Christ and that the faithful in this Sacrament are nourished and re-

147

freshed "with the spiritual food of the most precious Body and Blood of thy Son our Saviour Jesus Christ."[15]

The Anglican churches are likewise reluctant to make dogmatic and theological considerations and declarations that would seek to determine more closely how Christ is present and operates in and through the Sacrament, and how one should conceive the kind of nourishment that is received through His Body and Blood.

The vast majority of Anglicans believe that the doctrine of transsubstantiation affects too much the spiritual character of Communion and gives a too realistic and materialistic image of the mystery of the Supper. In this respect we may perhaps have great expectations from conversations between Anglican theologians and Roman Catholic theologians who belong to the *théologie nouvelle.* It seems to me that the concept of the Eucharistic Supper of the Dutch Reformed Church, as formulated by its General Synod of 1949,[16] could win the full agreement of the churches of the Anglican Communion.

As a consequence of the Anglican standpoint, the Anglican churches are not fundamentally opposed to admitting members of any other churches, whether they be of the Catholic or reformational or "free" type, to Holy Communion, if they have good reasons for making use of that possibility. Superficially speaking, this would seem to be rather strange and not quite correct: Anglicans are not supposed to receive Holy Communion in non-episcopal churches, whereas in certain cases members of these churches are supposed to wish to receive Communion in an Anglican church. However, when we look at it more closely, we

---

[15] *Book of Common Prayer,* Thanksgiving after Holy Communion.

[16] *Fundamenten en Perspectieven van Belijden,* pp. 26 and 48. Cf. the Prayer before the Supper of the Dutch Reformed Church: "We pray Thee that Thou shouldst work in our hearts in this Supper . . . , in order that our burdened and prostrate hearts may be nourished and comforted, through the power of the Holy Spirit, by His true body and blood, nay by Him, who is true God and true man, the only heavenly bread."

realize that this situation follows of necessity from the Anglican concept of office and sacrament. We may even say that this Anglican situation has a practical sigificance when a common service of the Supper is held during ecumenical conferences, and both episcopal and non-episcopal churches participate in it. Considering the ecumenical situation as it concretely exists today, this practice can be executed only when an Anglican church is the one that issues the invitation.

There is an added reason why we must attach particular importance, from the ecumenical standpoint, to the relations between Anglican and Reformation churches. It is precisely in those relations and the conversations that follow from them that the crucial problems of Christian unification will come in for consideration. One is justified in looking upon the relations between Anglican and reformational or "free" churches as the thermometer of the ecumenical unification. The worse it goes with those relations and discussions, the less chance there is for a unification of all churches of the entire *Ecumene;* the better the results of those conversations, the better in general will be the possibility of ecumenical unity.

If reunion between Anglican and reformational churches were to meet with insurmountable obstacles for which no solution can be found, it would then also be *a fortiori* impossible to arrive at a reunion between Rome and the Reformation. Anglicanism is in this respect a road-sign and a pace-maker. We shall deal with this matter more fully in the following chapter.

4. THE CHURCH OF ENGLAND AND THE "FREE" CHURCHES

Since the middle of the last century, the Convocations of Canterbury have occupied themselves with the problem of the reunion between the Church of England and the "free" churches that had separated from her, such as the Presbyterian, the

Congregationalist, the Methodist and the Baptist churches. Also in the Protestant-Episcopal Church of America means were considered that would foster contacts with the other churches.

A first result of the second Lambeth Conference of 1878 was its resolution to offer its five reports together with the accompanying encyclical for the consideration of all churches.

The first practical step was taken by the Great Convention of the Protestant-Episcopal Church of America in 1886. The latter sent a report concerning reunion to all denominations in the United States. In it appeared for the first time the basis of four points which, since the third Lambeth Conference of 1888, are usually called the "Lambeth Quadrilateral."[17]

In the following year the Convocations of Canterbury accepted a resolution in which the Archbishop was asked for the appointment of a "Joint Committee," namely a commission with Anglican and non-Anglican members, in order to discuss relations between the church and those which were estranged from her Communion in England and eventually to give a report about that matter. Similar joint committees were appointed by the synods of the Anglican churches in Australia, New Zealand and Canada.

The Lambeth Conference of 1888 devoted an extensive report to the reunion with the "free" churches in the English-speaking countries, Home Reunion. This report incorporated the Lambeth Quadrilateral and added to it:

The Committee believe that upon some such basis as this, with large freedom of variation on secondary points of doctrine, worship, and discipline, and without interference with existing conditions of property and endowment, it might be possible, under God's gracious providence, for a reunited Church, including at least the chief of the Christian Communions of our people, to rest.[18]

---

[17] Cf. above, p. 129.
[18] *The Lambeth Conference,* 1920, p. 160.

The Commission likewise expressed its opinion that:

With the chief of the Non-conforming Communions there would not only be less difficulty than is commonly supposed as to the basis of a common faith in the essentials of Christian doctrine, but that, even in respect of Church Government, many of the causes which had originally led to secession had been removed.[19]

This is a realistic remark which very exactly describes the actual situation. For, considering the faith and conduct of the large group of moderate Anglicans and adding to that the Anglicans who belong to the evangelical wing, it is certain beyond a doubt that there is a much greater common basis of agreement regarding essential points of Christian doctrine between Anglicans and reformational Christians than between Anglicans and Catholic Christians. Hence it should not astonish anyone when he reads the declaration of the Anglican missionary bishop Stephen Neill: "I sometimes ask myself what I would be, if I was not an Anglican. I think that the answer is probably: 'Presbyterian.' "[20] It follows that the question of the relations between the Anglican and the "free" churches deserves all our attention and that we can consider it a matter of the greatest importance.

The Lambeth Conference of 1897 expressed the wish that the various churches of the Anglican Communion would no longer content themselves with declarations of readiness but that every church should try to enter into official conversations with the non-Anglican churches in their own countries. The report of the ecumenical commission of the Lambeth Conference of 1908 mentions that in Australia such conversations had been held "between committees of the General Synod of our own Communion and of the General Assembly of the Presbyterian Church with a view to possible reunion."[21]

---

[19] *Ibid.*, p. 159.
[20] Neill, *Anglicanism*, Pelican ed., London 1958, Preface, p. 7.
[21] *The Six Lambeth Conferences*, p. 432.

We may see here one of the reasons why the ecumenical commission of 1908 concentrated its attention principally on the relations with the churches that belong to the Presbyterian Communion:

> Many circumstances have led your Committee to pay special attention to the relations between the Presbyterian Churches and the Churches of the Anglican Communion. To many Presbyterians we owe a deep debt of gratitude for their contributions to sacred learning. We are equally indebted to them for many examples of holiness of life. With regard to their Churches, although their characteristics appear to vary in different countries, they have in many ways a special affinity with our own Communion. Wherever they have held closely to their traditions and professed standards of faith and government, as formulated[22] at Westminster, they satisfy the first three of the four conditions of an approach to reunion laid down by the Lambeth Conference of 1888. Even as regards the fourth, though they have not retained the historic episcopate, it belongs to their principles to insist upon definite ordination as necessary for admission into their ministry. Their standards[23] provide that "the word of ordination" should be "performed with due care, wisdom, gravity, and solemnity" "by imposition of hands and prayer, with fasting" by the presbytery; they regard and treat ordination as conferred by those who have themselves been ordained and are authorised to ordain others.[24]

The group of churches to which these words refer have, since 1877, become united in the World Presbyterian Alliance. For various reasons a new reciprocal confrontation of Anglicanism and Presbyterianism is of the utmost importance. After a war that lasted about a hundred years, Anglicanism and Presbyterianism definitively separated in the middle of the seventeenth century. Both, however, are founded on a common

---

[22] The Westminster Confession dates from 1646. It was composed by a committee appointed by the Westminster Assembly, the synod which by order of the "Long Parliament" was charged to transform the Church of England into a Presbyterian church.

[23] From the confessional standpoint, these standards agree with the *Liturgische Formulieren* and the *Dienstboek* of the Dutch Reformed Church.

[24] *The Six Lambeth Conferences*, p. 431.

reformational basis which they have not renounced to the present.

The situation became confused through the development of the Oxford Movement into contemporary Anglo-Catholicism. However, leaving out of consideration the Anglo-Catholic minority, we must say that there are no church groups that are so closely related to one another, in regard to the interpretation of Scripture, theology and spirituality, as the Anglican and Presbyterian churches. The Presbyterian churches also stand midway between the Catholic churches on the one hand and the Methodist and other free churches on the other. This is evident from their concept of the ministry and their care to preserve continuity with the Ancient Church in their faith and church structure.

The questions that are at stake between Anglicanism and Presbyterianism now appear in a new light because of the results of modern exegetical, patristic and historical investigations. Considering this new light and the stage that has been reached today in the ecumenical movement, one must say that a continued dialogue between Anglicanism and Presbyterianism can make an important contribution toward the unification of the whole of Christianity. We will devote the entire seventh chapter to that question.

In regard to the Presbyterian and other "free" churches, the ecumenical commission of the Lambeth Conference of 1908 had not been able to go beyond this earnest recommendation:

Private meetings of ministers and laymen of our own and other Churches should frequently be held, such as those which have taken place under the auspices of the Christian Union Association in Scotland, in which, by common study of the Word of God, by frank and friendly discussion, and by united prayer, they could at once realise and deepen the sense of union in the fellowship of Christ.[25]

In proposing to the churches concerned an ideal of reunion,

---

[25] *Ibid.*, p. 433.

the ecumenical commission stressed that this ideal should include "all the elements of divine truth now emphasised by separated bodies; in a word, the path of efforts towards reunion should be *not compromise for the sake of peace, but comprehension for the sake of truth and the goal not uniformity but unity.*"[26]

The recommendation of the Lambeth Conference to foster spiritual relations between ministers and laymen of the Anglican and "free" churches was not without results. Common needs and cares often contribute toward a rapprochement between the churches. It was that way also during World War I. The relations between Anglicans and members of non-episcopal churches developed so rapidly that the bishops of the Lambeth Conference of 1920 saw themselves obliged to send out a warning to the effect that decisions regarding intercommunion and reunion should be made by the official church authorities.[27] (Let it be noted that these are the same bishops who wrote the Lambeth Appeal which was discussed in the previous chapter.) And they felt especially obliged, in view of an orderly ecumenical relationship, to give detailed and precise lines of conduct for church relations between members of the Anglican and non-episcopal churches.[28]

The report of the sub-commission for relations and reunion with non-episcopal churches took the first and the most important place among the reports of the ecumenical sub-commissions in contrast with what had been customary until then. It is easy to see that the bishops who wrote the Lambeth Appeal and addressed it to all Christian churches had principally in mind a rapprochement with the Presbyterian and other "free" churches in English-speaking countries. It begins by remarking that "The character of the movement towards reunion with non-episcopal

---

26 *Ibid.*, p. 433.
27 *The Lambeth Conference 1920*, Resolution 11, p. 30.
28 *Ibid.*, Resolution 12, p. 30.

154

Churches since the last Lambeth Conference has been dramatic and impressive."[29]

Almost all churches that belonged to the Anglican Communion seemed to have had conversations with other churches after 1908. According to the report of the sub-commission,

In not a few cases definite proposals have been made, and in others actual schemes set forth. Of this we have received striking illustrations. They range from simple conferences where differences have been discussed and lines of agreement indicated, to definite proposals where substantial agreement has been obtained.[30]

The following concrete proposals are expressly mentioned in the report:

In the United States of America a Concordat has been proposed by members of the Protestant Episcopal Church and Ministers of Congregational Churches. These proposals were presented to the General Convention of the Protestant Episcopal Church at Detroit in October, 1919. A series of resolutions was concurred in by both the House of Deputees and the House of Bishops, and a proposed canon has been drawn up. The whole matter is to be considered at the next General Convention which meets in 1922.

In South India a proposed union of the Anglican Church with the South-India United Church (which includes five separate non-episcopal missions) has reached a stage at which the proposals may shortly be brought before the Episcopal Synod of the Province of India and Ceylon.

In East Africa a Constitution of an Alliance of Missionary Societies has been adopted, and the Members of the Alliance declare that they "pledge themselves not to rest until they can all share one Ministry."

In Australia proposals, having as their object a union with the Presbyterians have been under consideration, and several conferences have been held with representatives of other non-episcopal churches. Much will depend upon the decisions of this Conference as to the possibility of further progress in this region.[31]

---

[29] *Ibid.*, p. 139. [30] *Ibid.*, p. 139.
[31] *Ibid.*, p. 140.

I still remember vividly the enthusiasm with which those events were greeted by many Anglicans, an enthusiasm which I too felt greatly. At the same time, the first preparations had begun for the World Conferences of Stockholm in 1925 and Lausanne in 1927. The air was full of ideals of unity. In this respect the Lambeth Appeal could not have been made at a more opportune moment.

But unfortunately dark clouds also appeared in the sky. My youthful and somewhat naive enthusiasm received its first shock when I learned to my surprise that some leaders in the Christian student organizations of that time made speeches in which they warned against the attempt to "build a new tower of Babel," and urged their audiences to use everything in their power to prevent the oncoming ecumenical movement from degenerating into an organized movement for unity.

Being a zealous reader of the *Church Times,* which was then rather extremely Anglo-Catholic in its views—today this weekly also accepts more moderate and evangelical Anglican views and contributions—I was dismayed at the sometimes violent reactions of some Anglo-Catholics against the proposals made for reunion with non-episcopal churches. Soon there appeared articles and pamphlets, written by such Anglican theologians as Gore, Williams, and Rawlinson, in which the authors maintained that no intercommunion and reunion with non-episcopal churches was possible except under the condition of episcopal reorganization.

Since that time the Anglican Communion has been faced with a dilemma: either let her recommendations and decisions take into account the standpoint of the Anglo-Catholic minority, thus endangering the success of reunion with non-episcopal churches, or achieve reunion with non-episcopal churches at the risk of causing an Anglo-Catholic schism. This dilemma forces the Anglican bishops to navigate the *Ecclesia Anglicana* safely between the Scylla of too one-sided evangelical Anglicanism and the Charybdis of too one-sided Anglo-Catholic principles, and pilot her to the haven of a reunited Church. The seamanship required by this necessity will undoubtedly be beneficial for the whole of Christianity in its attempts to achieve unity. In the reunited Church of the future, a synthesis will have to be reached between all those Catholic and Reformation elements of faith and church structure that in the coming dialogue between the churches will be seen to conform with God's Word in Holy Scripture and the Faith of the Catholic Church of all centuries that is based upon it.

The Anglican bishops constantly keep in mind the ultimate unity of the whole of Christianity. They cannot allow themselves nor do they wish to endanger the ultimate result for the sake of easy successes in one direction. Those who understand this position will not readily accuse the Anglican churches of being unjust and unreasonable in their actions and omissions. We have here a very real situation that deserves the attention of all who penetrate deeply into the problem of Christian unity and the divisions among Christians and seek for a way out of the impasse into which the churches have drifted in the course of centuries as a result of many conflicts and schisms, and in which all of us, as Christians, are involved.

It is easy to shake one's head in doubt and to criticize the Anglican searching and groping, with its failures and sometimes strange results, when we look at it from some particular standpoint. Such a view disregards the fact that the Anglican churches have had to fight in the front line for the ecumenical movement at a time when the other churches had not yet enlisted in an active struggle for unity. The thorny position in which the Anglican bishops often find themselves from the ecumenical standpoint is something that concerns us all, for it is precisely this situation, more than any other, that is symptomatic of the actual condition of affairs that exists in Christianity as a whole.

157

After these remarks we can now resume our story and trace the further developments of the relations between Anglican and non-Anglican churches since the Lambeth Appeal of 1920.

From the Church of Sweden came a lengthy reply signed by Nathan Söderblom, Archbishop of Uppsala, and a short but significant reply was sent from the General Council of the World Alliance of the Presbyterian Churches. Apart from these, the official reactions on the part of churches were principally confined to the various Protestant Churches of England, Scotland, the U.S.A., Canada, India and Australia, that is, to the English-speaking countries, or if we wish, to Anglo-Saxon Christianity.

The Lutheran and Reformed churches of the continent appear to have done little more than accept the Lambeth Appeal as a piece of information. In a certain sense this was an advantage, for by limiting the important discussion that followed upon the Lambeth Appeal to Anglo-Saxon countries, a survey of the problem was easier to make than it would, in all probability, have been otherwise. The most important material concerning those discussions was gathered by Dr. Bell, who at that time was still Dean of Canterbury and later became Bishop of Winchester:[32]

During the last four years a series of Appeals and Proposals for Christian Unity have been published, of a variety and importance remarkable in the history of the movement for the Reunion of Christendom. . . . And in particular, the "Appeal to All Christian People," issued by the Lambeth Conference in 1920, gave what may fairly be described as a new impetus to the whole cause in many directions.[33]

The third decade of this century will be known as the years during which the ecumenical dialogue between the churches definitively began to develop. Dr. Bell alluded not merely to

---

[32] *Documents on Christian Unity*, Oxford University Press, 4 series published, respectively in 1924, 1930, 1945 and 1958. A selection from the first two series appeared in 1955 in one volume.

[33] *Ibid.*, first series, 1924, p. VII.

the reactions to the Lambeth Appeal but also the great number of concrete proposals toward reunion of churches in various Anglo-Saxon countries and in India, to encyclicals of Rome and Constantinople, and to the preliminary conversations in view of the projects of World Conferences to be held at Stockholm and Lausanne.

The first official reaction to the Lambeth Appeal in England came from the Federal Council of the Evangelical Free Churches, which met for the first time in September 1920. The Council expressed its conviction that the question proposed by the Lambeth Appeal "affects the whole future of religion in this country and beyond it."[34] It therefore appointed a commission, in which all the member churches of Presbyterian, Congregationalist, Methodist and Baptist denominations were represented, with the charge:

> to submit the pronouncement of the Lambeth Conference . . . to a careful examination in the light of the principles of the New Testament and the evangelical conception of the Church and the ministry, and to prepare a statement thereon for the consideration of the Council, with the view of transmitting the results of their examination to the Authorities of the Free Churches, on which will fall the duty of dealing with the whole question.[35]

The Council did not wish to run ahead of that examination but confined itself to four preliminary suggestions.[36]

The "free" churches appear to have taken the Lambeth Appeal very seriously and to have expected great things from the practical results of the dialogue between the churches during the coming years. The text of the declaration composed by the appointed commission was accepted by the Federal Council. It was published May 22, 1921, and sent to the authorities of the churches that belonged to the Federal Council.[37] It is a lengthy

---

[34] *Ibid.*, p. 118.   [35] *Ibid.*, p. 118.
[36] *Ibid.*, pp. 118–119.   [37] *Ibid.*, pp. 120–141.

and theologically profound document, which carefully determines and justifies the standpoint taken by the "free" churches since that time in regard to the Anglican ecumenical proposals. It appears also to have served as a foundation for the replies to the Lambeth Appeal that were sent separately by many churches to the Archbishop of Canterbury.[38]

It became evident, from those official documents and from articles and pamphlets of individual theologians belonging to various churches, that the difficulties in the way of a real inter-communion or even of reunion were considerably more numerous and more serious than the bishops of the Lambeth Conference of 1920 might have foreseen. Professor Sundkler of Uppsala, in his standard work about the movement toward reunion in India, goes so far as to claim:

> Lambeth 1920 was the high-water mark of Anglican reunion endeavours towards the "non-conformists." After Lambeth 1920 the climate became cooler and at the following Lambeth Conference, 1930, home reunion had lost something of its first attraction. The leaders of the Churches had had enough of the great opposition on the part of various groups within their own Church. The chance for a reunion, which before 1920 had seemed so promising, diminished somewhat during the twenties.[39]

This observation is in itself correct. But the decline did not continue. The years between 1920 and 1930 showed that an ecumenical rapprochement easily becomes a new theological battlefield. In the Anglican churches it was principally the Anglo-Catholics who took a firm stand against all suggestions that were, or seemed to be, in opposition to their Catholic principles. In the "free" churches, both the orthodox Puritans and the followers of Karl Barth protested against what they considered to be a too human and unprincipled striving for

---

[38] *Ibid.*, pp. 104–117.
[39] Sundkler, *Church of South India: the Movement Towards Union 1900–1947*, London, 1954, p. 94.

unity.[40] Similar groups of opposition also exist in other countries. They certainly have the right to defend their most profound convictions and the principles that are rooted in them. The Roman Catholic and Eastern Orthodox churches act likewise.

In this respect there is a remarkable similarity between Roman Catholics and orthodox Presbyterians, especially in the matter of official ecclesiastical declarations about the unification of Christianity. Their ecumenical attitude toward one another and toward other churches comes down to this, that they are willing to engage in a dialogue with the others but they warn that there can be no tampering with, on one side, the episcopal office and the papacy and, on the other, with the full value of the presbyterial ministries.

This attitude is pre-ecumenical. It holds that there can be no other conversation than one of controversy, there can be no open dialogue; and it is established *a priori* that no rapprochement is possible concerning those points. The Anglo-Catholics are similarly inclined to take this pre-ecumenical attitude and the more extreme evangelical Anglicans are not differently disposed in that respect.

The official ecumenical standpoint of the Anglican Communion is different. From that standpoint the churches are not asked to sacrifice their convictions; they are asked to meet in an existential encounter, to examine together to what extent their grievances and arguments have a solid foundation, and to investigate together what must be done to attain intercommunion and reunion without having to sacrifice any elements of truth.

When that is done with openness and sincerity, it is possible that over and over again positive elements will be discovered in the testimony of the interlocutor and shortcomings detected in one's own belief and church structure. This procedure could

---

[40] Torrance, *Conflict and Agreement in the Church,* 2 vols., London, 1959, dedicated to Karl Barth, vol. I, pp. 23–75, 104–145.

then lead to real changes, to greater fullness and the bridging of gaps.

A church which *a priori* excludes the possibilities of new discoveries and profound changes and measures, which believes that it may and must withdraw from all ecumenical criticism—a criticism from the standpoint of the entire reunited Church of the future—cannot possibly participate in an ecumenical dialogue but is doomed to remain stuck in the isolation of its polemics. Ecumenical openness and readiness imposes no conditions, but desires precisely that the controversial elements in faith and church structure be examined once more by all together in the light of God's Word, the tradition of the undivided Church and the new acquisitions obtained by modern scientific investigations.

That is why it is not possible to call fully ecumenical the reaction of various "free" churches in regard to the ministry, as it was expressed in the above-mentioned reply by the General Council of the World Alliance of Presbyterian Churches. For this reply puts forward as a necessary condition:

> There will be substantial progress towards reunion only when the conferring Churches are ready frankly to recognize one another's Church standing, and to accompany words of unity by acts of unity in the fellowship of the Lord's Table and in co-operation in the Lord's work.[41]

The un-ecumenical character of this condition does not lie in the Presbyterian churches considering themselves true churches in the full sense of the term and their ministries authentic ministries, for all churches make similar claims. No church is asked to doubt herself. The un-ecumenical character of that condition is the demand which it imposes upon other churches, with different convictions, regarding what constitutes a true church and the true nature of a ministry. For, in

---

[41] Bell, *Documents on Christian Unity,* first series, p. 196.

advance and before the dialogue is initiated, those churches are told that they must sacrifice their own standards as being unecumenical and accept those of the Presbyterian churches as unquestionable standards.

When such conditions are required, it is indeed possible to have a dialogue between churches that are already totally in mutual agreement, but not between churches that are separated because of diverse concepts regarding the ministry, the Church and the sacraments.

That is why the ecumenical commission of the Lambeth Conference of 1930 gives once more a lengthy explanation of the principles which must lie at the foundation of every ecumenical encounter, if we wish to make such an encounter possible and meaningful. Such an encounter is always an encounter between churches that disagree in important points. It is precisely because they do not agree, that they want to enter into a dialogue. Their disagreement does not prevent them from looking upon the members of the other communion as believing and baptized Christians. Their willingness to enter into dialogue, however, implies that they may not anticipate the results of the encounter by establishing conditions which the others cannot fulfill as a matter of conscience, because of their religious convictions. Not only must every church acknowledge its share in the guilt and responsibility for the division, but every church should have the humility to listen to the grievances and arguments of the others: "The humility required must go further; it must lead to a readiness on the part of each church to admit that in some respects it may have been wrong."[42]

The report of the ecumenical commission of 1930 reveals clearly that the many conversations that were held from 1920 to 1925 between representatives of the Church of England and of the Federal Council of the Evangelical Free Churches of

---

[42] *The Lambeth Conference 1930,* p. 112.

England ran more or less aground on the difficulty of accepting or not accepting the historical episcopate as a necessary element in the structure of the future reunited Church. At the same time, however, it emphasizes the fact that a striking agreement was reached in regard to the essential points of the Christian faith: "It is upon the basis of this unanimity with regard to the Gospel Message that we are encouraged to go forward in the search for full organic union."[43]

5. RELATIONS WITH THE CATHOLIC TYPE OF CHURCHES

Some tangible results were achieved in the relations with churches of the "Catholic" type.

Present at the Lambeth Conference of 1920 was a delegation of the Ecumenical Patriarch of Constantinople. This delegation upon its return sent a lengthy report about its experience to the Holy Synod of the Greek Church.[44] One of its members, moreover, had published a study regarding the Anglican ordinations. This was followed in 1921 by a report composed by a commission, appointed by the Archbishop of Canterbury, in which the Anglican view was more fully explained in respect to a number of controverted points about faith and church practice.[45]

As a result of all this, the Archbishop of Canterbury was pleasantly surprised when he received a letter, dated July 28, 1922, from the Ecumenical Patriarch who "had the great pleasure" of letting it be known that the Holy Synod had carefully studied all the aspects of that matter; it had come to the conclusion that in the eyes of the Orthodox Church the ordinations of the Anglican Episcopal Confession of bishops,

---

[43] *Ibid.*, p. 113. [44] Bell, *op. cit.*, pp. 52 f.
[45] *Ibid.*, pp. 77 f.

164

priests and deacons have the same validity as those of the Roman, Old Catholic and Armenian churches, since they contain all the true elements which the Orthodox consider essential for the recognition of the Charism of the priesthood that goes back to the Apostles.[46]

However, the letter continues, the agreement of the whole Orthodox Church is required for accepting that fact as the basis for the creation of a full sacramental communion between the churches concerned. About the same time as that letter was sent to the Archbishop of Canterbury, the Ecumenical Patriarch wrote an Encyclical to all the "Presidents" of the particular Eastern Orthodox churches.[47] In it he explained the reasons that had prompted the examiners to declare the Anglican ordinations valid. In 1923, the Patriarch of Jerusalem and the Archbishop of Cyprus also spoke in favor of the validity of the Anglican ordinations.[48]

A similar progress was soon witnessed in the relations between Anglican and Old Catholic churches. Lockhart, in his biography of Gordon Lang who was then Archbishop of Canterbury, went so far as to say that "with the Old Catholics the road was easier and the pace faster."[49]

In June 1925 the Archbishop of Canterbury received a letter from Francis Kenninck, Old Catholic Archbishop of Utrecht, in which the latter made it known that, after a lengthy examination, earnest reflection and deliberation with the clergy, the conclusion had been reached that their former doubt regarding the validity of Anglican orders was unfounded. The conclusion read as follows:

We believe that the Church of England has wished always to maintain the episcopal rule of the Church of antiquity, and that the

---

[46] *Ibid.*, p. 93.
[47] *Ibid.*, pp. 94 f.
[48] *Ibid.*, pp. 97 f. Cf. Ramsey, *Constantinople and Canterbury, a Lecture in the University of Athens on May 7th 1962*, London, 1962.
[49] Lockhart, *Cosmo Gordon Lang*, London, 1949, p. 356.

Edwardian formula of consecration must be accounted valid. We therefore declare, without reservation, that the apostolic succession has not been broken in the Church of England.[50]

In Bern that same year, this decision was subsequently confirmed by the Conference of the Bishops of all Old Catholic churches that are in communion with the Church of Utrecht. The way was thus opened for negotiations in view of an official intercommunion of Anglicans and Old Catholics. They were stimulated by the Society of St. Willibrord, an association of Anglicans who, under the devoted direction of its former secretary Reverend C. Beaufort Moss, worked hard for the reunion with what they used to call "the Church of Holland." The desired intercommunion was realized already in 1931 at Bonn. The Anglican deputation was under the leadership of A. C. Headlam, who was at that time Bishop of Gloucester. Agreement was reached on the following points:

1. Each Communion recognizes the catholicity and independence of the other and maintains its own.

2. Each Communion agrees to admit members of the other Communion to participate in the Sacraments.

3. Intercommunion does not require from either Communion the acceptance of all doctrinal opinion, sacramental devotion, or liturgical practice characteristic of the other, but implies that each believes the other to hold all the essentials of the Christian faith.[51]

After World War II a shadow was cast on the propitious development of relations with the churches of the Catholic type. The Moscow Conference of the heads of the Orthodox churches in communion with the Patriarch of Moscow accepted a lengthy resolution in 1948 in which they made the following declarations:

---

[50] Bell, *Documents on Christian Unity,* second series, p. 64. Cf. Moss, *The Old Catholic Churches and Reunion,* London, 1927, and Moss, *The Old Catholic Movement, Its Origins and History,* 1948.

[51] *Report of the Meeting of the Commission of the Anglican Communion and the Old Catholic Churches held at Bonn on Thursday, July 2nd, 1931,* London, 1931. Cf. Bell, *op. cit.,* third series, p. 60.

1. The official doctrine of the Anglican Church differs greatly from the dogmas, doctrine and tradition of the Orthodox Church. The recognition of the validity of Anglican ordinations should be based on an essential agreement about the fundamental principles that govern the sacraments. One must not start, in this matter, from the personal interpretation of some (namely, Anglo-Catholic) members of the Anglican Churches. The Orthodox Church cannot recognize the validity of Anglican ordinations unless a complete and official agreement is reached regarding the doctrine concerning the sacraments in general and the nature of the ministries and the ministerial ordinations in particular. The favorable expressions of individual Orthodox churches must therefore be considered as conditional.

2. It is necessary therefore to wait for an official and authoritative declaration of a Council of the entire Anglican clergy, confirmed by the head of the Anglican Church and based on a substantial review of the whole doctrine regarding ministries and sacraments.

3. Only a Council of the entire Holy Orthodox Church has the authority to declare that the Anglican orders are valid on the principle of "Economy," and then only after a formally expressed unity in faith and confession between the Orthodox and Anglican churches has been attained.[52]

In practice all this comes down to the conclusion that the Russian Church will not recognize the validity of Anglican ordinations unless the Anglican churches officially revoke and reject all Protestant and Reformation doctrines regarding the Church, her ministries and sacraments, insofar as they are contrary to Orthodox Catholic doctrine.

In spite of the reserved attitude of the Russian Church, it is a fact that a remarkable ecumenical pattern has appeared in the whole of the Christian *Ecumene,* and it will gradually

---

[52] For the complete text see Bell, *op. cit.,* fourth series, pp. 35 f.

become evident that it could be very significant in the process of the unification of the whole of Christianity.

In the first place, the problem of the validity of Anglican orders has been placed in a new light. At least it is surprising that the orders which the Church of Rome declared invalid in 1896 were, without difficulty, accepted as valid by Old Catholic and a part of the Eastern Orthodox churches. Moreover, we may legitimately ask ourselves whether those ordinations will eventually not be recognized as valid even by the Church of Rome, if systematically an Old Catholic bishop acts as consecrator or co-consecrator in all Anglican consecrations of bishops.

Secondly, it is of great importance that the intercommunion —which since 1958 is called "full" communion—between Anglicans and Old Catholics has become possible in spite of the reformational past of the former and the Roman Catholic past of the latter. It is undeniable that Rome and the Reformation have met here, though only in a certain sense and in an unusual and provisional way. It is also true that those who have striven most zealously to obtain that result were Anglo-Catholics. Yet the fact remains that there now exists full communion between the whole Anglican Communion and the whole Old Catholic Communion. We must keep in mind that, of the whole Anglican Communion, most bishops, clergymen and faithful are without any doubt on the side of the Reformation in their concept of the Gospel, their exegesis of Sacred Scripture, their method of theology, their devotions and spirituality and finally the entire pattern of their Christian life; and that they know they are one in mind with the "free" churches which for accidental, though very serious reasons, have separated from the Church of England.

From the standpoint of Christianity in general and of theology, the relation between Anglicans and Presbyterians remains the closest of all. Both the Old Catholics, on the outside, and the Anglo-Catholics, inside the Anglican Communion, would not understand their ecumenical vocation properly if they showed apprehension and offered objections to the continued efforts of the Anglican churches to eventually attain to a full communion with the reformational and "free" churches. For the special significance of Anglicanism, from the ecumenical standpoint, lies precisely in its orientation toward the positive witness of both the Catholic and the reformational past.

One who wishes to get an idea of the extensive work that has been done to reach intercommunion with reformational and "free" churches, should study the material which the former Bishop of Chichester has collected and published in the four volumes of his *Documents on Christian Unity.* We shall confine ourselves here to the two most important events, namely, the plans for reunion in India and the renewed conversations between Anglicans and Presbyterians. To each of these events we shall devote a chapter. However, it should be kept in mind that there are also relations and conversations between Anglican, reformational and "free" churches in Canada, the United States and Australia; these are in part the result of common membership in the World Council of Churches. Since 1958, there are also in England conversations with Anglicans and Methodists, in view of an eventual intercommunion.[53]

---

[53] *Conversations between the Church of England and the Methodist Church.* An Interim Statement dated April 16th 1958, London, 1958. Its compilers declare that "while the road towards fuller unity is sometimes hard and tortuous we believe that if there is an invincible will to unity the obstacles can be surmounted" (p. 44). Meanwhile the final report has been published: *Conversations Between the Church of England and the Methodist Church,* London, 1963.

CHAPTER SIX

Reunion in India

1. THE EVANGELICAL CHARACTER OF THE ANGLICAN CHURCH OF SOUTH INDIA

IT is not difficult to claim that the division of Christians is a disgrace and to see that that division has many disastrous consequences. It is easy to reach the conviction that the division must come to an end. It is not even difficult to reach an agreement among Christians regarding the final goal to which all ecumenical endeavors must be directed.

It seems extremely difficult, however, to effect a reunion of churches, even when these have close historical and dogmatic connections and belong to the same country.

Nevertheless, there exists one country in which such a reunion has been realized. On September 27, 1947, there took place the inauguration of the new Church of India in the St. George Cathedral of Madras. Half a century of difficult labor and study, and countless conversations and discussions, had been necessary before the final goal was reached. First, in 1928, the United Church of South India arose from various Presbyterian and Congregationalist churches. Since 1919 there were regular conversations between representatives of this church and the Anglican Church of South India. From 1925 on representatives of

170

Methodist churches joined them, though at first with great reserve.[1]

From these diverse churches there developed finally the Church of South India. It is most captivating to read the detailed history of that difficult unification. If anyone wishes to understand how an organic unity of churches gradually comes about and the numerous and varied difficulties that have to be overcome in the process, let him read the book of Sundkler, professor of missiology at the University of Uppsala. This work can unquestionably be considered the standard work regarding the reunion in South India.[2]

What makes the reunion in South India so important from the ecumenical standpoint is the fact that the Anglican Church was also involved in it. It appears, therefore, that the mission churches of South India have progressed farther in respect to reunion than their mother churches in England. It is easy to realize how much more difficult the situation in the mother country is, when we recall the objections and difficulties that developed when the question arose of a full communion between the Church of England and the new Church of South India.

It is unjust to attribute those objections to conservatism or to a want of ecumenical spirit. Those difficulties necessarily arise when one considers unification in the light of the whole *Ecumene,* and not merely according to a situation in a particular mission field.

If we wish to get a correct view of the projects of reunion in South India and their final and definitive realization, it is necessary to pay special attention to two facts.

First, we must note that all the churches involved were

---

[1] Concerning the origin, character and principles of Presbyterians, Congregationalists and Methodists, see the author's *Der Weltprotestantismus,* pp. 237 f.

[2] *Church of South India: the Movement towards Reunion 1900–1947,* London, 1954.

mission churches. Here then we have not only an example of reunion in general but at the same time a telling example of the connection that exists between mission and reunion. There are also other questions, such as the liturgy, which take on a special form and urgency in mission countries. But this special form arises most of all in connection with the Christian rapprochement, collaboration and reunion.

The second fact is that the Anglican dioceses which ceased to exist in South India, because they lost their identity and independence when absorbed into the Church of South India, had a clear evangelical-Anglican character. In other words, they were not fully representative of the Anglicanism of the Church of England and of the Anglican Communion.

It is particularly important not to lose sight of this second fact. The reunion in South India does not at all mean that the opposition between Anglican and "free" churches, and in particular between an episcopal and a presbyterial church order, has been definitively bridged. The bridging in South India would certainly not have taken place in the same way if it had been a question of reunion with the official Anglicanism of the Anglican Communion, or if Anglo-Catholics had been involved in the process. Sundkler touches the heart of the matter when he remarks:

> The fundamental fact about the work of the [Anglican] Christian Missionary Society, apart from which the union movements in South India cannot be understood, was its genuine *evangelical* character.[3]

This fact also explains why the Anglican Church could be absorbed in the Church of South India. But, on the other hand, it shows us that the reunion which took place in South India does not have the broad significance that it would have if there had actually taken place a reunion of "free" churches with the entire Anglican Communion.

---

[3] *Op. cit.,* p. 50.

What we are able to study in South India is how an actual synthesis between an Anglican-episcopal and a Presbyterian or even "free" church order could be accomplished if there had been no Oxford Movement in the Church of England during the last century, if Anglo-Catholicism did not exist, and if the Church of England as a whole adhered to an evangelical and reformational concept of the offices of the bishop and the priesthood as they were universally accepted in the sixteenth century; in other words, if there existed only an evangelical Anglicanism derived from a typically Reformation source.

Particularly the evangelical Anglicans, as a consequence of the revivalist movement of John and Charles Wesley and their spiritual adherents, manifest such a religious kinship with the spirituality and the ecclesiastical climate of the "free" churches, that they are able to agree with them regarding practically all points of Christian faith and church practice. That is why in the matter of reunion in South India it was not so much a question of solving problems concerning principles and doctrines but of practically adjusting and integrating diverse forms of church order and liturgy. Because of these circumstances the reunion in South India does not have the depth without which a reunion between Anglican, Presbyterian and "free" churches in England, and eventually in the whole of Great Britain, is positively impossible. This will be sufficiently evident from what will be said in the following chapter.

2. Principal Experiences and Discoveries Made in the South India Process of Reunion

The movement for reunion in South India had been going on for some time and had already led to the actual reunion of the Presbyterian and Congregationalist mission churches in 1908, when the Anglican Church in South India also became involved in it. The stimulus for this involvement had come from the International Mission Conference of Edinburgh in 1910, which many consider the most important pace-maker of the ecumenical movement. However, the Anglican contribution to the movement for reunion in South India would have been unthinkable without the inspiring and wise leadership of Henry Whitehead who had become Bishop of Madras in 1899.

When we survey the process of unification over half a century, we ask ourselves how it was possible to achieve unity between churches that were so diverse in nature and origin, and how this practically came about. We clearly see that some general factors played a role in the process without which the unity could not possibly have been attained. Here we are concerned with unforeseen factors which played a role but which no one had *a priori* demanded as a condition. These factors manifested themselves gradually as the process of unification went on.

The first significant factor is the fact that all the leading figures underwent a change when they became involved in the process of unification. It is remarkable that all those leaders began with a defense of their individual outlook, vision and conditions which they considered to be unquestionably necessary from the standpoint of their own religious and ecclesiastical milieu. However, they increasingly influenced one another's thinking until all, in one or another respect, changed their original conviction and gradually grew more closely together.

Bishop Whitehead, who had begun as a convinced Anglo-Catholic, was influenced by his contact with other churches and gradually shifted to the position of the evangelical Anglicans. K. T. Paul, an Indian Presbyterian, who had played an important role in the reunion of Presbyterians and Congregationalists, was originally opposed to any form of organic unity implying the acceptance of the episcopate, but in 1921 he renounced his opposition. At the General Synod of the United Church of South India, in the same year, he pleaded for a full communion with the Anglican Communion.

174

Philips, a Congregationalist, at first had reservations with respect to any kind of ecclesiastical office and every fixed form of liturgy. But through his contact with the Anglican Bishop Azariah, he discovered that the Anglican principles were not so unacceptable if they were applied by a man of stature. He ended by asking whether there were not present in the tradition of the Church certain inalienable Catholic elements that cannot be dispensed with in a "full-orbed" Christianity. As Sundkler says:

> Just as Henry Whitehead at the beginning of the century had moved from Tractarianism to a moderate Evangelicalism under the urge to unite the Church in India, so this same urge had led the Congregationalist missionary leader to a quest for Catholicity that was to bring him near to Whitehead's original position.[4]

If we add to this the great influence that was exercised during the period of growth by the visits or counsels and writings of a number of theologians, church leaders and missionaries of England, Scotland and America, it is difficult to avoid the practical conclusion that a process of Church unification is evidently unthinkable without unlimited openness for one an other's arguments and a profound mutual influence. We are in the presence of a process of development in which new insights are constantly acquired, new values are discovered, and no one remains what he was at the beginning of the ecumenical journey of discovery.

A second important factor is the fact that unification is impossible if one or the other insists on absolutizing a particular confession and liturgy, a particular theological system and particular conventional customs and institutions. Only God, His Word, and His Revelation in Christ are absolute. Church unification presupposes, on the part of all the churches involved, a readiness to listen to one another's testimony regarding that absolute truth and reality, and the willingness to sacrifice what-

---

[4] *Ibid.*, p. 274.

175

ever does not do full justice to the whole of revealed truth and the full intention of Christ with respect to his Church.

The principal obstacle that, at the beginning of this century, stood in the way of the unification of Presbyterians and Congregationalists was the fact that:

> They had been wedded so long to the Canons of Dort and the Westminster Confession, that they heartily believed that the organization which held those symbols of orthodoxy was the only true Reformed Church. Others who had been nurtured in Congregationalism and had tasted the sweets of local autonomy could hardly be prevailed upon, for the sake of their weaker brethren and a larger union, to surrender even a little of the personal liberty they had so long been enjoying.[5]

When one surveys the entire process of unification, it appears that the principal obstacle consisted in the tendency to hold fast to orthodox teachings and practices which were simply identified with absolute truth, with the exact interpretation of Holy Scripture and with the original intention of Christ. Since there are as many "orthodoxies" as there are churches and denominations, it will be impossible to reach unity as long as each church clings with might and main to its own orthodoxy and *a priori* considers the orthodoxy of every other church as an error. A study of the actual unification in South India shows clearly that progress was in direct ratio to the churches' willingness to take account of the views of others, to insist less on their own ways and to form a different and more positive judgment about things that had formerly been considered strange in the doctrines of others, or even to adopt such elements in their own church.

For this reason the reunion in South India must be looked upon as a victory over every species of stark and sterile orthodoxy. This does not mean there is a tendency here to modernism or liberalism, for the latter need not be feared in mission churches. But it became evident that unification is possible only

---

[5] *Ibid.*, p. 47.

if supposedly unchangeable positions are tested in common according to the Word of God and the sentiments and experience of the Christians of all the churches together. The churches will be able to unite only if they are ready to leave the ghetto of their isolation, in which they have been cloistered, and to enter the open space of a genuinely ecumenical encounter.

Dogmatic and theological considerations played no role in the conversations between the delegates of the various churches regarding the matter of the Church, the ministry, the sacraments and the liturgy. The question of the Church structure was approached from a purely historical and constitutional standpoint. The delegates asked themselves how the historical continuity of the Church, the ministry and the liturgy could best be preserved and how the Church could be organized if one tried one's best to adopt in her constitution and functioning all the elements of church order that had proved their practical value in the churches that were now uniting.

In this way it was possible to make the Congregationalists and Methodists accept the office of bishop by whom the historical continuity of the ministry is best preserved and expressed. It was expressly agreed that this acceptance did not necessarily imply the recognition of any divine authority or the belief that a supernatural grace is attached to that continuity of offices. The greatest possible liberty would be left in the reunited Church with respect to the theological interpretation of the ministry and office and regarding the effect of the ministerial and sacramental actions.

The only thing that was asked of all churches and their members was the conviction that the ministry and the sacraments go back to an institution of Christ, that they must be continued in the Church and must be conceived by every one, as best he can, as they were intended by Christ. In regard to differences about the latter point, each one's liberty of conviction would be safeguarded. It appeared that only this way would make it possible to form together a church order that would receive the

177

approval of all the churches concerned. In regard to liturgy there would exist the greatest liberty and possibility of variety within the reunited Church. Every congregation would have the power—if it so wished—to preserve its customary practices or to organize new ones.

A third factor of great importance seemed to be the application, on the one hand, of respect for the beliefs and moral conviction of all the faithful involved in the reunion; and on the other, respect for the doctrines and practices of the mother churches of the mission churches that were being united. That is why the constitution of the reunited Church contained rules that guaranteed to all the faithful concerned complete liberty of conscience, particularly regarding the concepts of the ministry and the practice of the sacraments

Greater difficulties presented themselves when there was question of taking account, in the construction of the church order, of the doctrine and practice of the mother churches in regard to the ministry and the sacraments. It stands to reason that none of the reuniting churches wished to achieve unity at the cost of losing ecclesiastical communion with their respective mother church. Hence the Anglican dioceses, for example, that were to enter into the Church of India counted upon the fact that their clergy would continue to be recognized in all the churches of the Anglican Communion and that they would also remain able to exercise their ministry in those churches. Strictly speaking, they even counted upon a full communion between the churches of the Anglican Communion and the new Church of South India. The difficulties that arose were connected with the fact that the churches of the Anglican Communion were not able to agree in every respect with what the evangelical Anglicans had accepted for the sake of unification.

A last factor that seemed unavoidable in that unification was the factor of patience. Churches that have been separated from one another for a long time gradually develop their individual

178

character, mentality and identity. It seemed, therefore, that if they wished to unite, there should elapse an intermediary period between the time of their former isolation and the time of eventual ecclesiastical communion. During this interval various transitional measures would be taken to facilitate the passage from the time of planning to that of the final execution of the project of reunion. It is not possible to construct a church artificially and expect that the faithful of the merging churches will suddenly and in one day adopt a totally different church pattern. But neither can one wait until the merging churches agree regarding the most minute details. For such a moment never arrives as long as the churches consider things from their own individual standpoint and do not think and live from the standpoint of the larger community.

It is true, of course, that there must exist a common basis in essential points, upon which the churches can unite without doing violence to their deepest convictions. If, however, such a basis is present, the reunion itself is the principal condition promoting further integration. It is only within the reunited Church that the faithful, who have come from diverse churches, can acclimatize themselves, can gradually learn to better know and appreciate one another and, finally, to grow together in a new and living communion of faith, prayer and sacraments.

In every reunion the Church will have to exercise patience with her members; she will have to give them plenty of opportunity to develop themselves in the direction of a true, non-artificial, unforced and not externally imposed unity and communion. The unification must be seen and experienced as a steady process of growth and maturation that requires understanding and forbearance and, above all, much patience on the part of all concerned.

We have sketched some of the most important discoveries and experiences which half a century of striving for unity in South India has yielded as practical results. For the remainder

179

of this chapter we shall confine ourselves to the examination of the Anglican contribution to the movement for reunion in India. In this connection we can distinguish three phases: a phase of preparation until 1919; a phase of negotiations with representatives of the other churches involved in the movement concerning the organization of a project of reunion (1919–1929); and a phase of conversations within and without Anglicanism which led to six revisions of the project, until the final realization of the reunion (1929–1947).

3. THE PREPARATORY PHASE

Whitehead, the Anglican Bishop of Madras, in a pastoral letter of 1909, had given the following direction for the creation of the Christian Church in India:

We are founding and building up a Christian Church in a new country; we cannot simply accept the traditional ideas and institutions of an old established church like the Church of England and ask no questions. When we transplant from West to East forms of worship, methods of administration and formulae of doctrine, we are forced to ask ourselves what must be preserved and what must be changed, what is or is not essential, what is purely Anglican and what is Catholic.[6]

Palmer, who from 1908 to 1929 was the Anglican Bishop of Bombay, was the great church organizer of those days. He saw that a reunited Church could be built up only if the old episcopal church structure was developed in a modern direction, namely, by adopting all valuable elements of the structure of the reformational and "free" churches, and especially by insuring a large place to lay representation. Under his leadership the Bishops' Synod of 1912–13 decreed the creation of a Synod of the whole Province of South India. This was composed of sixty representatives of the clergy and also of sixty representa-

---

[6] *Ibid.*, p. 56.

tives of laymen, each of these two categories constituting a separate "house" beside that of the bishops, and which held meetings at the same time as the latter.

The Church of England itself, in 1919, initiated a drastic reorganization of her structure by the creation of a Church Assembly, to which also belongs a House of the Laity, beside the old "Convocations" comprising the House of Bishops and the House of the Clergy. Moreover, church boards were created in the parishes, in imitation of the boards existing in the parishes of the "free" churches.

These were radical changes in the administration; by them, as in modern states of the free world, an absolute form of government was replaced by a constitutional order; and the "free" churches did not fail to take notice. Generally this was seen as a first step on the part of Anglicanism in the direction of a new concept of the Church, which might serve as a basis for closer deliberations with non-episcopal churches regarding reunion.

4. The Development of a Project for Reunion

The second phase was that of the development of a project for reunion. At the beginning of this phase we find the Tranquebar Manifesto. It was composed during the Tranquebar Conference of 1919, which was the first conference of delegates of the United Church of South India and of the South India Province of the Anglican Communion. The Anglican deputation was under the leadership of Azariah, the Indian Bishop of Dornakal who, as Sundkler remarks, "embodied in his person the main streams of the development in India."[7]

Before his appointment as Bishop of Dornakal in 1913, he had worked in close cooperation with the missionaries of all

---

[7] *Ibid.*, p. 97.

reformational "free" churches for the evangelization of India. Until his death in 1945 he remained the soul and the leader of the movement for reunion in India. He died two years before the definitive inauguration of the Church of South India: "By faith he looked from afar into the Promised Land."[8]

The Manifesto first recalls that unity is the will of God according to Holy Scripture and that it is the explicit intention of Christ; it is therefore high time to build up one Church of Christ in India from the many and diverse mission churches. It continues:

In this Church we believe that three Scriptural elements must be conserved:

1. The *Congregational* element, representing "the whole Church," with "every member" having immediate access to God, each exercising his gift for the development of the whole body.

2. We believe it should include the delegated, organized or *Presbyterian* element, whereby the Church could unite in a General Assembly, Synods or Councils in organized unity.

3. We believe it should include the representative, executive, or *Episcopal* element.

Thus all three elements, no one of which is absolute or sufficient without the other, should be included in the Church of the future, for we aim not at compromise for the sake of peace, but at comprehension for the sake of truth.

In seeking union, the Anglican members stand for the one ultimate principle of the *Historic Episcopate*. They ask the "acceptance of the fact of episcopacy and not any theory as to its character." The South India United Church members believe it is "a necessary condition that the Episcopate should reassume a constitutional form" on the primitive, simple, apostolic model. While the Anglicans ask for the Historic Episcopate, the members of the South India United Church also make one condition of union, namely the recognition of *spiritual equality,* of the universal priesthood of all believers, and of the rights of the laity to their full expression in the Church. They ask that this principle of spiritual equality shall be maintained throughout at every step of the negotiations.[9]

[8] *Ibid.,* p. 349.

[9] *Tranquebar Manifesto 1919;* text in Sunkler, *op. cit.,* pp. 101 ff.

With this presupposition, and after accepting the Lambeth Quadrilateral as a foundation for future reunion, the Manifesto adds once more a passage expressly regarding the sense in which the historical episcopate must be understood:

We understand that the acceptance of the fact of the Episcopate does not involve the acceptance of any theory of origin of episcopacy nor any doctrinal interpretation of the fact. It is further agreed that the terms of union should involve no Christian community in the necessity of disowning its past, and we find it no part of our duty to call in question the validity of each other's orders.[10]

Finally the Manifesto gives a provisional description of the way in which the churches concerned could bring about their union:

After full deliberation, let the South India United Church [i.e., the Presbyterian-Congregationist] if it desires union [with the Anglicans] choose from its own members certain men who shall be consecrated as bishops. In the consecration of these first bishops it is suggested that three or more bishops of the Anglican Church shall lay their hands upon the candidates, together with an equal number of ministers as representatives of the South India United Church.

As soon as the first bishops are consecrated, the two bodies would be in intercommunion, but the further limitation of existing ministers with regard to celebrating the Communion in the churches of the other body might still remain. As one possible solution, we would suggest that a special Service of *Commission* should be held. All ministers of both bodies desiring authority to officiate at the Communion throughout the whole Church should present themselves to receive at the hands of all the bishops of the United Churches a commission for such celebration of the Communion. Ministers of either body not desiring to officiate at the Communion in the other Church would be under no obligation to present themselves. Full liberty would be claimed for individuals on the extreme wing of each body to maintain their present views and practices.[11]

---

[10] *Ibid.*   [11] *Ibid.*

This was the starting-point in 1919. The purpose is clear. The existing differences between the churches that were striving for union were not considered obstacles to reunion. An attempt would be made to build up a church structure that would incorporate and preserve all the characteristic elements belonging to the diverse church orders concerned. This, however, would result in difficulties for the ministers involved, especially because, on the one hand, an episcopal ministerial order would be considered necessary in the future whereas, on the other hand, no one would be forced to renounce the ordination which he had received previously.

For ten years official delegates of the United Church of South India and of the Anglican Church Province regularly met as members of a Joint Committee to discuss that first project of reunion. The first of those meetings took place in Bangalore even before the Lambeth Conference of 1920; the second, likewise in Bangalore, was held immediately after the Lambeth Conference. The Lambeth Appeal, which we have dealt with in Chapter Four, seemed to contribute more to a clearer perception of all the difficulties than to their solution. Non-Anglicans were unable to shake off the impression that the Lambeth Appeal practically denied the full validity of non-episcopal ministerial ordinations; and this they fought with might and main.

Bishop Palmer finally assured them that he and his fellow bishops of the Anglican Church in South India would be willing to receive a Presbyterian ordination, if the reunion in India were made dependent upon the condition that the ministers of non-episcopal churches be obliged to receive an episcopal ordination for the sake of unity. In this way, by means of a mutual complementary ordination, the ministries in the newly reunited Church would be considered as having validity and full value according to everyone's conviction.

The Joint Committee finally adopted a resolution during its

second meeting in Bangalore in 1920. It stated that all ministers of the churches involved would be ministers of the whole Church of South India from the moment of the reunion. But everyone would be free to ask or not to ask for a complementary or new ministerial power from the bishops of the future Church, in order to be entitled to exercise his functions in the part of the reunited Church to which he did not originally belong. The scruples of conscience of those on either side who were affected by divergent opinions would be fully respected.

The vision of the reunited Church of the future stood out clearly before their minds. But the road that was to lead to an actual realization appeared strewn with traps and pitfalls. During the years that followed the Lambeth Conference difficulties piled up to such an extent that it seemed, more than once, that the project for reunion would suffer shipwreck. Six more meetings of the Joint Committee had to be held before the greatest difficulties were overcome sufficiently to proceed, during the eighth meeting in Madras in 1929, to the publication of a concrete plan of reunion.

In the meantime numerous specialists from England had aided the Joint Committee with their advice. The Congregationalist patristic scholar Vernon Barlet of Oxford offered important proposals in 1921; among them was the suggestion that a new *Ordinale* should be composed for the reunited Church in which all the characteristic traits of the rites of ordination of the reuniting churches would be gathered in one single rite.

Particularly important was the proposal of Bishop Palmer, during the fifth meeting in 1926 of the Joint Committee, to the effect that an interim period of fifty years (later changed to thirty years) should elapse between the first inauguration and the final definitive perpetuation of the reunion. The Church, during that interim, should be content with the unsatisfactory situation that not all ministers would accept the complementary ordination and that, on that account, some of the faithful would

185

not consider them as having the power to exercise their ministry in the entire Church. But all new ministers would henceforth receive an episcopal ordination according to the new *Ordinale*. In this way, after the elapse of thirty or fifty years, all ministers would be recognized by the faithful as having the necessary powers.

As a result of that proposal new life was injected into the deliberations, and the Methodist churches also seemed ready to name delegates for the Joint Committee. The Methodists, too, made an important contribution toward the construction of a plan of reunion that would win the approval of all. They wished to forestall the apprehensions of some Congregationalists and Anglo-Catholics who might fear that no consideration would be given to their feelings in the reunited Church. Hence they proposed that, apart from the intermediary period to be established by the Constitution, guarantees would also be given to all the faithful of the churches concerned for the time when reunion had become a reality:

> They therefore pledge themselves and fully trust each other that in the united church no arrangements with regard to churches, congregations or ministers will knowingly be made, either generally or in particular cases, which would offend the conscientious convictions of any persons directly concerned, or which would hinder the development of complete unity within the church or imperil its subsequent progress towards union with other churches.[12]

5. The Third Phase: Reunion

With the publication of the first concrete plan of reunion in 1929 began the third phase in the history of the South India movement for reunion.[13] The plan was submitted to the official authorities of the churches concerned and also to the churches of the mother countries. The two Lambeth Conferences of 1930

---

[12] Sundkler, *op. cit.*, p. 166.
[13] For the complete text of the project of 1929, see Bell, *Documents on Christian Unity*, second series, pp. 143–190.

and 1948 made a detailed study and appraisal of the plan for reunion. It underwent repeated changes on account of the many different evaluations and the difficulties that were encountered. The seventh and final wording was drawn up in a meeting of the Joint Committee, in December 1944, a few days before the death of Bishop Azariah.

After the final edition of the plan had been officially accepted by the churches concerned, but not without the necessary elimination of all sorts of objections, fourteen bishops of the new Church of South India were appointed during the twentieth meeting of the United Committee; of these eight were originally Anglicans, three Methodists, two Congregationalists and one Presbyterian. The latter was Bishop Newbegin, who occupies an important place in the World Council of Churches and has become famous through his book *The Reunion of the Church*.[14]

Bishop Jacob of Central Travancore was chosen by the churches to read the Act of Reunion at the inauguration service on September 27, 1947. It reads as follows:

Dearly beloved brethren . . . I do hereby declare that these three Churches, namely:

the Madras, Travancore and Cochin, Tinnevelly, and Dornakal Dioceses of the Church of India, Burma and Ceylon;

the Madras, Madura, Malabar, Jaffna, Kannada, Telugu and Travancore Church Councils of the South India United Church; and

the Methodist Church of South India comprising the Madras, Trichinopoly, Hyderabad and Mysore Districts;

are become one *Church of South India,* and that those Bishops, Presbyters, Deacons and Probationers who have assented to the Basis of Union and accepted the Constitution of the Church of South India, whose names are laid upon this Holy Table, are Bishops, Presbyters and Deacons of this Church; in the name of the Father, and of the Son, and of the Holy Spirit. Amen.[15]

14 J. E. Lesslie Newbegin, *The Reunion of the Church. A Defense of the South India Scheme,* London, 1948; revised ed., 1960.

15 Sundkler, *op. cit.,* p. 343.

The final goal had been achieved. It soon appeared that it was only a first beginning. Now came the experiences and discoveries which were the necessary consequences of the common church life of Christians who came from different bodies and had grown up in diverse Christian traditions, doctrines and practices. The intermediary period, which will end in 1977, seems to be a period of genuine growth. The experiences of a church like that of South India, which arose from the fusion of churches that completely sacrificed their former independence and identity for the sake of unity, have a universal significance. New endeavors to achieve unity can benefit by those lessons.

6. Ecumenical Progress in North India, Burma and Ceylon

The significance of the South India experience manifests itself clearly in the extension of the reunion movement to the whole of India. For the first time Anglican dioceses that are not distinctly evangelical but to some extent even openly Anglo-Catholic have become involved in the movement for reunion. On the other hand, churches that are pre-eminently "free," such as the Baptist, and essentially reformational churches, such as the Lutheran, agreed to take part in the negotiations. Now for the first time the ecumenical movement in India is undergoing a true ordeal of fire. Time will show whether it will be possible to devise a plan of reunion that will prove acceptable to all those churches.

Bishop Newbegin relates that the conversations with delegates of the Lutheran churches introduced a totally new theological element into the discussions. It is becoming more and more evident in India that a confrontation of Anglican ecumenism with Lutheranism opens up an entirely new and vast complex of questions. It is also due to the Lutheran churches that theological reflection has developed greatly in the churches of India.[16]

One practical result of the ecumenical pioneer work in South India is that the negotiations which are going on all over India, from Pakistan to Ceylon (Lanka) inclusive, have progressed much more quickly than was the case in South India; and this, in spite of the fact that the differences and difficulties that presented themselves between the churches concerned are considerably greater.

Actually there are two separate efforts for reunion, one relating to North India and the other to Ceylon. In North India the first unofficial contacts between representatives of the various churches date from 1929; in Ceylon from 1934. The first official conference of delegates of all the churches concerned met in Ceylon in 1945; in North India they met in 1951. In about ten years and after several revisions, the two reunion committees of delegates managed to prepare (respectively in 1955 and 1957) a definitive and fully detailed plan of reunion. This was then communicated to the highest authorities of the churches concerned.

The Anglican Church that is involved in those plans is the *C.I.P.B.C.*, the independent Church of India, Pakistan, Burma and Ceylon. As we have seen, this church in 1947 lost four of her dioceses when they entered the newly inaugurated Church of South India. When both projects in question are realized, it will mean that then there will no longer be an Anglican Church in India and that the Anglican Communion, for the first time, will have "lost" one church. If similar plans of reunion are achieved in other countries in the future, the Anglican Communion will gradually shrink until it finally disappears altogether.

On the occasion of the creation of the Church of South India in 1947, the then Archbishop of Canterbury, Geoffrey Fisher,

[16] Newbegin, *op. cit.,* p. XXVIII.

gave a speech in which he expressed his joy at the sight of that event; for it showed that churches can be willing to sacrifice their identity and independence for the sake of a complete restoration of Church unity. The Archbishop expressed the hope that the ecumenical efforts will finally result in a total disappearance of a separate Anglican form of Christianity following upon the entrance of all Anglican churches in the future reunited Church of Christ.

It seems to me that this Anglican vision of reunion is the only one that is realistic and hence deserves to be called fully ecumenical. There is often too much Platonic thought and discourse about reunion without willingness to follow the ecumenical road until its goal is reached. Even some delegates, upon their return from New Delhi, declared that reunion in no case implied the sacrifice of one's own identity and independence.

In this respect the thinking in India is fully ecumenical. A "full communion without loss of one's independence" is a contradiction in terms. Whence comes that explicit desire for self-preservation at any cost? Is "full communion" not the same thing as a complete restoration of the community in Christ through love? Does not the love of Christ, which is the mainspring, necessarily imply a complete self-sacrifice, a readiness to relinquish one's independence, privileges and pretensions? How can the Church ever become truly one, if all churches stubbornly cling to their selfish ecclesiastical Ego? Should not our criterion for recognizing with certainty which churches are earnest in their ecumenism be precisely whether they are ready and able to sacrifice themselves for the benefit of a complete restoration of the unity and communion of all Christians in the One Church of Christ?

The ecumenical problematics begins only when the churches seriously strive for unity in that sense. This is most evident from what has been taking place in and around India in this matter of ecumenism. The fact that representatives of so many, and in

190

some respects so diverse, churches succeeded in reaching an agreement concerning a detailed plan of reunion is in itself a very significant achievement. But the dominant question remains: How will this plan be judged by the churches concerned and what will be the consequences of an eventual acceptance in regard to the connections which they have with related churches in the whole world?

The titles of the Indian plans read: *Proposed Scheme of Church Union in Ceylon* and *Plan of Church Union in North India and Pakistan.*[17] In the construction of the Church of Lanka (Ceylon), five different types of churches are engaged: the Baptist churches in Ceylon, the Methodist Church in Ceylon, the Presbyterian churches in Ceylon, one Anglican Diocese of the Church of South India, and the *C.I.P.B.C.* In North India and Pakistan no less than seven mission churches are involved: the United Church of North India, which sprang from a reunion in 1924 of Presbyterian and Congregationalist churches; the Methodist (episcopal) Church of South Asia, which is of North American origin; the (non-episcopal) Methodist Church, of English and Australian origin; the *C.I.P.B.C.;* the Baptist churches in North India, of English origin; the Church of the Brethren in West India and the Disciples of Christ in Central India, both of American origin. With respect to the Anglican Church we must add that in both cases it is a question of participation not only of dioceses that profess a moderate form of Anglicanism but even of those that are predominantly Anglo-Catholic.

Both projects are true masterpieces of church organization. Those who are familiar with the opposition between the Dutch Reformed Church and the reformational churches, or between various types of the latter, experience one surprise after another as they study the projected constitutions of the two churches of

---

[17] Complete text in Bayne, *Ceylon, North India, Pakistan. A Study in Ecumenical Decision,* London, 1960, pp. 15–178.

India. They have a solution for every difficulty that would prevent any one of the churches from entering into the new church. This is especially true in regard to the ministry in the new church; it will have both an episcopal and a synodal structure. At the same time the solutions are such that no church concerned nor individual believers are asked to sacrifice theological convictions or to accept any form of authority, liturgy or spirituality against which they would have an objection. In both projects there is a remarkable order and harmony in the many things that will obtain for all members of the whole Church following the unification; and combined with it is the greatest possible comprehensiveness and complete freedom of professing and practicing the entire faith of the Church according to the conviction of individual consciences.

That kind of reunion is something entirely new in the history of twenty centuries of Christianity. It is not based on a new understanding of the content of God's Word and the Gospel. It rests on the conviction that all sincere and believing Christians fundamentally agree in their understanding of the Word of God and the Gospel; and that, to the extent that this is not so, they are ready to help one another in obtaining an ever purer, fuller and deeper understanding. In this respect the churches concerned have placed all their hope and confidence in the process of growth which the Church will experience after the unification, under the guidance of God's Spirit.

An intellectualistic distinction between truth and error and the heresy-hunt resulting from it is rejected as fundamentally non-scriptural. The churches believe rather that the pure and full truth in the biblical sense will come to light only in a frank dialogue and in lovingly working and living together in the spirit of mutual helpfulness. The history of theological controversies, of schisms and persecutions, is thought to be contrary to the intention, the will, the spirit and the love of Christ and to result from an apostasy from faith in the biblical sense of the term, in favor of faith in a pagan-intellectualistic sense.

It stands to reason that this does not mean that some groups in the churches involved are not seriously concerned about the consequences of the unification. We can even say that every one of these churches realize that they are engaged in a risky affair which can be undertaken only with a strong faith and great trust. These churches count upon the fact that this will be understood by the churches of their mother countries.

To prevent a break with the Anglican Communion in consequence of the reunion in India, the General Council of the *C.I.P.B.C.* accepted two resolutions, in January 1960. Their consequences will be decisive for the success or failure of unification. In virtue of those resolutions both projects were sent for consideration to all independent churches of the Anglican Communion; they were asked to examine those plans and to send word concerning their willingness to enter into full communion with the future reunited Church from the very beginning of its unification. In North India and Pakistan the plans were sent also, for consideration, to the various dioceses of the Anglican Church province. In Ceylon, too, this was done after the replies of the churches of the Anglican Communion had been received.

It is evident that the definitive decision of the Anglican Church of India, Pakistan, Burma and Ceylon regarding the joining or staying out of the reunited churches of North India and Ceylon, will be influenced by the attitude of the other churches of the Anglican Communion. An unfavorable answer not only would put the Anglican Church in India in a difficult situation but it would probably also have a bad influence on the other churches concerned with respect to a complete union with the Anglicans of India.

The attitude of the Lambeth Conferences of 1948 and 1958 regarding the Indian proposals justifies in any case the hope of a

193

favorable answer. The Lambeth Conference of 1948 declared explicitly that the project of Ceylon and the results of the first unofficial deliberations in North India showed a considerable improvement over the plan and the constitution of the Church of South India:

> In respect of all the more disputable points in the South India Scheme which have caused difficulty to many Anglicans, it is, from the Anglican point of view, a decided improvement.[18]

A similar remark was made in the paragraph concerning North India.

This real progress, according to the report of the ecumenical commission of 1948 concerning the plan of Ceylon, is particularly evident from the following points:

1. The pronouncements concerning the sacraments are theologically better justified.

2. The plan sufficiently safeguards the position of the episcopal office and declares that it is the intention of the uniting churches that the office of bishop, as it was known in the undivided Church, will form a part of the united Church of the future.

3. It is stated explicitly that those of Baptist origin are not obliged to accept infant baptism and that a Baptist minister may let another replace him, if he has some scruple of conscience regarding infant baptism.

4. The project avoids the introduction of an interim period with its related difficulties as in the South India plan; namely, that the ministers who had not received any complementary ordination might not be found acceptable by all the members of the new Church of South India. Hence, the constitution foresees a unification of the ministries of the various churches from the moment of unification. On the day of the inauguration of the New Church of Ceylon, all the newly named bishops would first receive the episcopal consecration and after that the

---

[18] *The Lambeth Conference 1948*, II, p. 57.

solemn commission for the exercise of their office in the entire reunited Church. After that every bishop in his own diocese would administer a complementary ministerial ordination to all presbyters, without prejudice to a previously received ordination, using the following formula:

Forasmuch as you were called and ordained to the Ministry of the Church of God within the . . . Church, and are now called to the Ministry of the Church of God as Presbyter within this United Church; receive from God at my hands the power and grace of the Holy Spirit to exercise the wider ministry of this office, and to nourish by Word and Sacraments all the members of Christ's flock within this United Church, in the name of the Father and of the Son and of the Holy Spirit. Amen.[19]

We note that the term "priest" is avoided, and that it is said that the power and grace are received not "through" or "by" but "at" my hands. The report remarks prudently:

In general it would appear to satisfy the requirements for making the orders of the unified Ministry acceptable as valid without offence to the consciences of Anglicans.[20]

The first project for the constitution of the Church of North India likewise had provisions to the effect that the continuity with the historical episcopate would be "effectively" preserved from the very beginning. Here also there is question of the unification of ministries in a manner similar to that of the projected constitution of the Church of Ceylon. At the same time, however, the project gave to the members of the non-Anglican churches involved in the unification the following guarantee:

The acceptance of this provision does not involve any judgement upon the validity or regularity of any other form of the ministry, and the fact that other Churches do not follow the rule of episcopal

19 *Ibid.*, II, p. 58.   20 *Ibid.*, II, p. 59.

ordination shall not in itself preclude the united Church from holding relations of communion and fellowship with them.[21]

The Lambeth Conference of 1958 devoted much consideration to both Indian projects of reunion. The report of the ecumenical commission said:

Both the *Scheme* and *Plan* under consideration constitute a great and significant step towards the healing of divisions and the recovery of the visible unity of the Church Universal according to the will of Christ. What has been achieved is especially impressive in view of the number of the Churches to be brought together, the variety of their policies, and the consequent complexity of the problems involved.[22]

The report notes with satisfaction that later revisions of the plans took serious consideration of the principles by which the continued efforts toward unity ought to be conducted in accordance with the directives of the Lambeth Conference of 1948. It was also noted with satisfaction that no Anglican needs to entertain any fears regarding the orthodoxy of the two Indian churches. Neither is there any need to doubt about the right intention in the ministerial ordinations in the united Church of North India and of Ceylon. Both projects expressly say that care will be taken to secure a ministerial service which fully harmonizes with all the demands of the members and, as far as possible, with the demands of all the churches of the whole world. The preface of the projected Ordinale for the Church of Ceylon states explicitly:

It is the intention of this Church to continue and reverently to use and esteem the threefold ministry of Bishop, Presbyter and Deacon which existed in the undivided Church.[23]

Both projects evidently aimed at avoiding the difficulties that resulted from the creation of the Church of South India. In

---

21 *Ibid.*, II, p. 60. Cf. Bayne, *op. cit.*, p. 128.
22 *The Lambeth Conference 1958*, II, p. 31.
23 Bayne, *op. cit.*, p. 37.

1958, the report of the ecumenical commission of the Lambeth Conference could name only five Anglican churches that had recognized the bishops and episcopally ordained presbyters and deacons of the Church of South India as true bishops, presbyters and deacons in God's Church and that had engaged in a limited and carefully regulated intercommunion with that church during its interim period of thirty years. The Anglo-Catholic minority in those five churches, which include the Church of England, continued to oppose that intercommunion.

The Anglican Church in India wishes to prevent such a development of affairs when the reunion in Ceylon, North India and Pakistan takes place. It wants to make sure that the ministries in the united Church will be acceptable by the Anglican Communion as fully valid ministries and that a full communion will be possible between the reunited Church and the churches of the Anglican Communion. That is why the resolutions of the Lambeth Conference of 1958 regarding this matter are so very important. The principal resolution reads:

The Conference advises the Churches and Provinces of the Anglican Communion that they should be willing to enter into full communion with the resulting Church of Lanka on its inauguration.[24]

The Lambeth Conference showed some reserve, for it was not fully in accord with the religious service in which the unification of the ministries would be accomplished. It proposed some amendments and was ready to give the same advice as given for the Church of Lanka, if those amendments were accepted in India.

Until then the process for unification had seemed to progress favorably. The first difficulties occurred when the two provinces of Canterbury and York of the Church of England, the Church of Wales, and the Protestant Episcopal Church of America presented and put to a vote in their Convocations the proposition

---

[24] *The Lambeth Conference 1958,* Resolution 23, I, p. 36.

of immediately entering into full communion with the Church of Lanka after its inauguration. The Higher (bishops') House of Canterbury accepted the proposition unanimously in May 1961; the Higher House of York also accorded it a majority of votes. The Lower House of Canterbury, however, in October 1961, attached as a condition for approval the guarantee that the rite of unification of the ministries would include that all ministers of the uniting churches who had not received ordination from a bishop would be required to receive a complementary ordination through the laying on of hands of a bishop. At the same time the bishops of the Province of York seemed to have changed their minds. In October 1961, seven of the eleven bishops simply voted against an eventual full communion with the Church of Lanka, and the Lower House of York likewise rejected the proposal by forty-seven votes against forty-three.

It is clear that this created a grave situation; the more so because the Church of Wales also seemed to be ready to accept an eventual full communion only on the condition that all presbyters of the Church of Lanka would, if necessary, be ordained by a bishop.

In America the bishops were of the opinion that, as members of the Lambeth Conference of 1958, they had, as a matter of course, to adhere to the favorable opinion that had been expressed by that Conference. But the House of Deputies wished, at the most, to make a carefully defined concordat with the Church of Lanka until specific discrepancies and irregularities in the proposed practice of the Church of Lanka were eliminated.

In the meantime, at the beginning of 1962, a more favorable wind seemed to be blowing, perhaps under the influence of the Convention of New Delhi. The project for the Church of North India was more objectionable than that for the Church of Lanka, and yet this did not prevent both Houses of Canterbury and the Higher House of York from voting unconditionally in favor of an eventual full communion with that church from the moment

198

of its inauguration. Only the Lower House of York voted against it.

At this moment of writing it is not yet clear what decision the other churches and provinces of the Anglican Communion will come to. It is perfectly evident from the hundreds of proposals, discussions and decisions of the past half century that the Anglican churches are able to reach an agreement with the reformational and "free" churches on all points of doctrine, liturgy and church practice, or can leave an eventual agreement to the future.

All Anglican churches adhere with absolute firmness to the principle that the ministries in the reunited Church of the future must of necessity be in unbroken continuity with the ministries of bishop, presbyter and deacon, as the undivided Church of the first centuries knew, respected and preserved them, and specifically by means of an episcopal laying on of hands.

In any case, one thing has become perfectly evident in the practice of half a century of ecumenic efforts for reunion: no actual reunion of all Christian churches is possible without a full reestablishment of the continuity of the episcopal office wherever that continuity was violated or broken.

CHAPTER SEVEN

Episcopal and Presbyterial Church Order

1. PRELIMINARIES TO THE REPORT OF 1957

THE final goal toward which the ecumenical movement has been directed, at first in a more or less indeterminate way, has lately become gradually more precise. In most churches there is a growing realization that in the long run one cannot remain satisfied with longings, demonstrations and conversations about unity, but that the churches must engage in an active mutual planning for this purpose. The concrete final goal is nothing less than the complete restoration of the visible, sacramental and ecclesiastical unity of all Christians. Experience has taught that there are chiefly two sets of questions that come under discussion in that regard.

The first set comprises all the questions which the churches ask one another concerning the content of God's Word, of the Gospel and the Christian faith. The ecumenical question in this regard is whether—in spite of the many dogmatic and theological differences and ancient points of controversy—there exists sufficient agreement to serve as a basis for a fruitful dialogue, or for closer communion and cooperation.

In respect to that first set of questions, it appears, from the reports about the many and diverse conversations which the Anglican churches have conducted with churches of the Cath-

200

olic, reformational and "free" types, that the common acceptance of the same Holy Scriptures and the same ancient Christian creeds guarantees sufficiently that all churches want to profess the same Christian faith. As soon as the churches begin to see one another, not primarily as opponents, but as partners and fellows in Christ, closer discussions reveal that they often agree in many more points than one would have expected.

The second set comprises all the questions that concern the Church, which as the Body of Christ is, or is meant to be, the visible manifestation in the world of the unity and the communion that binds all believing and baptized Christians together in Christ. It is ultimately with this visible manifestation that the ecumenical movement and the ecumenical problematics are concerned.

Although the fact of Christian disunion is closely connected with the first set of questions, nevertheless, as soon as there is question of the restoration of visible unity and communion, the first and foremost question that comes up is that of the nature, the authority, the structure and the functioning of the Church.

The first question in this connection is whether the Church with its ministries and sacraments must possess objectively given and unchangeable characteristics that are based on an explicit institution, will and intention of Christ, or on the contrary, whether that is left to the talent of organization and the practical views of the members of the Church.

The most extreme of the "free" churches take the second standpoint. For them reunion is merely a matter of organization in accordance with the time and circumstances. On the other hand, in regard to reformational churches, especially in those that have a presbyterial church order and in the Anglican churches, a close connection is kept between Church, ministry and sacrament. They are convinced, moreover, that the manner of union should be in accord with Holy Scripture and the practice of the undivided Church of the first centuries.

Both the Anglican and the Reformation churches are convinced that their church order satisfies that requirement. Both assert most emphatically that the Word of God must be proclaimed and the two sacraments of baptism and the Lord's Supper administered by lawfully called and validly ordained ministers. Both recognize that the ministry from the beginning has had a threefold character, that is, that there have always existed three ministries in the Church, namely: *episkopoi* (bishops, overseers), *presbyteroi* (priests, elders) and *diakonoi* (deacons).

Just as explicitly as the Anglican churches, with their episcopal church order, the reformational churches possessing a presbyterial church order intended to restore, through their sixteenth century Reformation, the threefold ministry in accord with the witness of the New Testament and the practice of the primitive Church.

The difference between those two church orders is the result of a difference in method. The Anglican churches preserved intact the episcopal structure; but in regard to its dogmatic interpretation and practical functioning, they have applied the scriptural and ancient Christian principles that were considered normative by the Reformation. The Reformed churches, on the contrary, have followed a Puritan method. They considered the existing order so corrupt that they simply replaced it by a new one. And they thought the latter was the only one that could be rightly derived from the Scriptures.

Concerning the nature of the Church, the ministry and the sacraments, originally there existed no difference between Anglicans and Presbyterians. Both believed that medieval doctrine and practice in regard to that point were degenerate and unscriptural. It is only in consequence of the so-called Restoration Settlement of 1662, and notably under the influence of the Oxford Movement of 1833–1845 and the resulting Anglo-Catholicism, that the Anglican churches have emphasized the necessity of an episcopal church order and that an Anglo-Catholic ecclesiology has developed that is more "Catholic" than reformational. However, the new "Catholic" interpretation of the ministry based upon the latter has never been officially accepted in the Anglican churches as the only correct one.

As soon as churches cease to pursue purely dogmatic and theological discussions regarding the differences and agreements in the interpretation of Revelation and the profession of faith and make a real effort to restore Church unity and communion, the principal practical difficulty is of an ecclesiological nature. More than half a century of ecumenical experience bears witness to this fact. Although the diverse concepts about the Church and sacraments play a role here, though often unperceived, it seems that the heart of the difficulty is always in the ministry. A real reunion of the Church appears simply impossible unless the ministry that existed from the first beginnings in the undivided Church is restored in the reunited Church. And this in such a way that all churches involved and their members can, without scruples of conscience, consider all ministers as possessing the power of the ministry that has been continuously transmitted in the Church from the days of the Apostles until now through the laying on of hands of *Episkopoi*.

The difference of opinion between Anglicans and Presbyterians concerns their answer to the questions: which ministers must rightly be considered as *episkopoi* according to the New Testament and the practice of the primitive Church? and what norms can help to determine in concrete cases whether the historical continuity of the ministry was or was not preserved; in other words, whether or not the ordinations (eventually consecrations) were "valid"?

It is most important, of course, that Christians once more agree in their understanding of God's Word, the Gospel, Holy Scripture and the Christian faith. Nevertheless, every reunion of churches ultimately amounts to a common recognition and acceptance of the ministry, that is, the form, authority and functioning of the ministry, in the reunited Church. This is not an aprioristic and arbitrary statement; it merely expresses a fact

203

that has become perfectly evident during half a century of ecclesiastical negotiations between Anglican and every imaginable type of non-Anglican churches.

If, in this connection, we look at the entire *Ecumene*, we see that until now there has been no agreement between the Church of Rome and all the other churches collectively with respect to the origin, nature and authority of the specific Petrine office. This office according to Catholic belief will continue to exist until the Last Day as the office of the pope, that is, as the special office of Peter and his successors on the Apostolic See. Whether this See will always or of necessity be connected with the city of Rome is, in this connection, not an essential but only an accidental question.

When we leave the Petrine problem out of consideration, we see that the churches are concerned about another question, namely, whether the authentic ministry in its original form and significance is continued and preserved exclusively in episcopal churches or is also, wholly or in part, continued in non-episcopal churches. This problem comes to a head in the question whether Holy Scripture and the primitive Church reveal an episcopal or a presbyterial order.

Apart from the question regarding the Petrine office, there exist among the episcopal churches themselves no essential differences regarding the ministry, that is, regarding the structure of the episcopal ministry and the continuity of office that is connected with apostolic succession.

The Anglican Communion occupies a special place among the churches of this group for two reasons. First, the Anglican orders are, rightly or wrongly, considered invalid by the Church of Rome. Secondly, the Anglican Communion believes that it is not officially obliged to adopt a particular dogmatic interpretation of the ministry and of the relations between ministry and sacrament. More particularly, the Anglican Church abstains carefully from making any negative declaration concerning the relation between the validity or fullness of the ministry and the effect produced in the administration of the sacraments. Expressed in a "Catholic" manner, this means that the celebration of the Eucharist can produce the same "operation of grace" whether or not the minister is validly ordained according to "Catholic" standards.

Among the non-episcopal churches, a special position is occupied by the reformational churches possessing a presbyterial church order. Leaving aside catholicizing tendencies that manifest themselves in some Lutheran churches, we can say that the non-episcopal churches look upon the ministry as on a matter of order and organization that can be regulated according to the individual opinion of each church. Only the Presbyterian churches adhere to the view that the form and functioning of the ministry must be in accord with certain norms based on Scripture. The other non-episcopal churches are less exacting in that respect. They are ready, in a certain sense, to accept every church order and every structure of ministry provided no claim of divine authority is connected with it by which a distinction would arise between priest and layman, and provided such a church order and such a structure of ministry clearly is to be strongly recommended for purely historical and practical reasons.

The many ecumenical conversations between the "free" churches themselves or, as in India, between Anglican and "free" churches have shown that many Presbyterian churches have abandoned the claim that their ministry has a scriptural basis. Like other "free" churches, they have adopted the view that the ministry is a purely practical matter. Hence the question is no longer whether an episcopal or a presbyterial church order is the most scriptural, but how valuable elements belonging to the structure of diverse churches can best be combined in such a way that all churches involved can be satisfied with them. It was in that way that, for instance, in India, Presbyterian and other non-episcopal churches could be persuaded to accept an episcopal structure in the reunited Church.

If the crucial problem with respect to a reunion of churches is ultimately that of the ministry, the battle line runs along the frontier between Anglican and Presbyterian churches. Supposing that a full mutual communion could be reestablished among all episcopal churches, including the Anglican Church, and a similar communion among all non-episcopal churches, the problem of the reunion of all churches would then come down to the question of a possible reconciliation or re-integration of an episcopal and a presbyterial structure of the Church and the ministry.

If we do not limit ourselves to a part of the *Ecumene,* but reflect upon the restoration of the visible unity and communion of the whole, the core of the ecumenical problem appears to lie in the bridging of the chasm between an episcopal and presbyterial church order. In other words, if the Anglican and Presbyterian churches were able to reach a real solution of the theological and practical problems regarding the ministry, the ecclesiological part of the ecumenical problem would in principle be solved. (We abstract from the question concerning the Petrine office and the judgment of the Church of Rome concerning Anglican orders.)

For this reason we devote a separate chapter to the confrontation between the episcopal and presbyterial church orders, as it has evolved in recent years during the ecumenical deliberations between the Anglican and Presbyterian churches of England and Scotland. A settlement of the problem of the episcopal versus presbyterial church order would be very important from the ecumenical standpoint. It could very well be that here is the key to a complete reunited Church, the key which the churches of the whole *Ecumene* have been looking for consciously or unconsciously.

That is why the authors of the collective report *Relations between Anglican and Presbyterian Churches* (1957) had the impression that, as they expressed it:

The questions arising between Episcopalians and Presbyterians lay at the heart of the differences evidenced by other divisions in the

Body of Christ, and that a notable act of reconciliation between them could not fail to introduce a new and promising element into the whole field of ecumenical relationships.[1]

The first official relations between the Anglican Church of England and the Presbyterian Church of Scotland go back to the Lambeth Conference of 1930. One year before, the movement for reunion in the various Presbyterian churches of Scotland, that had separated one after another since the second half of the eighteenth century, was crowned with the successful reunion between the National Church of Scotland and the United Free Church which was itself a reunion of separated churches. Hence, since 1929, Scotland has a large Church of Scotland that embraces all Presbyterians. There exists, however, in Scotland also an independent Anglican Church which calls itself the "Episcopal Church of Scotland."

In connection with the memorable unification of the Presbyterian Church of Scotland, the Lambeth Conference of 1930 passed the following resolution:

> The Conference expresses its gratitude to the distinguished members of the Church of Scotland who accepted the invitation to confer with its Committee. It hopes that an invitation may soon be issued to the now happily united Church of Scotland to enter into free and unrestricted conference with representatives of the Anglican Communion on the basis of the Appeal to All Christian People issued in 1920.[2]

In 1932 for the first time, official delegates of the Church of England, under the leadership of William Temple, then Archbishop of York, and of the Church of Scotland met in a joint committee. After no more than four meetings, of which two took place in Lambeth Palace and two in Edinburgh, they were able to publish a collective report.

Its authors stated:

---

[1] *Relations Between Anglican and Presbyterian Churches,* London, 1957, p. 3.

[2] *The Lambeth Conference 1930,* Resolution 43, p. 53.

A period of two years is not a long time for the exploration of the measure of agreement existing in our Churches after more than three centuries of separation. Nevertheless it has been sufficient to reveal, beneath our differences, a remarkably wide area of common faith and common principle which should supply a strong foundation on which we and our successors may confidently build as we labour to promote the unity of our Churches and the furtherance of the cause of Christ at home and across the seas. Such a result calls for devout acknowledgment and thanksgiving to Almighty God.[3]

Unity in the mother country is here clearly placed in close connection with the missions in other parts of the world.

The end which the commission had kept in view was that of "an unrestricted inter-communion" among the members of the two churches and an equally "unrestricted fellowship" of their ministers.[4]

From the beginning it was evident that here, once again, it was a question of the ministry, how to restore the ministry in such a way that it would be acceptable to all the members of both churches and that all could without scruples of conscience recognize it as fully valid.

The committee went to work in a very methodical way. It began with determining the amount of agreement that already existed between the churches and to what extent cooperation could already be initiated with respect to particular objects on the basis of that agreement. Next, it examined the points in which they differed in order to reach a better mutual understanding. Finally the committee examined what could be done provisionally to create a closer fellowship.

When we examine the nine points upon which there was complete agreement according to the commission, and compare them with the principles of the sixteenth century Reforma-

---

[3] *Report of the Committee Appointed by the Archbishop of Canterbury to Confer with Representatives of the Church of Scotland,* London, 1934, p. 5.
[4] *Ibid.,* p. 5.

tion, it is evident that the Scotch representatives defended these principles and that the representatives of the Church of England expressed their complete agreement with them. Both the Anglican *Thirty-nine Articles* and the Presbyterian Westminster Confession were accepted by the entire commission as historical expressions of the Christian faith.

The report on the nine points of agreement uses the word "Catholic" in the new ecumenical sense of "all-embracing." It accepts Scripture as containing God's Word and as the final standard of faith and morals, which should therefore be placed within reach of everyone, but leaves room within a Catholic fellowship for diversity of interpretation. The divine instrument of individual as well as social rebirth is the Gospel of God's grace. The rebirth is conceived in an ethical and not in a sacramental and ontological way. The sacraments are not regarded as means of grace but as signs and seals of the saving grace of God, although they are also effective signs and seals. The efficacy is ethical; it does not belong to the ontological order of things and through the sacraments "members are admitted, renewed and strengthened within the Body of Christ to form one fellowship in Him of life and service in believing and thankful dependence upon His Spirit."[5]

In regard to the Church, ministry and sacraments, the report makes a sharp distinction between "that" and "how." The Anglican and Presbyterian representatives agree about the "that" but permit mutual freedom in the interpretation of the "how." They both agree *that* the sacraments incorporate the members into the communion of the Body of Christ, renew and strengthen them; *that* the ministry and ministerial services are a gift of Jesus Christ our Lord to His Church; *that* the Church has its foundation not in the will of men but in the eternal will of God; *that* the interior unity of the faithful in Christ, the one Head of the

---

[5] *Ibid.*, p. 10.

209

Church, must be made visible in a social church life and in a church fellowship; and, finally, *that* the Church manifests its continuity through the centuries and all over the world as one Body of which Christ is the Head. This manifestation of the continuity of the Church as the one Body is considered to be real in spite of the present external division.

The Anglicans and Presbyterians, according to the report of 1934, are agreed *that* all this is so, but admit mutually that there are diverse ways in which one can conceive *how* all these things come about, continue to exist and operate. Here again it appears, as in the conversations in India, that unification rests in the first place on the acceptance of facts and not on agreement in the dogmatic, theological and speculative interpretation of the facts.

In view of the remarkably wide area of common faith and common principle and agreement about facts of vital importance, the members of the commission insisted that that agreement should be publicly confirmed and made known as widely as possible. At the same time they proposed six points about which it was already possible to establish a real cooperation. Among these were the open pulpit and the admission of members of the other church to Holy Communion, if circumstances make it impossible for them to participate in services of their own church. This admission to Communion was based on the fact that all baptized Christians are members of the Catholic Church of Christ. Other points were of a Christian-social nature or were concerned with obtaining closer knowledge of one another through study and continued research.

The commission called the result of the common exploration a mere first beginning. It realized that this beginning demanded great efforts, for it considered it proper to advise the church authorities involved not to engage in further negotiations for the time being:

210

Meanwhile we propose that these conferences should for the present be suspended—to be resumed, we trust, when in God's providence the time shall appear opportune.[6]

This opportune time came after World War II. William Temple died in 1944 after being Archbishop of Canterbury for two years and was succeeded by Geoffrey Fisher. The new archbishop at first showed great preference for reunion with reformational and "free" churches. Personally he manifested no affinity with Anglo-Catholicism.

The relations between the Church of England and the evangelical "free" churches,[7] which had come to a dead end, entered an entirely new phase when the new Archbishop of Canterbury, on November 3, 1946, delivered his famous sermon at the University of Cambridge on the theme *A Step Forward in Church Relations*. A commission was organized consisting of representatives of the Archbishop of Canterbury and of the evangelical "free" churches of England. Its purpose was to examine the bearing and range of the suggestions made by the Archbishop in his sermon.[8]

Meanwhile, following the proposal of the ecumenical commission, the Lambeth Conference of 1948 adopted a resolution expressing its agreement for an early reopening of the conversations, interrupted in 1934, between the Archbishop of Canterbury and representatives of the Church of Scotland, "in view of the new situation created by the Archbishop of Canterbury's sermon at Cambridge, November 1946."[9]

---

[6] *Ibid.*, p. 6. Cf. Conclusion on p. 12.

[7] Counted as belonging to the evangelical free churches are the Presbyterian, Congregationalist, Methodist and Baptist churches and the Moravian Brethren.

[8] *Church Relations in England, being a report of conversations between representatives of the Archbishop of Canterbury and representatives of the Evangelical Free Churches in England, together with the sermon preached by the Archbishop of Canterbury on November 3rd, 1946, entitled A Step Forward in Church Relations*, London, 1950.

[9] *The Lambeth Conference 1948*, Resolution 60, I, p. 41.

It was the intention from the start to draw into the confrontation between episcopal and presbyterial forms of church order the Anglicans of Scotland, the Presbyterians of England, and ultimately also the whole Anglican Communion and the whole World Alliance of Presbyterian Churches. The meetings of the Joint Committee, formed in virtue of Resolution 60, were attended by observers of the Presbyterian Church of England and the Episcopal Church in Scotland. In 1951 the Committee was able to make its first report, which introduced a new distinction that has universal ecumenical importance. In connection with the fact that everyone who is actually engaged in ecumenical discussions and negotiations quickly becomes convinced that the road to the ultimate goal is long and difficult, the report made a distinction between two different procedures: a short-term policy and a long-term policy.

No one who is familiar with the subject still thinks that it is possible to find a theological solution of the ecumenical problem in a purely theoretical way. The unification of Christianity is a thoroughly practical matter; we shall be able to speak of progress only after many encounters and explorations, much searching and groping, of which no one can foresee the result. It is also becoming increasingly evident that unification can be attained only gradually and step by step. It is a matter of a slow process of growth on the part of all churches concerned, the Church of Rome not excepted; a long process that will bring with it radical changes, adjustments and, in a certain sense, concessions to the extent that these are in accord with the objective content of Revelation and the Christian faith that is based upon it. It is a question of a patient and carefully planned long-term procedure.

Meanwhile, however, the churches can investigate in what ways living and working together is already possible without delay. This is a matter of a more simple short-term procedure.

The report of 1951 was a first step on the road of the long-

212

term policy toward a final complete bridging of the, in some respects more seeming than real, opposition between the Anglican-episcopal and the presbyterial church orders. The report was received and judged favorably in the General Assembly of the Church of Scotland in May 1951. The proposal contained in the report of 1934 regarding the open pulpit and the mutual admission of members of the other church to Holy Communion in one's own church was accepted.

The General Synod agreed that it was its duty to strive, together with other Christian communions, for the fullness of the life of the Church in unity, according as the will of God will become manifest to the Church. It expressed its agreement with the two important ecumenical principles on which the report of 1951 was based, viz., 1. it recognized the sovereign freedom of God's grace in the history of the Church; 2. it approved the method of not beginning with a declaration about the validity of the ministry in one another's churches, but to begin instead with a joint investigation of what belongs to the full life of the Church, seen from the standpoint of the ultimate unity which God wills for His people.

Finally, the General Synod of the Church of Scotland, as well as the Convocations of Canterbury and York, expressed the wish that the conversations be continued and even assume a broader perspective. The official character of those conversations was particularly emphasized by the fact that the Anglican representatives of the Church of England would be named by the Convocations of Canterbury and York, and not by the Archbishop of Canterbury personally. Representatives of the Episcopal Church of Scotland and of the Presbyterian Church of England would take part in a broader Joint Committee. The members of this broader committee were named in 1953.

The Church of England expressed the wish that the report should be ready before the Convocations in May 1957; but added that after it had been presented it should not be discussed before the Lambeth Conference of 1958 had had the opportunity to form a judgment about the report and to propose it for consideration to the Church of England, the Episcopal Church of Scotland, and all other churches of the Anglican Communion. This procedure would best foster unity of judgment within the Anglican Communion. And this is what in fact took place. The report *Relations Between Anglican and Presbyterian Churches* was ready in time and in April 1957 was first published by the Society for Promoting Christian Knowledge (S.P.C.K.). This report deserves to be called one of the most sound and important ecumenical reports that has ever been published until the present.

2. THE 1957 REPORT "RELATIONS BETWEEN ANGLICAN AND PRESBYTERIAN CHURCHES"

The Joint Committee that wrote this report was composed of twelve representatives of the Church of England, twelve of the Church of Scotland, three of the Episcopal Church of Scotland and four of the Presbyterian Church of England. The president of the Anglican deputation was the famous dogmatist Rawlinson, who resigned as Bishop of Derby in 1959. Dr. Ramsey was also a member of this deputation until his appointment as Archbishop of York; and so was Dr. Tomkins, formerly secretary of the Faith and Order commission in the World Council of Churches. The Presbyterian deputation had as its chairman Dr. Craig, the present Moderator of the Church of Scotland. Members of this deputation were, among others, the dogmatist Torrance[10] and the church historian Burleigh, professor at the University of Edinburgh.

The Joint Committee described its aim in the following words:

---

[10] The principal eccelesiological studies of Torrance have been published in two volumes under the title, *Conflict and Agreement in the Church*, London, 1960. Concerning the relations between Anglicans and Presbyterians, see vol. I, pp. 104 ff.

The intention [is] to set about the preparation . . . of a draft outline of practical ways and means whereby, with some measure of mutual adaptation and modification of their respective traditions but without disloyalty to principles held to be essential, the Churches taking part in the Conversations might by God's grace be enabled to attain mutually a fuller manifestation of catholicity in faith and order than was exhibited by any of them in separation.[11]

Like any other significant ecumenical encounter this one was based upon the distinction between essential and accidental elements in the profession and practice of the faith. It was agreed that no one would sacrifice for the sake of unity anything he considered to belong to the unchangeable and inviolable essence of faith and church order. It is from this starting point that all ecumenical conversations must begin. They must also start with the conviction that no single church is capable of exhausting the full meaning and content of God's Revelation in Christ in its preaching and practice of the faith. Together, therefore, they must try to come nearer to full Catholicity. Neither should they cling to cherished practices that are only accidental, to the detriment of a communion of church life; but they must be ready to adapt themselves and, if necessary or desirable, to re-examine themselves.

In line with the report of 1951 the committee concluded unanimously that it should not seek its starting point in the question about the validity of ministerial ordinations but in the examination of what must necessarily and finally belong to ecclesial fullness in the reunited Church of the future. Only looking forward to the future can give freedom from too narrow and restrictive a bond with the past. In all ecumenical encounters, the churches must concentrate their attention not so much on the causes of the division as on the question what the reunited Church ought to be. The committee, whose members

---

[11] Published in 1955 and incorporated into the report, *Relations Between Anglican and Presbyterian Churches,* Preface, p. X.

had become acquainted in the World Council of Churches, wished to continue to build knowingly on the results that had been achieved by the ecumenical movement during the previous years. In this respect it started from four implicit presuppositions:

1. Unity is not an accidental but an essential mark of the Church. The Church must of necessity be one, since her existence is based on divine realities in which no division is conceivable. In spite of that truth, division remains a visible reality and this division, whatever its extent, is always contrary to the nature of the Church.

2. Division and disunion undermine the missionary activity of the Church in the world. The Church cannot properly fulfill her task of reconciling the world as long as she fails to cure and reconcile her own disunion. If it is desirable to have union in the countries of the ancient churches, it is imperative to have that unity in countries where the churches are young. Every step in the direction of unity is at the same time a step toward a proclamation of the Gospel which will exercise greater influence and power of persuasion.

3. The road of ecumenism, as was clearly defined during the Conference on Faith and Order at Lund, in 1952, begins with the unity of Christ. Starting from that unity, the Christians try to come together and reach a common understanding of the unity of the Church on earth; and, starting from the unity and bond of Christ with His Body, they reflect upon the means of manifesting that unity as a reality in the state of disunion that actually exists on earth. The committee refers to a passage in the report of Lund which emphasized that, if one wishes to foster the progress of ecumenical endeavors, it is of decisive importance to deal with the doctrine about the Church in close connection with both the doctrine concerning Christ and the doctrine concerning the Holy Ghost.

4. It is necessary, at every stage of the deliberations, to take

into account the fact that churches of the same type have, in other parts of the world, been successful in bringing about a union. In other words, whenever one wishes to take another step forward on the ecumenical road, one should make use of the achievements that have been attained elsewhere. In this way there will be no need to repeat the laborious work of others. In this matter the committee pointed to the experiences and discoveries produced by the efforts for unity in India. The fact that South India succeeded in achieving unity must serve as a spur. In other words, why maintain that what has been possible and has become a reality elsewhere cannot be achieved in one's own country?

There was complete agreement between the Anglican and Presbyterian members of the committee concerning these four points. They likewise agreed fully about the two fundamental conditions of every ecumenical encounter, namely, that Christ wills complete unity in His Church, and that no solution is conceivable without definite modifications in the two types of church order.

Every ecumenical discussion must keep away as far as possible from a preconceived "either/or," as if it were a matter of determining which of the parties is entirely right and which is entirely wrong. On the basis of a true faith in God's Word, in Christ and His Gospel, the churches should strive for the maximum of integration of whatever divine truth they, in their condition of division, have preserved. Every ecumenical encounter between churches that believe that changes must be made exclusively by the other party is *a priori* doomed to failure. Faults have been committed on both sides. Hence when they meet, it is meaningless to repeat the old reproaches.

In regard to the opposition between episcopal and presbyterial church orders, two facts must constantly be kept in mind, namely: first, that in both cases there is question of a one-sided development in which definite elements have appeared to full

217

advantage at the expense of others; and secondly, for the sake of attaining the full truth and reality, every church, while upholding her own positive values, must be willing to incorporate the elements which are lacking in her but which have been preserved in the other.

The ecumenical movement will advance only when the churches are primarily critical of themselves and full of esteem for the other. Destructive criticism must make room for reconstruction. What is out of date must be removed. All elements that have lasting value and significance, no matter where they are found, must be brought together to serve as building material from which the reunited Church of the future will be constructed.

The authors of the report of 1957 applied that ecumenical principle to the opposition existing between the episcopal and the presbyterial church order. All the members of the committee came to agreement in every detail about the modifications that would have to be made in the episcopal and the presbyterial church order. In the determination of those concrete changes, the entire commission unanimously started from the consideration of the following five Biblical and doctrinal points:

1. The whole Church as the Body of Christ participates in His threefold ministry as Prophet, Priest, and King, by serving Him as Lord. Sent from God it is rightly described as apostolic not only in its faith, doctrine and mission but also in its order.

2. (a) All ministry in the Church is to be interpreted as a ministry of Christ to the Church, that is from the Head to the Body as a whole.

(b) All ministry in the Church is to be exercised within the corporate priesthood of the whole Church.

3. Within this wider exercise of ministry there is a specific ministry of the Word and Sacraments to which by ordination some are set apart.

4. The unity and continuity of the Church includes the following points:

(a) The unity and continuity of the whole Body as baptismally incorporated into the royal priesthood of Christ.

(b) The unity and continuity therein of the ministration of the Word and Sacraments as means of grace in the Church.

5. Among the functions of the ordained ministry is that of exercising *episcopē* or oversight in the Church. Such *episcopē,* far from being exclusively concerned with administration, can be considered under five aspects:

(a) Apostolic mission and authority.

(b) The pastoral office.

(c) The continuance of the ministry of Word and Sacraments through ordination.

(d) Guardianship of truth and exclusion of error.

(e) Representation of the Church in its unity and universality.[12]

These points are more fully developed in the report. The Anglicans and Presbyterians agreed that the fullness of ministry rests pre-eminently in Christ. From that fullness of ministry Christ has called into existence the apostolic service of ministry and through the power of the Holy Spirit has given it to the Church as a whole, to function for the benefit of the whole Church "in order that He may increase and edify the Church through the means of grace, and keep it always in subordination to Himself."[13]

It is clear that the whole committee put all emphasis on the close connection of the ministry in the Church with its lasting dependence on Christ, for fear of a human independence of ministry and ministers with respect to Christ or with respect to the faithful:

Accordingly, when a man is ordained to the ministry, he does not act apart from the Body, but acts for the Head to the Body in particular ways.[14]

According to both Anglican and Presbyterian conviction, the ministry in the Church goes back to the ministry of the first Apostles. These are called the masterbuilders of the Church.

---

[12] *Ibid.,* p. 8.   [13] *Ibid.,* p. 9.
[14] *Ibid.,* p. 9.

The pastoral stewardship and the missionary service of the Word and the Sacraments are continued in the ministry and the ministerial service of the Church in a manner that corresponds with the apostolic testimony and within the apostolic tradition.

It is recognized that the continuity of the ministerial succession constitutes an element in the unity of the Church through the centuries, and that breaks in the unity have usually been coupled with more or less important breaks in an orderly succession of ministry. These breaks were usually connected not so much with different concepts regarding the nature of the ministry but with the development undergone by the ministry in later centuries and in particular regarding the manner in which the supervision and authority must be exercised in the Church.

In this respect the Anglican and Presbyterian members of the commission laid down a number of differences regarding the manner in which supervision functions in an Anglican-episcopal and a Presbyterial church order. The respective standpoints would come somewhat closer if the episcopate of the episcopal churches functioned more as a corporate episcopate within a synodal church representation.

A full bridging of the opposition between those church orders could be expected only from a unity through mutual adjustment. Both church types would have to receive from one another what each considers essential regarding the ministry in its own confession, but each would remain free regarding the theological interpretation of the additions and changes. Moreover, there should be no question of doing violence to the religious and ecclesiastical heritage and development of the other type of church, but only of healing the ministry together in such a way that a fully sacramental communion would become possible while each preserved its full spiritual liberty. The numerous modifications that would have to be introduced in both Presbyterian and Anglican churches are described in great detail.

With respect to the short-term policy, the report said, the Presbyterian and Anglican churches could meanwhile begin with making more frequent use of the open pulpit and, in particular circumstances, members of the Presbyterian churches could, if they desired, be permitted to receive Holy Communion in Anglican churches. The report finally mentioned various means for fostering contact between Anglicans and Presbyterians and an increasingly better understanding of one another's point of view.

The Lambeth Conference of 1958 studied and discussed the report very thoroughly and expressed its appreciation of the result that had been reached in the following resolution:

The Conference notes with satisfaction and thankfulness the remarkable measure of constructive theological agreement, which the theologians on both sides were able to reach and record, and expresses the hope that serious consideration may be given to the possibility of drawing the Anglican and Presbyterian traditions more closely together by a process of mutual assimilation of their respective Church Orders such as is suggested in the Report.[15]

The churches of the Presbyterian World Alliance have adopted a more reserved attitude regarding the report. There is as yet no question at all of a definitive solution, in virtue of which Anglican and Presbyterian churches would be able to enter into a full sacramental communion.

It would be an ominous sign for ecumenical prospects in general if the Anglican-Presbyterian deliberations remained stuck halfway, at the stage in which they are at present. As we said at the beginning of this chapter, the success or failure of the endeavor of Anglicans and Presbyterians to reconcile their respective church orders is decisive for the near future with respect to a complete restoration of continuity of the ministry with the ministry of the undivided Church of the first centuries, and with respect to a consequent restoration thereon of the

---

[15] *The Lambeth Conference 1958*, Resolution 28, I, p. 37.

visible unity and communion of all Christians in the one Church of Christ.

There are indications that the Assembly of New Delhi has contributed toward a greater rapprochement between the stands of the Anglicans and the Presbyterians. The Assembly has given various representatives of non-episcopal churches greater understanding of the importance of an episcopal ministerial succession. Hopes are also founded on the ecclesiological results of the fourth World Conference on Faith and Order that took place, under the auspices of the World Council of Churches at Montreal in 1963.

3. CONCLUSIONS FROM THE ANGLICANS' ECUMENICAL EFFORTS

Surveying once more all the discoveries and experiences that have resulted from the ecumenical efforts of the Anglican Communion in its dialogue with the most diverse churches during the past half century, it seems to me that we are permitted to draw from them at least the following important conclusions:

1. The restoration of the visible unity and communion of all Christians, within the One Catholic and Universal Church of Christ implies *de facto* principally a complete restoration of the ministry in the Church. This restoration must be in accord with the data of Holy Scripture and with the development of the ministry by the apostles and the tradition of the primitive Church, in such a way that all Christians, according to their deepest religious convictions, are able to recognize the ministry as Christ intended it for His Church, as He has given it to her, and maintains it in His Church through the power of the Holy Spirit.

2. There seems to exist perfect agreement between Anglican and Presbyterian churches regarding the nature of the ministry. In the "free" churches in which the ministry is approached and

conceived as not being scriptural and dogmatic but purely a matter of human organization, there is, under the influence of the ecumenical encounter, a growing conviction of the indispensable place, profound meaning and significance of the ministry in the Church. Without becoming over-optimistic, we can even expect that ultimately—speaking globally—there will appear to be a great measure of agreement about the nature of the ministry between the Anglican and Presbyterian churches on the one hand, and the Catholic churches on the other.

3. On the basis of a common conviction regarding the nature of the ministry, there seems to remain principally three points concerning the ministry about which no sufficient clarity and agreement has been reached. They are the following:

a. The diverse ways in which the Church perpetuates itself through the centuries and the marks by which the continuity of the ministry can be recognized.

b. The form and the manner in which the *episkopē* and *exousia* (the "overseeing" and authority) instituted by Christ must be exercised in the Church according to His intention.

c. The efficacy of the administration of the Word and the sacraments in the heart and the life of the faithful, and the extent to which that efficacy depends on the validity of ministerial ordinations.

d. If the signs are not misleading, we stand at the beginning of a truly existential ecumenical dialogue between the Church of Rome and all other churches, and not in the presence of a dialogue that is chained to *a priori* conditions and restrictions. In this encounter the problem of the ministry, and in connection with it the question about the continuity of the Church, will ultimately take the central place in the dialogue. In it the important results obtained through the conversations, between the churches of the Anglican Communion and practically all other churches during the last twenty-five or fifty years, will undoubtedly offer fruitful suggestions.

223

e. There remains a lacuna in the Anglican efforts in the ecumenical field. They have not yet come to a serious confrontation with Karl Barth's vision of the Church and the *Ecumene* or with World-Lutheranism.

CHAPTER EIGHT

Catholicity and Ecumenicity

1. ECUMENISM, CHURCH AND GOSPEL

As experience shows, ecumenical negotiations have rarely led
to a satisfactory solution of the dogmatic and theological
questions that lie at the foundation of Christian disunion. This,
however, does not mean that ecumenical encounters have
produced no important results. In many cases they have clarified
a confused ecumenical situation. They have resulted in unforeseen experiences and discoveries that can be significant for the
future. It is becoming gradually clearer by what road visible
unity can be reached.

The participants in ecumenical conferences have been able
to know and understand one another much better. They have
learned to put themselves as much as possible in one another's
place. When there was sufficient openness, it appeared possible
to appreciate the positive value of the other's ecumenical contribution and to realize one's own one-sidedness and shortcomings. Ecumenical encounters have contributed to a deeper
and more thorough understanding of the seriousness and true
nature of the difficulties. All kinds of incidents, situations and
decisions which, in the past and today, have promoted estrangement between Christians appear now in another light and are
found to be, if not acceptable, at least more understandable.

225

Many encounters have thus had a liberating effect. They have contributed toward a wholesome reappraisal of the past in the sense of making it easier to let it rest and to deliberate together about what can and ought to be done in view of the future. Particularly the many relations and negotiations of the Anglican churches in the most diverse directions have gradually made it clearer which practical and theological problems, precisely, must be solved if we wish to see the eventual restoration of the visible, sacramental and ecclesial unity of all Christians.

In the preceding chapters we have discussed the results to which the ecumenical endeavors of the Anglican Communion have led until now. At first sight these results seem disappointing. The Anglicans have been successful only in establishing complete intercommunion, now termed "full communion," while maintaining each one's independence with the small group of Old Catholics. True, this "full communion" may become more important for the unification of the churches in the future than presently appears. Nevertheless, when it is seen against the background of the energy and perseverance with which the Anglican churches have striven for unity during more than half a century, that result looks very poor. Probably this is due to the fact that the Anglican churches have been ahead of all other churches in the field of ecumenism. Only now does the time seem ripe for a better understanding and appreciation of the practical methods which the Anglican churches advocate and apply on the basis of their ecumenical principles.

In this connection it might be useful to devote a few words to two misconceptions from which the ecumenical activity of the Anglicans has undeservedly suffered.

In the first place, one might hear the remark that the ecumenical activity of the Anglicans is possibly only an expression of the inborn imperialistic instinct of Englishmen; it would thus be an endeavor to acquire a central and leading position in the World Church of the future. Anyone who has had personal and sufficient contact with one or more pioneers of Anglican ecumenicity, or has made a proper study of their writings, will be forced to testify that there is no foundation for such a supposition.

A second misconception is more serious because it concerns fundamentals. It consists in saying that the Anglicans are essentially only an ecclesiology, hence a mutilated form of Christianity. This mistaken idea results from the fact that the Anglicans, by their manifold contacts with other churches, have learned that projects for intercommunion or reunion always get stranded on difficulties that are of an ecclesiological nature. That is why Anglicans have been forced by the circumstances to concentrate their principal attention on ecclesiological questions.

One who knows Anglicanism exclusively through its ecumenical activity could indeed get the mistaken impression that Anglican thought, belief and life is principally concerned with the Church. If, on the contrary, we approach Anglicanism from the standpoint of liturgy, spirituality and theology, we recognize that one of the most striking characteristics of Anglicanism lies precisely in the desire and endeavor to express, live and give deep theological consideration to the whole of the manifold riches of God's revelation in Christ. Hence also comes the ecumenical principle of Anglicanism that the reunited Church of the future will have to express and render the totality of Christ in a rich variety of forms.

The reports of the Lambeth Conferences likewise reveal that these have increasingly raised precisely non-ecclesiological questions. Thus, the principal theme of the Conference of 1930 was the Christian doctrine about God; that of the Conference of 1948 was the Christian teaching about man; and in 1958 there was the important subject of the Bible, its authority and message which, among other things, is of particular ecumenical importance. Without exaggeration one can say that lately there has

227

appeared in Anglicanism a shift of accent from the Church to Holy Scripture and the Gospel. This change is coupled with a growing appreciation of the spiritual heritage of the Reformation.

In this connection we shall now first examine a group of questions that are addressed to the ecumenical movement by modern theologians, prophets and seers who see a need for a total and radical renewal of the Church and Christianity, of theology and preaching, of liturgy and pastoral care. Such questioners include Barth, Bonhöffer, Niemöller, Kraemer and their many kindred spirits, among whom there are also Roman Catholics.

When we listen to their biblical and prophetic testimony, we cannot help asking ourselves whether perhaps we should not adopt a totally different view, even in regard to unification, than the one we have hitherto entertained on account of our conventional connection with the past. Has the question concerning the restoration of unity not been overshadowed for a long time by a more pressing one: What must be done if we do not want to witness the total collapse of the Church and if we wish to make it possible for future mankind to listen to, understand and believe the Gospel? Are we not worrying too much about questions concerning ecclesiastical organization, canon law and liturgy that are essentially out of date?

Will the unification of the Christians not come about of itself if all churches adopt a totally new way of preaching the Gospel to a totally changed and still constantly changing world and especially of living that Gospel in that world? In any case, should we not put the principal emphasis on the close and important connection between reunion and reform? Does this not mean that we should have the intelligence, the will and the courage to break radically with many conventional meanings, practices, attitudes and conditions of the past? Is it not ten times more necessary, before we attempt to unite the churches, that they be awakened and be made aware of the urgent necessity of a new reform and of a total renewal all along the line? Isn't the principal question what must be done against the apathetic defection from the faith, against growing irreligion, against religious indifference? Must we not say that Henry Kraemer is right when he declares that communication is no longer possible between the old tumble-down Church and the modern world?

These and similar questions are constantly asked by Christians who, possessed of the necessary sense of reality, are involved in the life of the present time. No one can silently evade those questions without showing a serious want of responsibility toward modern man and the future.

Connected with that sense of responsibility are, among other things, the high hopes with which many look forward to the results of the second Vatican Council. Will the Council understand the signs of the time? Will it make a genuine contribution toward the renewal of the Church, the restoration of the communication between priest and laymen, between the Church and the world, and finally also toward the restoration of Christian unity?

As a matter of fact all those questions are most closely interconnected. It is not merely a matter of restoring Christian unity. Much more is at stake. It is above all a question of a new proclamation of the Gospel, of a new way of preaching the faith, a new form of ecclesial worship, a new way of being a Christian, a new communication between the Church and the world, a new response of modern man to the Gospel and a new understanding of Sacred Scripture. It is then a matter of renewal. One of the many results of the renewal must be the restoration of the visible, sacramental and Church unity of the Christians.

It is with the latter theme that we deal in this book. This does not, in the least, imply an undervaluation of the importance of the questions we have just now proposed. We need nevertheless to be on our guard against one-sidedness. However

229

great the need of giving serious attention to the various questions we have put forward, the theme of the restoration of the visible unity of Christianity thereby loses none of its proper and distinct meaning and significance.

The possibility of a certain one-sidedness, which is proper to all prophetism and idealism, is not excluded; a false antithesis might be created between two different endeavors that are both equally necessary: the endeavor to make modern man open to the Gospel and the effort to restore the visible unity of the Christians. In the first case it is principally a matter of renewal, in the second, of restoration. In one case it is a question of creating a new communication; in the other a matter of restoring the visible, sacramental and ecclesial communion that was lost.

There is question here of two different objectives, hence also of two different approaches. But the two objectives and approaches are not in the least opposed to each other. It is not a matter of choosing either one *or* the other, but of both the one *and* the other. It is a question of two different concerns but these must constantly interact. The renewal of the outward involvement will foster the restoration of unity and the restoration of unity will exercise a favorable influence upon the outward involvement.

That is why it is greatly desirable that an end be put to the clearly noticeable tendency to play the two sides of the full reality against each other. On the one hand is the static and on the other the dynamic element in the announcement of the Gospel and in the life of the Church; on the one side are the traditional institutions that have a permanent validity and significance and on the other new ways in which the Gospel must be brought to men and in which the Church must function, in order to correspond to the demands of a new humanity in a totally changed world. It is necessary to watch lest history repeat itself and, as in earlier times of reformation and renewal, true values be sacrificed.

In view of the restoration of the visible unity of Christians, it is therefore most necessary that all churches should strive for an integration of the Church and the Gospel, as this accords with the apostolic testimony of Sacred Scripture and the Church Fathers of the undivided Church. The churches in our time are faced with a twofold task, namely, to reflect again upon the core and the proper purport of the Gospel and to reach a new understanding of the nature of the Church in the full and true sense of the Word.

It is indeed a question of the Gospel, but it is also a question of the Church. It is a matter of the exact relation and connection between the Gospel and the Church. It is a matter of the Church which is expressly the Church of the Gospel, that is, the Church which is announced and supposed by the Gospel. But it is also a matter of the Gospel that is expressly the Gospel of the Church and not the Gospel of this or that prophet, reformer or religious party. It is a matter of the whole Gospel of the whole Church in the inseparable connection and mutual interaction that exist between both. Only on the foundation of a complete integration of the whole Gospel and the whole Church can a complete restoration of the visible unity of all Christians be achieved.

In spite of all the radical changes that are taking place in our time and the reforms and renewals that necessarily result from them, man's nature remains unchanged. Changes and renewals always take place on the surface, in the sphere of what is not essential. But this does not at all mean that those changes and renewals are unimportant and meaningless. They are in many cases inevitable and urgently necessary.

The same is true also of the Gospel and the Church. With respect to the most profound nature of the Church and the Gospel there can be no more question of change than in God, "with whom there can be no change, no swerving from his

231

course."[1] No doubt, the preaching of the Gospel and the function of the Church have also a human and therefore relative and defective aspect. But just as the Gospel is not subject to change, so there can be no change in the nature of the Church with its ministries and sacraments that go back to an institution by Christ.

Both the Gospel and the Church owe their authority and power to the living Lord, who is the Head, and the Holy Spirit, who is the Soul in the Church. The Church's ministerial services are signs and external visible means of a supernatural operation of grace or, which comes down to the same thing, of a divine operation of the Holy Spirit. To the extent that the Church expresses itself in human opinions and conduct, no divine character can be attributed to her. But neither may we reduce her to the human level when there is question of what Christ Himself does and brings forth through His Word and Spirit by means of His Church.

If it be permitted to use Greek philosophy—although Sacred Scripture does not express itself in the same words—to clarify the relation between the unchangeable, inviolable essence and the changeable, violable human exterior, we could say that underneath the Heraclitean flux there always remains the permanent foundation, the being of that which is as it is. According to the famous word of Parmenides, "being is"; and it always remains the foundation of any philosophy that is faithful to truth and reality. If this is true of natural things, how much more must it be true of the inscrutable mystery of God Incarnate, Jesus Christ, and of His Body, which is the Church.

This idea explains the strong emphasis the churches of the "Catholic" type have always placed on the ontological character of the Church, the ministries, the ministerial ordination and the sacramental ministrations. The reformational churches, reacting against the unscriptural, wholly or partly pagan, sacramental

---

[1] James 1:17.

practices of our medieval ancestors who had been too quickly and superficially converted, put the emphasis principally on the connection between sacrament and the Word and on the scriptural manner in which the sacraments should be administered. The churches of the "Catholic" type, on the other hand, principally emphasize the mysterious nature of the sacraments and of the supernatural gifts which the Holy Spirit through the sacraments imparts really (ontologically) and *per se* to the believing recipient.

Here we are in the presence of merely seeming contradictions. For the benefit of reunion between the churches of the "Catholic" type and the churches that have sprung from the Reformation, all churches, in the measure in which it is needed, must rediscover the connection between Church and Gospel that was intended by Christ; and they must reestablish it in the purest form in the way they function. The ecumenical effort can be greatly aided in this respect also by the churches of the Anglican Communion. For the Anglican churches have been successful in gradually introducing a balanced integration between the Catholic view of the Church and the Reformation view of the Gospel whereas no other church has been able to realize that ideal.

The Church is truly an "established institution," at least if the expression is not taken in a political, social and cultural, but in a theological-ecclesiological sense. Within the Church there exists a *koinonia*, a community and mutual service, a *communio sanctorum*, a "communion of saints," in which all share in the same faith, the same sacramental life, the same public worship and the same salvation, in spite of the variety of forms that may have been adopted on account of different circumstances of place and time.

However, it is not a good thing for the projected restoration of unity among Christians if an opposition is created between the Church as a static institution and the Church as a dynamic fellowship. The fact that the Church has established itself in the world is not in contradiction with the fact that she is and will remain, until the Last Day, a pilgrim-Church or, to use the words of Kraemer, an "Abrahamitic adventure of faith." Whoever sees a contradiction between "being established" in the world and the dynamic "pilgrimage" can hardly avoid approaching ecumenical efforts with reserve, for the first and principal purpose of ecumenism is to unite all churches within an all-embracing World Church. This reserve and caution is clearly expressed in Kraemer's warning:

> It would mean a spiritual catastrophe if, for instance, the World Council of Churches in fact became mainly the organized effort for reunion and mobilization of the separated Churches, thereby forgetting its true inspiration, that is to say, being an Abrahamitic adventure of faith towards a still unknown country, which God will show us.[2]

It is incorrect to suppose that those who pray and work for a complete restoration of the visible unity of the Church look upon it as the product of an organized effort. It is rather a question of a rediscovery of the nature of the Church in its most profound and most complete sense and significance, that is, as the one visible expression on earth of the mystical (that is, hidden and supernatural and yet sacramentally visible in earthly forms) Body of Christ. We face here a reality of faith which has been obscured, as a consequence of conflicts and schisms in the course of the centuries, and which can be perfectly realized only when all who believe and are baptized in Christ are again restored in the unity of the one Church of Christ.

When looked at from the ecumenical standpoint, there is a danger in an excessive emphasis on the Bible as the Book of personal piety, vocation and responsibility. In the Bible we meet not only prophets sent by God, who announce God's judgment and call for repentance and conversion, but there are also kings anointed by God who administer order and law, priests anointed

---

[2] Kraemer, *The Communication of Faith,* Philadelphia, 1961, p. 10.

by God who daily offer public worship, and men versed in the Scriptures who are enlightened by God and, as servants of the divine Word, instruct the people in Sacred Scripture.

The Bible is as expressly concerned with preserving and keeping alive what God has given and commended, as with prophetic revival movements, reforms and renewals. It is even permissible to say that in periods of dynamic revolutions it is fundamentally a matter of returning to and restoring what God has given and instituted but which through misuse or negligence has lost its original meaning and significance. Dynamic movements presuppose precisely that there is something static to which people must return and that must be restored to its original "state" or position.

In Holy Scripture the static and dynamic are not mutually exclusive but rather mutually inclusive. Hence also the dynamic element in the ecumenical movement must be directed to a complete restoration of the visible unity of the Church as a static reality that is willed and given by God.

The penetrating, shocking, frightening and sometimes even sensational words of revivalists and critics may meet the need of some people for emotional piety, but in the long run it is not possible to build, restore and preserve a Church with such means. The ecumenical movement must be fostered rather by a steady will, purposeful effort and perseverance in continuing to build on the foundations that were laid centuries ago. The ecumenical effort would tend rather to a systematic restoration of everything that, according to a tradition and experience of almost twenty centuries of Church and Christianity, truly gives "firmness to God's edifice." In other words, we should not build on the precarious ups and downs of the subjective inspiration of prophetic seers and theologians but on the firm foundation of the divine economy of salvation as revealed in Christ and the Church.

2. CATHOLICITY AND "COMPREHENSIVENESS"

The preceding remarks were intended to clear the way for a good understanding of the principles, purposes and manifestations of Anglican ecumenism.

This ecumenism, no doubt, is in some respects typically British. This is an advantage. The sober realism of the Englishman is reserved, if not distrustful, when faced with excessively spontaneous, enthusiastic, exuberant, sensational and pressing manifestations of religiousness. The Englishman is aware of the relativity which permeates all human undertakings. He dislikes the individual prophet who raises himself above the time-tested customs, institutions and norms of the community. He expects more from slow improvements as the fruit of mutual deliberation than from sudden and radical revolutions. Although he is interested in desirable renewals, he is rarely a radical who sees nothing good in what already exists and wants to make everything different. He pleads for moderation and wants things done in a gradual way. He attaches little importance to abstract and theoretical considerations, however penetrating they may be, if they cannot be put into practice or if it appears that they do not work. He wants action, not words. That is the reason why English ecumenism dislikes paper solutions of the ecumenical problem which appear flawless from a dogmatic and theological standpoint, but don't work in practice. It is perhaps even more averse to all sorts of pious, seemingly very scriptural remarks about sin, the inevitability of divisions, the impossibility of attaining perfection, and the necessity of waiting peacefully for the last times. All such things often simply camouflage an unwillingness to do what can and should be done to restore unity.

Anglican ecumenism goes straight to its goal. It does not allow itself to be led astray by deviational maneuvers that constantly call attention to a new ecumenical problem but neglect the one and only important issue, namely, the restoration of unity. Anglican ecumenism is thoroughly realistic and practical. It sees the unification of the Christian churches as a process of growth that requires time and patience and that must not be forced, but also should not be blocked and disturbed by considerations and undertakings that are not to the point or by premature and ill-considered resolutions and actions that, in relation to the whole, are doing more harm than good.

As a consequence of all that, Anglican ecumenism puts the principal emphasis not so much on the relation between renewal and reunion as on the inseparable connection between catholicity and reunion, between catholicity and ecumenicity.

The growth of Christian unification is fundamentally a question of a process in which all churches individually and together gradually grow in catholicity; in other words, a process in which they gradually embrace and express ever more clearly and universally the whole fullness of Christ. All churches have fallen into one-sidedness and excesses in one or more theological, liturgical and spiritual aspects by a too exclusive emphasis on particular truths and values. By meeting one another and openness toward the contributions of others, the churches will assimilate and manifest externally in an ever wider, fuller and richer manner all that Christ is and signifies. They will thereby become more and more alike; they will come closer to one another and become more conscious of their connection and communion. The more catholic a church becomes, the more ecumenical will be its thought and activity; and the more ecumenical a church's thought and activity, the more catholic it will appear to be. Catholicity and ecumenicity presuppose each other and are inseparable. A pretended ecumenicity that is not based on a real, broad and full catholicity is only a sham ecumenicity.

Anglican ecumenism can be understood only from the standpoint of the Anglican concept of catholicity. This catholicity is not only meant formally as an attitude that shows broadness, openness and breadth, but it is very explicitly and materially one that embraces the total fullness of Christ as it wishes to manifest itself visibly in and through the Church.

No single church in its isolation can claim to be fully "catholic." Absolute catholicity remains always a project, an ideal, an exemplar and prototype. This ideal will be most closely approached when the visible unity of all churches is restored and every church has contributed its treasures to the service of the entire Church. In their state of separation all churches are only on their way to full and perfect catholicity, although one church is closer, another less close to the realization of catholicity, and one church realizes the ideal more in one point, and another in some other matter.

Well-known is the definition of catholicity that was given by Vincent of Lerins in the fifth century namely: "*quod ubique, quod semper, quod ab omnibus creditum est,*" "what is believed by all, everywhere and always." In this definition the accent is placed on extent or universality. The catholic faith then is the faith of the whole *Ecumene,* and the word "catholic" is practically synonymous with "ecumenical." That is why the term "catholic" is often translated by "general" or "universal."

However, this purely formal definition of a concept points toward a definition that is more "material." For in the definition we have given there is question of "something," of "what is believed," of "all that," of a whole, of a totality. This too is an element of the word "catholic." The Greek word *katholikos* signifies "that which forms a whole," that which belongs together, so that something is "catholic" when it has its place in a whole in which nothing is missing. The concept "catholic" is opposed to the concepts "heretical" and "sectarian" (a selected and separated part). "Catholic" indicates an all-embracing fullness.

When this aspect of "wholeness" is stressed, we come close to the Anglican "comprehensiveness." So long as a concept of faith, a theological interpretation, a liturgical form, an expression of spirituality, so long as a system, a school, a tendency, a current, a party is not in conflict with the evident message of Holy Scripture and the evident intention of Christ, we must see to it that there is room for it in the Church. For the Church is a "whole"; nothing should be lacking in it of all that really has a place in the fullness of Christ. Universality and totality, generality and "all-embracingness" constitute together the two complementary facets of the Anglican catholicity which must be conceived in a concrete, and not in an abstract, way.

Anglican ecumenicity is an endeavor to apply that catholicity, which has the total fullness of Christ with all its powers, implications and consequences, for its final purpose as perfectly and completely as possible, not only to its own members but to the whole ecumenical situation. It rests upon the conviction that if the churches grow in that catholicity, they will necessarily also grow together toward the totality of faith and life, as it will be fully realized some day in the one, completely and sacramentally reunited Church of Christ. That is why the ecumenical efforts of the Anglican churches always start from that totality. The churches can unite only when they are willing to remedy their one-sidedness, shortcomings and defects, and work together toward a re-integration of their seeming contradictions in the great totality.

3. THE REPORTS "CATHOLICITY" AND "THE FULNESS OF CHRIST"

We must now return to the above-mentioned reports *Catholicity, a Study of the Conflict of Christian Traditions in the West* and *The Fulness of Christ, The Church's Growth into Catholicity*,[3] and examine them more closely.

---

[3] The report *Catholicity* is published by the Dacre Press, Westminster, 1947, *The Fulness of Christ* by the S.P.C.K., London, 1950.

Each of these two reports is the work of a number of Anglican theologians; the first was composed by theologians belonging to the Anglo-Catholic wing, the second by theologians of the evangelical wing of Anglicanism. Although the second report is meant as a critique of the first, the two reports belong together. Taken together they give a rather complete picture of Anglican catholicity.

The first report, according to its critics, is wanting in understanding of the most profound principles of the Reformation. The second, on the contrary, puts all emphasis on relationship with the Reformation and the necessity of maintaining the Reformation witness in the Church. The second report has apparently given up the possibility of arriving at a positive relationship with the present Church of Rome. The first report, on the contrary, makes efforts to draw the Church of Rome into its own perspective; it stresses the relationship with the Catholic Church of all centuries and the need of preserving Catholic continuity. Nevertheless, the difference between the two reports seems to come down to a mere diversity in emphasis. Both reports desire a synthesis of the Catholic and the Reformation witness, and the construction of a Church and theology in which the fullness of Christ is more completely expressed in the preaching and the practice of the Church than is usually the case.

It is evident from both reports that Anglicanism itself is still trying to realize the catholicity that it advocates and wants to attain. At the same time it is clear that the fullness of catholicity can hardly be achieved by one particular wing or even one particular church. Both reports lack certain elements that other churches would consider essential doctrines of a reunited Church. Only all the churches together will be able to reach the fullness of faith and life without which a complete reunited Church will not be possible.

Precisely because the second report gives a full and authentic witness of the Reformation in connection with Anglican catholicity, it is particularly capable of giving a clear picture of the latter, provided some of its traits are emphasized by means of the first report. On the basis of both reports it is possible to describe as follows the typically Anglican concept of catholicity, which is the foundation of the ecumenical efforts of the Anglican Communion.

The final goal to which the churches' growth in catholicity must be directed is the complete construction and unfolding of the total fullness of Christ in the preaching, the liturgy, pastoral care and spirituality, in short, in the whole faith and life of the Church. No single church has achieved that ultimate end in its isolation. But the important point is that the churches are on the way to that ultimate goal. They are not wandering blindly in their pilgrimage, nor are they fighting "as one beating the air," but they are, even in their mutual conflicts, on the road to a concrete and clearly defined final goal: the manifestation of the total fullness of Christ in and by the One Catholic and Apostolic Church.

The growth in catholicity and ecclesiastical unity is unthinkable without the salutary "tension in unity," which stimulates this process of growth. Here it is necessary to distinguish between what is of capital importance and what is accidental. If all churches accepted the Lambeth Quadrilateral (the same Holy Scripture, the same ancient Christian Creeds, the same sacraments of baptism and the Lord's Supper, and the authentic apostolic ministry), and if in addition, they were willing to strive in common for an interpretation that in no respect discards anything that was believed by the Catholic Christians of the undivided Church, how could there still remain serious differences and oppositions? And if some differences in interpretation and theological forms still remained, would they be so serious that a sacramental and ecclesiastical communion would remain impossible? Are differences and oppositions not, in a certain sense, precisely the means by which Christians together penetrate more

241

deeply into the fullness of Christ? In any case should they not suffer those differences with patience and love, according to the words of St. Paul: "If in any point you are minded otherwise, this also God will reveal to you. Still in what we have attained let us be of the same mind and let us also continue in this same rule."[4]

Anglican catholicity stands firmly against any shifting of the accent from the living proclamation of the faith to a dead and intellectualistic orthodoxy. It believes that this shift is one of the causes of the schisms that have occurred in the past centuries. These schisms rest to a great extent on the confusion of the living Word of God with a theological system, and of the unity of faith with uniformity in doctrine and practice. In this way there arose a petrified catholicity based on a rationalistic orthodoxy. As a result, a number of diverse churches claim that they are, individually, the only orthodox and true Church; the other churches are accused of heresy and sectarianism, although they profess the same faith in the Triune God, in God's Revelation in Jesus Christ, and in the operation of the Holy Spirit.

The churches will free themselves from that impasse only by a living catholicity and a real authentic ecumenicity. Starting from the acceptance of the existing "tension in unity," the churches will gradually grow together in the direction of an ever more genuine unity. But even if the most complete and perfect unity were attained, a "unity in tension" will always be necessary in order that the living unity and communion of fellowship which constitutes the Church may not degenerate once more into dead uniformity, into a dead service of the letter and the dead legalism of a petrified institution. Again, according to the words of St. Paul: "The letter kills, but the spirit gives life."[5]

The report *The Fulness of Christ* clearly reveals that the Anglican concept of catholicity and ecumenicity has nothing in

---

[4] Phil. 3:15–16.   [5] 2 Cor. 3:6.

242

common with dogmatic indifferentism. On the contrary, it is concerned precisely with the fullness of faith and church order, and not with an arbitrary and one-sided choice and interpretation. The Church should know what it professes and guarantee what it proclaims. That is why the exercise of church discipline is unavoidable. But this discipline must always wield the living Word of God as a standard, as it has always been clearly heard and understood by all the faithful on the basis of Holy Scripture. This discipline, moreover, must be founded on the wisdom, the patience and the love which Christ has shown toward all who sought Him and sincerely believed in Him.

It is not surprising that the report *The Fulness of Christ* looks upon the Reformation itself, in view of the future reunion of all Christians, as "an unresolved issue," although the report appreciates the value of specific Reformation principles and doctrines which it considers scriptural. It is an inalienable mark of Anglicanism that it attributes an absolute character to the Body of Christ as a manifestation of the total fullness of Christ, but has never absolutized the Reformation or any other movement in the history of the Church.

The Reformation, too, is a past phase in the history of the Church as the community of all believing and baptized Christians. The churches have, in our own time, entered a truly new phase in their mutual attitudes namely, the ecumenical phase of reunion. Only now does the time seem ripe for taking up again the thread that was broken in the century of the Reformation. But this must not degenerate into a renewal of ancient enmities and make the churches again cling stubbornly either to an exclusive defense of, or an exclusive attack upon, the Reformation. On the contrary, the churches must meet on the spot where they separated. Together they must examine, in the light of the total fullness of Christ, the questions which the Reformation has raised; and together they must try to restore the unity in faith and church order that was lost at that time.

The witness of Scripture and the witness of the Church must

243

be reintegrated. The witness of the churches that are now separated must be tested by that of Scripture, but also every individual interpretation of Scripture must be tested by the common faith of the undivided Church. The ecumenical task, before which all churches are placed in a completely open dialogue, presupposes, on the one hand, that all churches have the duty and the right to testify openly and freely concerning what they in all earnestness and sincerity consider to be revealed Truth. On the other hand, they should also be willing to submit fully to God's Word and the guidance of the Holy Spirit.

To give witness to the Truth is, however, not the same as prescribing beforehand to other churches how they should submit to God's Word and to the guidance of the Holy Spirit. In this respect every church and every believer should be given freedom to give an account for himself to God, according to the word of St. Paul: "Let everyone be convinced in his own mind,"[6] or as another version has it: "Grant to every man his own conviction."

Only on this condition will the churches truly meet one another and will the full truth become manifest from the conflict of sentiments and opinions, under the guidance of God; and only thus can unity be restored on the basis of the whole truth.

---

[6] Rom. 14:5.

CHAPTER NINE

Ecumenical Evaluation of the Situation

1. THE CRUCIAL ISSUES
OF GOAL AND METHOD

IN this final chapter we shall try to make an evaluation of the ecumenical situation on the basis of the facts and data we have collected in the preceding chapters. Our account will be a summing up of questions rather than of answers. To be sure, the solution of the ecumenical questions must be left to the churches themselves in close cooperation. The ecumenical problems will be solved only when the churches earnestly and perseveringly cooperate in a true dialogue. That is the reason why we confine ourselves to drawing up an account of the ecumenical experiences and discoveries that have resulted from ecumenical efforts in general and those of the Anglican Communion in particular. These experiences and discoveries have gradually revealed what questions the churches will have to deal with when they seriously engage in the endeavor to restore visible unity. Hence we shall not offer here a personal view regarding the unification, but merely a synthesizing conclusion from the experiences gathered by the churches in their striving for unity.

We do not intend to look for errors and heresies nor for means to defend any particular religious conviction. We only ask ourselves what practical and concrete possibilities are contained in

245

the escape from the impasse, which the Anglican Communion believes to have found; an ecumenical impasse in which the churches, in a certain sense in spite of themselves, are caught as a result of events that have occurred in the past.

Now that the ecumenical movement begins to gain momentum, the first question which all churches that take part in the movement must ask themselves, in all earnestness, is whether they fully realize what it is they have begun; how new and hitherto unheard-of the genuine ecumenical endeavor is; what implications and consequences are contained in the ecumenic purpose and methods. These questions must be asked if we do not wish to be satisfied with vague desires for unity or more or less unrealistic manifestations of such desires, but if, as we say in conversational English, we "really mean business."

Let us suppose that the churches have jointly come to the conviction that the concrete final goal of the ecumenical movement, as was generally accepted in the report about unity at New Delhi, is and cannot be anything but the final and complete restoration of the visible, sacramental and ecclesiastical unity of all who believe in Christ and have been baptized in His Name. What then, we ask, must take place, what must be done in order to reach that final goal together in mutual consultation and a united effort?

In the first place it is necessary, of course, that the churches should truly agree about this final goal. They must really desire to reach it, under God's guidance, without any hesitation or reservation; they must be ready to modify and complement their teaching and practice if necessary. They must be willing to adopt all conclusions and measures which, after mutual deliberation, are seen to be necessary and are, at the same time, in accord with the intention of Holy Scripture and the general sentiment of the primitive undivided Church. It is very important not to minimize those implications and consequences for the various churches with their different viewpoints. Ecumenically

246

speaking, the churches are still far from having reached a broad and well-paved road. On the contrary, they should expect and be prepared for a long and difficult climb along steep and rocky paths.

We sometimes hear the remark that it is the theologians and ecumenical experts who create the difficulties that slow up the process of unification. This is a great mistake. They expose the situation as it really is and express the ecumenical problem as it presents itself in reality to them. They do not make this situation and the problem more difficult. In fact, the ecumenical problem is so difficult that it is practically insoluble unless God takes a hand in it, performs a miracle and so greatly enlightens the minds of all who guide and represent the churches, so moves their wills and fills their hearts with so much love and goodwill, that the complete restoration of the visible sacramental and ecclesiastical unity becomes possible and finally attains fulfillment.

Let us suppose that all churches, in spite of all the difficulties, are mutually agreed regarding the final goal and truly desire to attain it. We are then faced with the second question, namely, that of the method. On the basis of the ecumenical experiences acquired thus far, the churches could ask one another whether it would not be possible for them to engage themselves on the road which the Anglican Communion has indicated for half a century through her Lambeth Conferences.

In itself this proposal does not say anything about any particular point of faith nor about the final form of the reunited Church. It is formally concerned only with the most appropriate method that could lead to the proposed final goal. If the encounter of the churches is expected to be meaningful and to lead to practical steps and tangible results, they must reach an agreement among themselves regarding the method they will jointly follow.

As has been made plain in the preceding chapters the method

used by Anglican ecumenicity comes down to the following. It starts from the fact that all believing and baptized Christians, who desire to profess and live the faith in no other way than Christ intended, belong to the mystical Body of Christ. True, the churches that are now disunited do not agree at present regarding the way in which the Body of Christ has a visible form in the Church, regarding the relation of the existing churches with the Body of Christ and with one another, and regarding the implications and consequences of baptism and of being part of the Body of Christ. However, this difference of dogmatic and theological interpretation cannot simply destroy the fact of being-baptized and being part of the Body of Christ.

The ecumenical effort would be meaningless and would, moreover, immediately degenerate into purely apologetic contentions if it were not possible to start from an already existing unity, from a communion and relationship of all Christians concerned, in the mystical Body of Christ. The question is not *whether* baptized Christians belong to the Body of Christ. The question which the Christians together must ask anew is what consequences flow from this fact for the existence of the Church in general and for all churches and individual Christians in particular.

Starting from this fact the Anglican method implies that particular churches which deliberate together concerning consensus, full communion or reunion, must at the same time consciously and explicitly keep in mind the final goal and, beforehand, aim at it in their project for reunion. This aim is the ultimate, complete and visible reunion of all Christians and all churches without distinction. In accidental points unity must not at all be confused with uniformity; the churches should aim rather at unity within variety, which, at the same time, leaves plenty of room for a wholesome tension between diverse insights, forms of expression and ways of religious life.

Hence in bringing about a partial Church reunion, nothing

should be done or omitted that would do harm or make impossible the final unification of the whole. In particular, thought must be given to the Church of Rome and an eventual restoration of communion with the Apostolic See. However numerous and great the problems which this idea may suggest to most churches, the possibility and even necessity of reunion with Rome may not be excluded beforehand. It was in this sense that Dr. Ramsey, the present Archbishop of Canterbury, wrote as early as 1936:

Hence it seems possible that in the reunited Church of the future there may be a special place for a *'primus-inter-pares'* as an organ of unity and authority. Peter will be needed as well as Paul and Apollos, and like them he will be chastened and repentant.[1]

The churches must ask one another once more in joint consultation whether and in what respect the Petrine office that has been continued historically in the Apostolic See is indeed an institution that goes back to Christ; and also in what sense and in what manner this office and this see are necessary in the reunited Church, as the center, norm and guarantee of the unity and communion of the one Church of Christ.

If ever there was a victory won by Satan, it seems to be because he managed to make the papacy unrecognizable through its degeneration in the late Middle Ages and the Renaissance. If anything requires face-lifting so that it will be able once more to exercise its original function in the reunited Church, it is the papacy. To the papacy also in general can be applied what Christ Himself said to Simon Peter: "Simon, Simon, behold, Satan has claimed power over you all, so that he can sift you like wheat; but I have prayed for thee, that thy faith may not fail; when, after a while, thou hast come back to me, it is for thee to be the support of thy brethren."[2]

---

[1] Ramsey, *The Gospel and the Church,* London, 1936, 1959 ed., p. 227.
[2] Luke 22:31–32.

This searching of the heart and renewal is in full swing in our time. It is one of the many indispensable preparations for the complete restoration of the visible unity of all believing and baptized Christians in the one Church of Christ. The Petrine office must first be cleansed and restored to its true form and must then be integrated again in the whole of the reunited Church. This integration must not be imposed as a demand from above but must be the fruit of a process of maturation in which all churches are jointly involved. According to the final conclusion of Dr. Ramsey:

> In this Body Peter will find his due place, and ultimate reunion is hastened not by the pursuit of "the Papal controversy," but by the quiet growth of the organic life of every part of Christendom.[3]

We are not concerned here with the dogmatic aspect—which certainly must come in for consideration in due time—but about the way in which the churches will grow gradually and together in the direction of a common view regarding the place, the function and the authority that, according to the intention of Christ, belongs to the Petrine office and the Apostolic See in the completely reunited Church.

2. THE FOUR PRINCIPAL DIFFICULTIES AGAINST CHURCH UNITY

Many a reader may have the impression that things are becoming very difficult if not unacceptable. Let us not delude ourselves nor one another. If the churches earnestly strive for the attainment of the final goal and seriously use the method we have described, it is perfectly clear that much patience, charity and prayer will be necessary to overcome the enormous difficulties that are in the way. These difficulties are not arbitrarily invented by this or that church as road blocks preventing

---

[3] *Op. cit.*, p. 228.

unity, but flow of necessity from the historically grown given ecumenical situation. The main difficulties are, I think, the following four.

1. *The Roman Catholic Claim of Infallibility.* The greatest difficulty for all the churches that are not in full communion with the Church of Rome lies in the fact that this church is convinced that she is the bearer of an infallible teaching authority, that this authority has its highest exponent in the infallible teaching authority of the pope as successor of St. Peter, and that, consequently, no doctrinal pronouncement or proclamation of a dogma based on this infallible teaching authority can ever be retracted or revoked.

When we look at this fact from the purely human side, we could say that no church places greater and more insuperable difficulties in the way of reunion than that church. She is the chief culprit with respect to both the origin and the continuance of church division. This is the firm conviction of practically all reformational Christians, the Anglicans not excluded.

The difficulty is not solved but it is in any case made more understandable and bearable if one bears in mind and accepts that there is here, on the part of the Church of Rome, no purely human pretention; it is on the contrary a question of religious conviction which a Roman Catholic cannot and may not renounce, no more than one can or may expect other Christians to be unfaithful to convictions that, according to them, belong to the content of faith.

In this connection, it is also important to remember that dogmas are not held to be inviolable by the Church of Rome on the basis of a subjective understanding that is derived from exegetic and theological considerations. The Roman Catholic Church holds them to be inviolable because they are related to an objectively given supernatural order of reality and salvation that was revealed in Christ and His Church, and that order is what it is independently of any human understanding or

251

desires. The formulation of the faith can be clarified and adapted in the course of the centuries; but a dogma itself is as inviolable as any declaration in the natural order that is based on an established fact.

In the field of the natural order of reality, certitude and the irrevocable character of ascertained facts rest on experience, on the question whether something really has or has not been observed. In the supernatural order of things, or, if one prefers, in the field of mysteries of faith, certitude and irrevocability rest on revelation. Hence, a question which the churches on their way to reunion will meet is concerned with the nature, the form, the knowability and the inviolability of the whole of revealed reality.

All the ancient Christian dogmas, but also all later dogmas, have reference to that whole of revealed reality. A dogma never says anything new. It merely expresses in words a special aspect or element that has always belonged to the full reality of revelation. That is why all dogmas, whether trinitarian, Christological and pneumatological, or soteriological, mariological and ecclesiological, are most closely interrelated; they presuppose one another and are so inseparable that it is not possible to discard some while retaining others.

For a Christian of the "catholic" type, it seems somewhat strange that the orthodox reformational Christian accepts matter of factly the trinitarian, Christological and pneumatological dogmas that were formulated in the first centuries, whereas he objects to soteriological, mariological and ecclesiological dogmas that were formulated at a later time.

2. *The Positive Value of the Reformation.* The second difficulty encountered by the churches, as soon as there is question of complete restoration of visible unity, is the positive content and value of the witness of the Reformation. The Reformation and reformational Christianity are too exclusively looked at by Catholic Christians as being the result of a negative

252

attitude of protest against Roman abuses, as the fruit of mis-understandings and prejudices, and as the product of individu-alism and subjectivism. If the abuses which mar the face of the Church could be abolished and the misconceptions and prejudices could be overcome by suitable enlightenment, then, Catholics think, the way would be open for a return of the Protestants to the Church. This is an illusion that rests on a misunderstanding of the inner meaning and most profound nature of the Reforma-tion as a religious and ecclesiastical movement.

The Reformation is, before all else, a positive witness. It was indeed directed first of all against Rome, but it retains its positive and lasting meaning and value even if Rome is left out of consideration. It is not possible to summarize that witness in a few words. In any case this witness aims only at expressing and proclaiming the full riches of the Gospel as they are found in the whole Bible. Where this Gospel is announced, understood and believed in all its purity, one can speak of a true Church. The witness of the Reformation rests upon principles and contains elements that no reformational Christian will ever renounce or sacrifice for the sake of achieving unity.

In a previous work[4] I have placed great emphasis on that point; it was not in order to suggest that on that account Christian unity will ever be attained. On the contrary, I wished to insist that that unification can be realized only if the Church that is in communion with Rome and the other churches of the "catholic" type are willing to take that positive witness of reformational Christians most seriously. They must stop inter-preting it in a one-sided manner; and finally, they must be willing to integrate that witness in the faith and life of the future reunited Church to the extent that, after mutual considera-tion and reflection, it is seen to be truly in accord with the witness of Holy Scripture.

---

[4] Das Zeugnis der Reformation, Essen, 1963.

When, thanks to the growth of the ecumenical movement, the polemical attitude and monologues have been replaced by an existential encounter and a fundamental dialogue between Rome and the Reformation, it will not be merely a matter of integrating the Catholic dogmas into the whole of the reunited Church; it will be decisively and emphatically also an integration of the positive and biblical witness of the Reformation. This, like the first-named difficulty, might appear to be an insurmountable obstacle. But this difficulty too is a concrete and given fact.

We should not underrate the difficulty created by Catholic dogmas, nor those of the positive witness of the Reformation. If we wish to see the realization of a true restoration of visible unity, both kinds of difficulties must be examined, clarified, reflected upon and finally "solved" by the churches together. The Old Catholic and Eastern Catholic churches should also keep this point in mind. Let us add that there is, until now, no church in which the integration of the catholic and the reformational ways of understanding the faith of the Church and the message of the Gospel has made as much progress as within the Anglican Communion.

3. The Ministry and the Sacraments. The third difficulty is one that is eminently practical. That is why it is necessary to point out beforehand that a real elimination of this difficulty cannot be achieved by itself alone; nor will the solution be found on the purely practical and organizational level. An eventual solution of this difficulty can be thought of only in direct connection with the solution of the first two difficulties.

This difficulty is concerned with the different persuasions regarding the nature, authority, functioning and "efficacy" of the ministry and the administration of the sacraments. For some churches this question, if not entirely devoid of importance, is at most a purely practical and organizational matter. They regard it, therefore, as something that is to be regulated or modified by each church in view of the best advantage of the life and order of that church. For them it is easy to pass over this difficulty.

However, there are also reformational churches which base the ministry explicitly on Scripture. The churches of the "catholic" type are even convinced that this is a matter of inalienable and essential elements belonging to the essence of the Church; these elements are so anchored in the given reality of revelation that the churches have no power to do with them what they want in view of varying circumstances. It stands to reason that the churches that consider the ministry as an absolutely necessary condition for the being of the Church, cannot disregard that difficulty for the sake of ecumenical agreement and harmony. Other churches should not expect them to make such a sacrifice.

Although this third difficulty, too, is fundamentally of a dogmatic, exegetical and theological nature, we can, nevertheless, call it eminently practical. As the preceding chapters have abundantly made clear, the numerous deliberations between the churches of the Anglican Communion and other churches concerning intercommunion, or even reunion, have repeatedly led to the often unforeseen experience and unexpected discovery: that the principal difficulty against the practical execution of reunion nearly always comes down to the difficulty caused by different views regarding the ministry. One repeatedly notices how difficult it is for the partners in the dialogue to show sufficient understanding of one another's standpoint precisely in this matter.

It would be unjust and a proof of superficiality to blame the failure of conversations about intercommunion and reunion on the church which caused the difficulty by clinging to a particular concept of the ministry. The blame could be laid equally at the door of the churches that believe that the question of the ministry is something that does not matter, and that it is not necessary in this respect to take account of the tradition of almost twenty centuries of Church and Christianity, to which

255

the churches of the "catholic" type appeal in defending their attitude. A rapprochement in this matter will be possible only if all churches take this difficulty seriously and are willing to solve it on the basis of the tradition of the undivided Church.

In this connection it may be useful to make a remark about the presently mooted question of the inter-church celebration of the Lord's Supper. To my mind, the churches that are members of the World Council of Churches are presently dealing with that problem in a way that does not seem proper. The question is asked whether common celebration of the Lord's Supper by the members of different churches should be introduced at the beginning or at the end of the process of unification. In other words, is the celebration of the Lord's Supper a means by which full communion and reunion must be achieved, or is the Supper in which all Christians can participate to be considered as the mature fruit that should not be gathered before the restoration of visible, sacramental and Church unity is an accomplished fact?

The very fact that even members of one same church have different ideas about that dilemma shows that the question is not put properly. It seems to me that it is not possible to give a general answer as to which of the two procedures is the right one. The reason is that, if the question is asked that way, one of the principal factors is lost sight of, namely, the fundamental opposition in religious persuasion that exists between the catholic and reformational (including the "free") churches with respect of the nature, validity and efficacy of the ministry and the administration of the sacraments.

In this respect there exists no essential difference between the various churches of the catholic type. If Christians belonging to the Roman Catholic, Eastern Orthodox and Old Catholic churches abstain from a common celebration of the Lord's Supper, the reason lies purely in the disciplinary order. Here one could indeed advocate the removal of such disciplinary rules

256

in order to facilitate a first practical step in the direction of the restoration of full Church unity and fellowship.

It is likewise my firm conviction that the various reformational (and "free") churches do not essentially disagree about the concept of the Church, ministry and sacrament to such an extent that a common celebration of the Lord's Supper is impossible. It is true that extreme orthodox Lutherans and Calvinists might object to that proposition. Nevertheless, in general, the differences regarding the concept of the Supper between reformational Christians are more a matter of terminology than of radically different persuasions.

Hence, in spite of accidental differences in the way of celebrating the Lord's Supper, I believe that there are no fundamental difficulties with respect to the inter-church celebration of the Supper in which Lutherans, Reformed Christians, Presbyterians, Congregationalists, Methodists and even evangelical Anglicans, and eventually, Baptists, Mennonites, and Remonstrants could not take part. In this case too an ecumenical celebration of the Supper could be a first practical step and an important means toward attaining a full fellowship and finally achieving complete reunion.

In all such cases one could agree fully, on both the catholic side and the reformational side, with the opinion of Professor Hoekendijk that frequent ecumenical and inter-church celebration of the Lord's Supper constitutes one of the most important and sure means for finally attaining complete unity.

There is one exception, however. It would be most contrary to the ecumenical spirit and be a proof of a poor understanding of the problem, if reformed Christians expected that Christians who belong to the catholic type of church should take part in the reformational Supper or if, in reverse, the latter admitted reformational Christians to their Holy Communion. Such an expectation would show that reformational Christians do not take a serious view of the religious persuasion of the catholic

257

Christian regarding the nature of ministry and sacrament, and look upon the latter's objections as unecumenical narrow-mindedness.

According to the catholic Christian, Church, ministry and sacrament are *ontological* elements of the supernatural reality of Revelation. Where there exists no ministry in the catholic sense of the word, there can, according to the catholic, be no valid and authentic sacramental service of the Lord Supper; hence the supper has an essentially different character. Hitherto the churches of the catholic and the reformational "types" have not succeeded in restoring together the ministry, in the sense of the ministry of the primitive undivided Church, based on an ordination by which it is taken up in the apostolic ministerial succession. (As we have seen, the Anglican and "free" churches are trying to do this.) As long as they do not succeed in this, there can and should be no question of an ecumenical celebration in which members of the reformational and catholic churches can take part.

Such a *communio in sacris* (participation in sacred things) disturbs consciences; it creates a new distance between those who do participate and those who don't; it presupposes a unity of faith and fellowship which in reality have not yet been achieved; it can lead to a crooked and false relation between those who participate in such a Communion and the churches to which they belong; and it runs ahead of a solution that can only be obtained by means of serious and patient deliberation. It is also not excluded that such a Communion might be advocated most strongly by Christians who secretly are in no way ready to cooperate toward a real reunion of reformational and catholic churches. In such a case sincerity and honesty could easily be jeopardized.

Experience has taught that until now there has not taken place any celebration of the Supper at ecumenical conferences in which all the members of the conference were able to participate. A celebration of the Supper that can be called ecumenical, in the full sense of the word, will be possible only when ministry and sacrament in all churches are in accord with the original standards of the undivided Church.

Now that the churches have become sufficiently acquainted with one another in the ecumenical movement, we must object to the celebration of a Supper that is open to all but in which the "lead" belongs to one church whose ministry can and should be fully recognized only by related churches. Such a celebration would give the impression that there is an ecumenical celebration of the Supper, whereas in fact a particular concept of the Supper is assumed to be the only one that is correct and based on Scripture. No account is taken of the religious persuasions of a particular group of members present, and, imperceptibly, an odium is cast upon the latter as not being as yet sufficiently ecumenical.

An inter-church celebration of the Supper, that comes as closely as possible to having a true ecumenical character, must not be based implicitly on the point of view of reformational and "free" churches; it should, on the contrary, start from the actual situation as it is found to exist today. The question that must be asked, is not which churches are ready to take the "lead" in the celebration of a Supper that is open to all, that is, a Supper in which all those present, whatever church they may belong to, are allowed to receive Holy Communion. For it is not a question of "being allowed" but of "being capable of." Hence it must be asked whether there are churches whose ministries and sacraments can be recognized by all the churches present as valid ministries and sacraments; and whether, among these churches, one can be found that can take the responsibility —in accord with its own religious views—of admitting all baptized Christians without exception to her celebration of the Supper.

In view of the present situation of the churches, this line

259

of thought is the only one that can be called truly "ecumenical." In this line of thought there is no anticipation of a stage that is not yet attained; no single church is faced with an unpleasant choice; and the question which concept of the Supper is the best and the only true one is completely left out of consideration. Now it is hard to see on what grounds a member of a reformational church could imagine that an essential obstacle prevents him from receiving communion in an Anglican celebration of the Supper. For it is perfectly clear from the *Book of Common Prayer* that the Anglican communion service contains no prayer, action or reading that is in conflict with the original witness of the Reformation. Neither is anything demanded of reformational participants that is not in accord with that witness. On the other hand, it is not only possible, but something that stands to reason, that all Anglican participants, Anglo-Catholics not excluded, might go to communion in such a service. Moreover this applies also to the members of Old Catholic and all other churches of the catholic type that can accept the Anglican ministries and ministerial services as fully valid in the ancient Christian and catholic sense of the word.

Hence the situation seems to be such that, when one really wishes to celebrate an "open" Lord's Supper, one that can be called truly "ecumenical," there exists as yet no other possibility than the Anglican communion service. That is why the celebration of the Supper that took place at New Delhi is, looked at objectively, the first "ecumenical" celebration of the Supper in the history of the ecumenical movement. Of course it was not yet "fully ecumenical," for the Roman Catholic observers and also no doubt a number of Eastern Orthodox members were not able to participate because of their religious convictions; but in any case it can be called truly "ecumenical." This fact shows that a task and function in the process of unification is reserved to the Anglican Communion which no other church can assume. The reason is that the Anglican churches alone are in accord

260

with the catholic and Reformation norms in respect to ministries and ministerial services.

4. Communication. Finally, there is still another serious difficulty of a totally different nature. Lately much attention has rightly been given to the non-theological factors that make the unification more difficult. It is clear that these difficulties in no way touch anything that belongs to the essence of things. We could name many of them. Perhaps we can sum them up in the word "communication."

One of the most striking characteristics of our time is a lack of communication, of contact, of ability to understand one another. The fact that the subject of "human relations" is very much in the air nowadays is a proof that we are struggling with a communication crisis. No true, intimate and lasting communion is achieved because there is no possibility of communication, because men do not know how really to reach and contact one another. Many on that account withdraw into involuntary isolation or suffer from an increasing loneliness. No community, no communion, is conceivable when there is no communication.

In our time communication seems to suffer from interference in every field. It is as if men, and in particular those of the older and those of the younger generation, the "reactionaries" and the "progressives," those who live in the past and those who live in the future, no longer understand one another. There exists once more a Babel-like confusion of tongues.

Here lies the reason for innumerable oppositions, tensions and conflicts in marriage between man and woman, in the family between parents and children, in the school between teachers and pupils, in the state between rulers and people, in business between employers and employees, in the world between East and West, between white and colored. Frequently the most that can be reached is so-called "peaceful coexistence." That coexistence, however, does not yet constitute a community, it is not a genuine and healthy togetherness.

261

In the religious and ecclesiastical field we behold the same disturbance of communication. There are increasing tensions and oppositions between ecclesiastical authorities and the faithful, between priest and layfolk, between preacher and congregation, between ultra-orthodox and ultra-liberal faithful, between believers and unbelievers and particularly between the Church and the world. It suffices to read the characterization given by Kraemer in his book *The Communication of the Faith,* to see how serious this lack of communication is.[5]

It seems undeniable to me that the principal reason for this tense situation lies in the radical and unheard-of material and spiritual revolutions that are taking place in our days with rapid acceleration and in which the whole of the inhabited world is involved, whether it wishes it or not. Never before has there been such a general awakening and self-consciousness, nor so rapid a development of maturity and independence in the whole of mankind as we are witnessing today. Never before have there been such profound changes in thought, in the way of representing things, and in the attitude of life. Many certainties of the past have suddenly collapsed. Forms of exercising authority, methods of education, attitudes of man toward man, which a short time ago were considered self-evident, have suddenly and definitively been discarded. In the "free" world, leadership is accepted but only on condition that that leadership rests on a constant consultation of those who are led.

We stand at the beginning of a new cultural period that is characterized by a new all-human mentality and way of life. In particular, the last remnants inherited from a primitive stage of culture are being done away with. Even the connection with the classical culture that lies at the foundation of Western civilization is greatly loosened. Interest in Greek and Roman writers is fading. Greek is disappearing or has already disap-

---

[5] Philadelphia, 1961.

peared from the curriculum of studies. During the last century scholars still looked upon Latin as a useful and ready means of communication. Today there are very few left who are able to express their learning in Latin and expect to be understood by others. The spiritual structure, the forms of thought and the methods of investigation are changing, so radically that only a living language which spontaneously adapts itself to those changes can serve as a scientific and general cultural medium of communication.

Although Latin may be considered a necessary means of communication with the Church insofar as it is in full communion with the Church of Rome, yet one must ask whether it will be possible to maintain knowledge of Latin at a sufficiently high level even among priests in non-Latin countries. For the laity in general that level is certainly out of the question. Hence, it is to be feared that too exclusive and widespread a use of Latin within the Roman Catholic Church will prevent communication between the church authorities and the faithful, the priests included, rather than foster it.[6]

The ecumenical movement has already achieved a great deal regarding a better communication between churches that became estranged from one another during the past centuries. A remarkable interaction manifests itself here. The improvement in communication promotes rapprochement and unification; but, at the same time, the rapprochement and frequent encounters are instrumental in removing and eliminating the disturbances of communication.

When we survey the whole *Ecumene,* nowhere are the disturbances of communication so serious as between the Church of

---

[6] The recent decree of the Roman Sacred Congregation for Seminaries and Universities concerning the use of Latin has no other purpose than that of preventing the loss of proficiency in handling this language, which is regarded as an indispensable means of communication within the Church. This purpose differs completely from another necessity, viz., how to counteract the ecumenical obstacles which a too exclusive use of Latin implies.

Rome, on the one hand, and all the other churches, on the other. This is not due only to Latin. The reason lies incomparably deeper.

In the first place there exist regulations—in part determined by Canon Law—that date from the time when schisms arose. These regulations were designed to safeguard the frontiers of the Roman Catholic Church. Now, however, the churches are seriously striving to become better acquainted with one another, and at the same time aim at an eventual reunion. The old saying may be true, that "Catholic books are not read by non-Catholics" (*catholica non leguntur*). But it is equally true that there is little opportunity for Catholics to read non-Catholic books so long as Canon Law forbids it. There are also other regulations that impede the spiritual and religious communication between Roman Catholics and other Christians.

In the second place, in spite of the progress of the "new theology," the character of Roman Catholic theology constitutes an almost insuperable obstacle to a smooth communication between Roman Catholic theologians and those of all other churches. Not only is Roman Catholic theology still based too little on Scripture, but it rests on philosophical postulates, works with medieval forms of thought, and makes use of a scholastic terminology that is no longer accepted, applied and understood in our century, outside the small circle of Roman Catholic theologians. When we step over from the field of Roman Catholic theology to that of any other Christian theology of our time, and vice versa, we get the impression not so much that we are faced with another faith but that we have drifted into another world and another century. This disturbance of communication becomes very serious whenever one tries to initiate a dialogue between Rome and the Reformation.

Thirdly, the communication in the religious field between Roman Catholic and reformational Christians is made difficult because of the many primitive forms of expression and representations that our pagan ancestors introduced, imperceptibly and unavoidably, into the practice of religious thought, but which the Reformation radically cast out. It is a question whether the ideas entertained by many "ordinary" Roman Catholic believers regarding the ministry, ordinations, sacramental actions and devotions are not in some respects partially vitiated by a heritage of pre-Christian notions and associations.

3. THE IMMEDIATE FUTURE

We now finally come to the question of what should be done in the near future if Christians do not want to confine themselves to Platonic desires for unity but "mean business" in their striving for Church unity. The suggestions presented here are not based on the author's particular—Roman Catholic—religious persuasion, but on the discoveries and experiences that have been obtained in the pursuit of ecumenical endeavors in general and more concretely and particularly by the Anglican Communion. Hence the same suggestions could be made also by representatives of other churches. Moreover, we must state emphatically that they are merely suggestions presented for consideration. They are like small balloons released to find out how the wind is blowing. It stands to reason that it belongs to the churches concerned to decide whether and in what measure the suggestions that follow deserve serious consideration.

When we survey the entire ecumenical situation, there seem to exist two groups of churches that could, without fundamental difficulties and in a short time, reach full communion and eventually complete reunion.

The churches of the catholic type have no difficulty in accepting the validity of one another's ministries and sacraments and understand these in the same dogmatic sense. They could begin by doing away with the disciplinary regulations that, until now, have made it impossible for the members of these churches to

265

receive the sacraments outside their own church. This suggestion applies to the Church of Rome, the Eastern Orthodox and the Old Catholic churches viewed as a catholic whole.

The restrictive discipline in question dates from the time when the schisms arose. But the churches have now reached a totally new and diametrically opposite stage. They are no longer in a separatist but an ecumenical stage; which means that they are striving earnestly for reunion. But this reunion can result only from mutual deliberation and in no case from a capitulation of one church to another.

True, dogmas like those of Transsubstantiation, the Immaculate Conception, Papal Infallibility, and the Assumption of Our Lady cannot be revoked by the Church in communion with Rome. But they can be clarified, scrutinized and interpreted. Since the Church has been able to live for ten centuries without these explicit and "official" dogmas, is it not possible for the Church of Rome to wait with love and patience for the moment when the other churches of the catholic type will agree with her regarding those points? Even if there is still little hope for such an agreement in the near future, would it not be possible for the churches of the catholic type to do away right now with the disciplinary regulations that prevent sacramental intercommunion, for the sake of the ecumenical endeavor and in view of ultimate complete reunion?

It cannot be denied that the catholic churches during the cold centuries of their estrangement became icebound in their own harbors. Why cannot the warmth of the ecumenical encounter effect a thaw that will enable the churches to move in the direction of an early reunion?

With respect to the churches that sprang from the Reformation, a similar kind of patience could be exercised regarding points of theology and church practice about which they have different persuasions. It should not be difficult for them to reach a common consensus that would make possible a full ministerial and sacramental communion, by means of a joint examination of the positive and lasting elements in the original Reformation witness, by striving for the unity in variety which was so much insisted upon by Luther, Melanchton, Calvin, Bucer, Bullinger, Cranmer, Whitgift and other reformers. In the end efforts could be made toward a complete reunion such as has already been achieved in India between different reformational churches.

It could not be asked of the Anglican Communion that it should renounce the integration of catholic and reformational principles, which it has obtained through so much patience and perseverance and that are based on the principles of continuity, moderation and comprehensiveness, and which are still the characteristics of the Church of England and her daughter-churches. To make such a demand would mean that one fails to recognize an ecumenical result of major importance. From the ecumenical standpoint it would mean a retrogression if the Anglican churches were asked to sacrifice that achievement for the sake of hastening intercommunion with reformational churches. The special vocation of the churches that are in communion with the See of Canterbury is precisely to help the reformational and "free" churches find the way to the restoration of a complete apostolic office and the apostolic succession of office. Without that restoration, as is taught by the experience and tradition of almost twenty centuries of Church and Christianity, the final goal of ecumenism cannot be attained.

In the reunions in India the Anglo-Catholics and the churches of the catholic type have not sufficiently been taken into account. The reunions that have taken place in India are not yet sufficiently in accord with the typically Anglican standard, which implies that in every reunion attention must be given to the ultimate unity of the whole, and that nothing should be undertaken that would impede or frustrate the final reunion of all churches.

Hence the difficulties in the Church of England regarding

267

full communion with the reunited Church of India must not be ascribed to the Convocations of that church, but to the fact that the unifications in India are not yet in every respect in accord with the standards of full ecumenism. Those reunions are based too one-sidedly on the ideas of evangelical Anglicans concerning the Church, the ministry and the sacraments and those of the "free" churches engaged in that reunion.

From the ecumenical standpoint it is most necessary that, in the process of reunions in which Anglican dioceses are involved, efforts should be made to strive for as complete an integration as possible of the positive truths and values derived from the catholic and the reformational traditions, for the sake of an unimpeded and full communion with the entire Anglican Communion and in view of the future reunion of all churches. A crucial point will be to restore completely the ancient Christian ministry in such a way that the entire unified Church will be able to accept it.

In particular circumstances the only possible course will be a "conditional" episcopal consecration. Just as a conditional baptism, administered in cases of doubt, does not disregard the validity of the previously received baptism if the latter really was a baptism, so the conditional consecration does not disregard a previous call and ordination. It is of the greatest significance that the churches of the Anglican Communion have never denied the spiritual meaning of the reformational ministry and its administrations. This fact makes it possible for reformational and "free" churches to accept an Anglican consecration or ordination conditionally, if that seems necessary for the sake of a full communion with episcopal churches and for the final and complete reunion of churches.

Such a consecration or ordination does not mean a renunciation of one's own call and ministry, but an insertion of these into the ministry of the whole Church and in the full ministerial continuity with the pre-Reformation and undivided Church.

268

Only in this way can a reunion of all reformational churches be attained in such a way that the entire Anglican Communion can also be taken up in it.

This brings us to another point that is of pressing importance from the ecumenical standpoint. One of the most serious obstacles on the way to the restoration of unity lies in the declaration of nullity of Anglican orders by Leo XIII in the Bull *Apostolicae curae* of 1896. This obstacle should, for the sake of unification, be put out of the way as soon as possible. But how? How can this be done without derogating from the element of truth in the point of view of the Vatican and from the element of truth in the point of view of Canterbury?

If it is correct that the concluding paragraph of said Bull,[7] quoted above in Chapter Two, must be understood not as an infallible declaration but as a disciplinary measure, the question of Anglican orders could once more be brought up. At the present stage of ecumenism this ought, of course, to take the form of a dialogue. The preparatory examination ought to be made by a joint committee, half of whose members would be appointed by the Pope and half by the Archbishop of Canterbury.

Particular attention should then be given to the *Preface* of the Anglican *Ordinale* of 1549 and the therein clearly expressed intention of continuing the three offices that have existed in the Church from the time of the Apostles, namely those of bishop, priest (presbyter) and deacon.

Attention should also be paid to the fact that the Old Catholic and Greek churches, whose ordinations are considered valid by Rome and that hold the same doctrine as the Church of Rome regarding the nature, form and function of the ministries, have declared that Anglican orders are valid and that, because of this, the Old Catholic Church has entered into full communion with the Anglican Communion.

---

[7] Cf. p. 58.

One may even legitimately question whether the Roman "certainty" about the invalidity of Anglican consecrations of bishops and ordinations has not been changed into a "doubt," in view of the fact that Old Catholic bishops participate in the consecration of Anglican bishops. Finally, a new examination of the validity of Anglican orders might indirectly bring favorable results in view of a more positive appreciation of these ministries by reformational churches.

Many questions regarding the ministry could thus be brought under discussion for the first time in the form of a dialogue between Rome and Canterbury, and hence indirectly between Rome and the Reformation. There could be questions such as these: What foundation can be found in the New Testament for the ministry? Is it truly evident that there existed a hierarchy of bishops, presbyters and deacons in the time of the Apostles, or is that a construction of later times? Are the terms "bishop" and "presbyter" not two different words for one same ministry? What does Paul mean in 1 Tim. 4:14, when he speaks of "the laying on of hands of the presbyterate"? How did the monarchical episcopate develop? Is it not possible that in many cases the bishop was chosen from among the presbyters without receiving a new consecration? Were not both the bishops and presbyters, at the beginning, "successors" of the Apostles in the sense that their commission in both cases was traceable to the laying on of hands with which the Apostles appointed presbyters (or bishops) from town to town? Do we not have too simplistic an idea of the apostolic succession? In what did this succession consist in the first centuries? Did the apostolic succession of the bishops rest on the fact that the latter were lawful successors of their predecessor in some particular episcopal see, or on the fact that they had received some "grace of ministry" from a previous validily consecrated bishop who, being in "possession" of this "grace of ministry," was able to pass it on to another? Does the consecration or ordination owe its "efficacy" to the latter fact or immediately to the prayer by which the laying on of hands is accompanied?

Could not a general picture of the actual course of things in the New Testament and post-apostolic times, resting on the most complete historical examination, lead to a sharper distinction between the essence of the ministry and the accidental form of the ministry? What is the meaning of the fact that, in an ordination to the priesthood according to the Roman Catholic rite, the priests who are present also lay their hands on the candidates? Is this an empty ceremony or does it indicate that the priests, too, in virtue of their priesthood can transmit "something" namely a "grace of ministry"? And if this is true, can we hold that the laying on of hands in reformational churches, that points at least to a presbyterial ministerial succession and that has its origin in the pre-Reformation Church, remains entirely without "effect," taking this term in the Catholic sense?

Moreover, in regard to ordinations and consecrations of ministers, must we not consider that God, as Catholic doctrine expressly teaches, is not bound to sacramental actions and hence could "effect" the same things that are effected by Catholic means by making use, if He so wished, of reformation ministries and ministerial administrations? Must we not agree with the Anglican Communion and conclude that the ministerial services and administrations of reformational churches are obviously blessed by God? Should we not be prudent in branding things as "wholly null and void"? Is the question of validity of a ministry not primarily a matter of legality, that is, whether the office or ministry was received within a particular church order? We could ask further what the nature is and what the consequences are of the changes introduced in the Middle Ages into the rite of ordination, and what connection there is between priesthood and the offering of the Holy Eucharist.

These and similar questions are concrete questions which, as we can judge from past ecumenical experience, will inevitably

271

come up for discussion, if conversations concerning unity take place in an authentic encounter and an open-hearted dialogue between the churches. Too long have the churches been hypnotized by abstract theological constructions. They should follow the serious advice of Norman Sykes and be on their guard lest the unification of the Church be impeded by abstract reasonings based on a starting-point that, ultimately, seems to have no foundation in historical facts.[8] Ecclesiological speculations must rest on facts and not on theoretical, unfounded premises and suppositions.

Let us suppose that a new examination were made concerning the validity of Anglican orders on the basis of certain arguments which the Anglican Communion would not accept but nonetheless respect. The result of such an examination could be that the invalidity of the Anglican orders cannot be established with certainty. In that case, according to the standards of the Church of Rome, the validity of these orders would be a matter of doubt. It would then be difficult to believe that there would exist any different relationship between the Church of Rome and the Anglican Communion than that which now exists between the Anglican Communion and the reformational and "free" churches. As we have seen in the preceding chapters, the principal difficulty in the way of an eventual reunion between Anglican churches and reformational and "free" churches is the uncertainty on the part of the Anglicans regarding the "validity" of the ministry in reformational and "free" churches.

On the basis of historical facts, the Anglican Communion is convinced that no reunited Church is conceivable without a restoration of the historical episcopate based on apostolic succession. She asks the reformational and "free" churches concerned to accept a regulation in virtue of which the ministry can be considered authentic and valid by the whole Church. She asks

---

[8] Sykes, *Man as Churchman,* Cambridge, 1960, pp. 1 ff.: Church History, History and Theology.

them, for the sake of unity, to be willing to remove the uncertainty which exists, justly or unjustly, on the part of one or more of the churches that seek reunion, with respect to the ministry and ministerial administrations in non-episcopal churches, by accepting a complementary ordination or a conditional ordination. If the Anglican Church can justly make such proposals to other churches for the sake of reunion, may we not expect that she would likewise be willing to consider seriously similar proposals that might be offered by the Church of Rome?

Everyone who is not concerned with his own church alone but with the present situation of the whole of Christianity will easily realize that the recognition of the validity of Anglican orders by the Church of Rome would constitute an important and decisive step on the road to Church unity. Such a recognition would open the road toward reunion at least of the churches that are in communion with the now disunited episcopal sees of Rome, Constantinople and Canterbury. A complete reunion will be possible only by stages. A beginning could be made by admitting one another to the reception of the sacraments; this leads to what Anglicans and Old Catholics call "full communion." But this is not yet reunion in the fullest sense of the word. A full reunion is not possible without agreement regarding the function and authority of the Apostolic See; nor is it possible without a full integration of the witness of the Reformation to the extent that this witness in a dialogue between the churches will be seen to agree with Holy Scripture and the right interpretation of the faith of the Church.

The importance of Anglicanism lies precisely in the fact that it has digested and assimilated the contribution of the Reformation. The Anglican Communion has bishops, priests and church members according to evangelical principles as well as bishops, priests and church members according to catholic ideas. That the Anglican Communion brings with it the Reformation and introduces it into the whole Church, if and when through an

273

ecumenical encounter it enters into sacramental communion, full communion and eventually reunion with Rome and Constantinople, is more an advantage than a disadvantage. At the beginning, the dialogue might thereby be made more difficult and more complicated, but in the end it will be seen to be advantageous for a reunion of the whole of Christianity, the reformational churches not excepted.

The contribution of the reformational churches to the process of unification will become real and effective only when these churches, on their part, become open toward the catholic contribution. For it is not self-evident in the least that the latter contribution is in conflict with the intention of Christ, the Apostles and the undivided Church, and with the complete and true sense of the witness of Holy Scripture. The churches should be willing to keep up a sincere dialogue among themselves; this will help them gradually to separate chaff from wheat in the doctrines and practices of the various churches.

If it ever becomes a fact that the Anglican Communion is once more a part of one large community together with Rome and Constantinople, she will then stand out as the one that could best serve as a connecting link between that large Communion and the community of reformational and "free" churches. On the basis of the many reunions that have already been achieved between churches that sprang from the Reformation, it is safe to hold that we can expect them to make constant progress toward reunion. Ultimately here also, it will be a question of a fuller fellowship and of a reunion between the catholic and the reformational parts of Christianity.

Certainly we have not yet reached this stage. It would not even surprise me if many a reader were shaking his head, saying to himself that the suggestions we have presented must be the fruit of utopian dreams. That we must deny, however. They are born from sober realism, a realism that asks itself: what is the use of starting a dialogue that should lead to the restoration of visible unity if we shrink from asking ourselves what concrete implications and consequences are implied in that ecumenical pursuit?

4. CONCLUSION

The suggestions presented here flow from the ecumenical situation as it really is; they rest on the concrete discoveries and experiences to which ecumenical endeavors have led thus far. They are intended solely to awaken or strengthen the realization that we have not advanced far when we have done nothing but hold conversations, although they are the things we must start with. At the end it will be a question of taking real steps on the ecumenical road; it will be a question of making decisions, of doing things that will gradually lead to the real and full restoration of visible unity.

Whoever is earnest about that final goal and truly hopes and prays that it will be achieved some day must be ready to make radical changes and to meet with events that cannot as yet be imagined. Those who desire *a priori* that everything should remain as their own church has always taught and done, who do not want to accept anything except a development that is in accord with the tradition and customs of their own church, would do better to abandon the ecumenical road and return to the old, well-trodden way of polemics and apologetics.

The suggestions and conclusions of this final chapter are not meant to serve as specific, definitive proposals. As such they would necessarily be premature. They are meant exclusively as results of an impartial phenomenological examination, with the hope that these results will prove useful once the dialogue between the churches begins in earnest. What we have principally in mind here is the future unity of the whole *Ecumene* and not an actually existing situation in any particular country.

A recent visit to England has convinced me that, in spite of certain expressions of friendship over and across separating church walls, a true ecumenical attitude is still hard to find. A question like that of Anglican orders, whose solution would be so important for the whole of the *Ecumene,* is not ready by far for re-examination.

The majority of Anglicans consider the idea of valid or invalid ordinations as simply unscriptural. The moderate Anglo-Catholics, who expressly appreciate "valid" orders, don't allow the smallest doubt regarding the validity of Anglican orders. The (Roman) Catholic hierarchy, on the contrary, tolerates no doubt about the invalidity of those orders, among other things, because the work of conversion among Anglicans would thereby lose one of its strongest arguments.

Hence it has not been my intention at all in this book to awaken unfounded expectations regarding what is presently possible or not in England in the ecumenical field.

Ultimately everything in this matter depends on the questions whether the churches really believe that Christ desires the restoration of the visible unity and are truly willing to enter the road on which unity can be gradually attained. Here no single church or group may beforehand prescribe what another church ought to do. Unity will be born only from an encounter, a dialogue and reflection, in which all together pray for and submit obediently to the guidance of the Holy Spirit.

Such an attitude is not in conflict with the abstract axiom that error has no equal rights with the truth. For those that meet are not errors and truths, but true, believing Christians, and churches and communions, that have grown historically; and all of them are still convinced that they know, love and serve the Truth. These Christians and Christian churches have positively the same rights when they meet in an ecumenical encounter that desires truth and not error, reunion and not separation.

Neither can one refuse an ecumenical dialogue on the ground that one is not permitted to deal with truth as if it were disputable, or to make it appear that one is doubting about the faith.

276

For the fact is precisely that each church positively witnesses to what she believes to possess as a truth, even if she thinks herself to be the only church that "possesses" truth in all its purity and completeness. For only in this way will it be possible to see clearly, under the guidance of the Holy Spirit, what is the pure and complete Truth, and what is Christ's real intention with respect to the complete and visible restoration of the unity of all Christians.

In the first chapter of this book we quoted a passage from the report concerning unity made by the third section of the Assembly of the World Council of Churches that was held at New Delhi in 1961.[9] This passage contains a description of the vision of a future and completely restored unity of all Christians in a universal Christian fellowship.

The Christians belonging to all churches, who were assembled at New Delhi, had a clear view of that ultimate goal. All of us without distinction should examine *ourselves,* and not the others, and ask ourselves if, behind beautiful and otherwise well-intentioned manifestations of desires for unity, there is not a secret unwillingness to engage effectively in what Christ demands of us. Before all else it is a matter of a firm will and sincere readiness.

The way of ecumenism is for all churches and all individual Christians a way of conversion. Conversion always implies the necessity to break an interior opposition, a secret unwillingness. To the extent that we are responsible for the continuance of Christian disunity because of our unecumenical or pre-ecumenical attitude, the words of the Savior addressed to the people of Jerusalem, will be applied to all of us:

Jerusalem, Jerusalem. . . . How often would I have gathered thy children together, as a hen gathers her young under her wings, but thou wouldst not![10]

---

[9] Cf. p. 10.   [10] Matt. 23:37.

APPENDIX

An Appeal to All Christian People

from
the Bishops assembled in the Lambeth
Conference of 1920

WE Archbishops, Bishops Metropolitan, and other Bishops of the Holy Catholic Church in full communion with the Church of England, in Conference assembled, realizing the responsibility which rests upon us at this time and sensible of the sympathy and the prayers of many, both within and without our own Communion, make this appeal to all Christian people.

We acknowledge all those who believe in our Lord Jesus Christ, and have been baptized into the name of the Holy Trinity, as sharing with us membership in the universal Church of Christ which is His Body. We believe that the Holy Spirit has called us in a very solemn and special manner to associate ourselves in penitence and prayer with all those who deplore the divisions of Christian people, and are inspired by the vision and hope of a visible unity of the whole Church.

I. We believe that God wills fellowship. By God's own act this fellowship was made in and through Jesus Christ, and its life is in His Spirit. We believe that it is God's purpose to manifest this fellowship, so far as this world is concerned, in an outward, visible, and united society, holding one faith, having

278

its own recognized officers, using God-given means of grace, and inspiring all its members to the world-wide service of the Kingdom of God. This is what we mean by the Catholic Church.

II. This united fellowship is not visible in the world today. On the one hand there are other ancient episcopal Communions in East and West, to whom ours is bound by many ties of common faith and tradition. On the other hand there are the great non-episcopal Communions, standing for rich elements of truth, liberty and life which might otherwise have been obscured or neglected. With them we are closely linked by many affinities, racial, historical and spiritual. We cherish the earnest hope that all these Communions, and our own, may be led by the Spirit into the unity of the Faith and of the knowledge of the Son of God. But in fact we are all organized in different groups, each one keeping to itself gifts that rightly belong to the whole fellowship, and tending to live its own life apart from the rest.

III. The causes of division lie deep in the past, and are by no means simple or wholly blameworthy. Yet none can doubt that self-will, ambition, and lack of charity among Christians have been principal factors in the mingled process, and that these, together with blindness to the sin of disunion, are still mainly responsible for the breaches of Christendom. We acknowledge this condition of broken fellowship to be contrary to God's will, and we desire frankly to confess our share in the guilt of thus crippling the Body of Christ and hindering the activity of His Spirit.

IV. The times call us to a new outlook and new measures. The Faith cannot be adequately apprehended and the battle of the Kingdom cannot be worthily fought while the body is divided, and is thus unable to grow up into the fullness of the life of Christ. The time has come, we believe, for all the separated groups of Christians to agree in forgetting the things which are behind and reaching out towards the goal of a reunited Catholic Church. The removal of the barriers which have arisen

279

between them will only be brought about by a new comradeship of those whose faces are definitely set this way.

The vision which rises before us is that of a Church, genuinely Catholic, loyal to all Truth, and gathering into its fellowship all 'who profess and call themselves Christians', within whose visible unity all the treasures of faith and order, bequeathed as a heritage by the past to the present, shall be possessed in common, and made serviceable to the whole Body of Christ. Within this unity Christian Communions now separated from one another would retain much that has long been distinctive in their methods of worship and service. It is through a rich diversity of life and devotion that the unity of the whole fellowship will be fulfilled.

V. This means an adventure of goodwill and still more of faith, for nothing less is required than a new discovery of the creative resources of God. To this adventure we are convinced that God is now calling all the members of His Church.

VI. We believe that the visible unity of the Church will be found to involve the whole-hearted acceptance of:—

The Holy Scriptures, as the record of God's revelation of Himself to man, and as being the rule and ultimate standard of faith; and the Creed commonly called Nicene, as the sufficient statement of the Christian faith, and either it or the Apostles' Creed as the Baptismal confession of belief:

The divinely instituted sacraments of Baptism and the Holy Communion, as expressing for all the corporate life of the whole fellowship in and with Christ:

A ministry acknowledged by every part of the Church as possessing not only the inward call of the Spirit, but also the commission of Christ and the authority of the whole body.

VII. May we not reasonably claim that the Episcopate is the one means of providing such a ministry? It is not that we call in question for a moment the spiritual reality of the ministries of those Communions which do not possess the Episcopate. On the contrary, we thankfully acknowledge that these ministries have been manifestly blessed and owned by the Holy Spirit as effective means of grace. But we submit that considerations alike of history and of present experience justify the claim which we make on behalf of the Episcopate. Moreover, we would urge that it is now and will prove to be in the future the best instrument for maintaining the unity and continuity of the Church. But we greatly desire that the office of a Bishop should be everywhere exercised in a representative and constitutional manner, and more truly express all that ought to be involved for the life of the Christian Family in the title of Father-in-God. Nay more, we eagerly look forward to the day when through its acceptance in a united Church we may all share in that grace which is pledged to the members of the whole body in the apostolic rite of the laying-on of hands, and in the joy and fellowship of a Eucharist in which as one Family we may together, without any doubtfulness of mind, offer to the one Lord our worship and service.

VIII. We believe that for all the truly equitable approach to union is by the way of mutual deference to one another's consciences. To this end, we who send forth this appeal would say that if the authorities of other Communions should so desire, we are persuaded that, terms of union having been otherwise satisfactorily adjusted, Bishops and clergy of our Communion would willingly accept from these authorities a form of commission or recognition which would commend our ministry to their congregations, as having its place in the one family life. It is not in our power to know how far this suggestion may be acceptable to those to whom we offer it. We can only say that we offer it in all sincerity as a token of our longing that all ministries of grace, theirs and ours, shall be available for the service of our Lord in a united Church.

It is our hope that the same motive would lead ministers who have not received it to accept a commission through episcopal

281

ordination, as obtaining for them a ministry throughout the whole fellowship.

In so acting no one of us could possibly be taken to repudiate his past ministry. God forbid that any man should repudiate a past experience rich in spiritual blessings for himself and others. Nor would any of us be dishonouring the Holy Spirit of God, whose call led us all to our several ministries, and whose power enabled us to perform them. We shall be publicly and formally seeking additional recognition of a new call to wider service in a reunited Church, and imploring for ourselves God's grace and strength to fulfil the same.

IX. The spiritual leadership of the Catholic Church in days to come, for which the world is manifestly waiting, depends upon the readiness with which each group is prepared to make sacrifices for the sake of a common fellowship, a common ministry, and a common service to the world.

We place this ideal first and foremost before ourselves and our own people. We call upon them to make the effort to meet the demands of a new age with a new outlook. To all other Christian people whom our words may reach we make the same appeal. We do not ask that any one Communion should consent to be absorbed in another. We do ask that all should unite in a new and great endeavour to recover and to manifest to the world the unity of the Body of Christ for which He prayed.[1]

---

[1] *Report of the Lambeth Conference 1920,* London, 1920, Res. 9, pp. 26 ff., cf. pp. 133 ff. and Bell, *Documents on Christian Unity,* First Series, Oxford University Press, 1924, pp. 1 ff.

Bibliography

THE list of studies presented here is not intended to be a record of the works consulted in connection with the writing of this book, but a first orientation for those who wish to become better acquainted with Anglicanism and want to study it more systematically. With this aim in mind, the present bibliography offers a choice of the most suitable books. Their selection has been restricted to recent works which 1. are the result of a first-hand investigation of the sources; 2. do not have an apologetic character; 3. and throw light on an important aspect of Anglicanism in an impartial and well-informed fashion.

It stands to reason that anyone who wants to study Anglicanism should be in possession of the *Book of Common Prayer*, and for historical reasons preferably in an edition of the Church of England (Oxford University Press and other publishers).

Introductory Books

Sykes, *The English Religious Tradition*, S.C.M. Press, London, 1953, rev. ed., 1961.

Moorman, *A History of the Church of England*, Black, London, 1953, 4th ed., 1961.

Neill, *Anglicanism*, Penguin Books, 1958.

Rawlinson, *The Anglican Communion in Christendom*, S.P.C.K., London, 1960.

Ramsey, *An Era in Anglican Theology*, Scribners, New York, 1960; in England published by Longmans, 1961, under the title, *From Gore to Temple*.

283

Ratcliff, *The Booke of Common Prayer; Its Making and Revisions 1549–1661*, S.P.C.K., 1949 (Published on the occasion of its fourth centennial).

History

Sykes, *Man as Churchman*, Cambridge, 1960. Four lectures delivered in 1959 at the University of Belfast to illustrate the necessity of familiarity with Church history for a good understanding of dogmatic issues.

Ollard-Crosse, *A Dictionary of English Church History*, Mowbray, London, 1912.

The Oxford Dictionary of the Christian Church, London, 1957.

Wakeman-Ollard, *An Introduction to the History of the Church of England*, Rivingtons, London, 1914.

Malden, *The English Church and Nation*, S.P.C.K., London, 1952.

Kemp, *Council and Consent*, Aspects of the Government of the Church as exemplified in the History of the English Provincial Synods, S.P.C.K., London, 1961.

Carpenter, *The Church in England 597–1688*, Murray, London, 1954.

Hughes, *The Reformation in England*, Hollis and Carter, London, 1954, 3 vols.

Bromiley, *Thomas Cranmer, Archbishop and Martyr*, London, 1956.

————, *Thomas Cranmer, Theologian*, London, 1950.

Rupp, *Studies in the Making of the English Protestant Tradition* (Mainly in the Reign of Henry VIII), Cambridge, 1949.

Meyer, *Elizabeth I and the Religious Settlement of 1559*, St. Louis, U.S.A., 1960.

Kressner, *Schweizer Ursprünge des anglikanischen Staatskirchentums*, Gütersloh, 1953.

Woodhouse, *The Doctrine of the Church in Anglican Theology 1547–1603*, S.P.C.K., London, 1954.

Dawley, *John Whitgift and the English Reformation*, Scribners, New York, 1954.

Sykes, *Old Priest and New Presbyter*, Episcopacy and Presbyterianism since the Reformation with Especial Relation to the Churches of England and Scotland, Cambridge, 1957.

Stranks, *The Life and Writings of Jeremy Taylor*, S.P.C.K., London, 1952.

284

BIBLIOGRAPHY

Charles and Katherine George, *The Protestant Mind of the English Reformation 1570–1640*, Princeton, U.S.A., 1961.

Bosher, *The Making of the Restoration Settlement*, The Influence of the Laudians, Westminster, 2nd ed., 1952.

Cragg, *From Puritanism to Reason*, A Study of Changes in Religious Thought Within the Church of England 1660–1700, Cambridge, 1950.

Sykes, *William Wake, Archbishop of Canterbury 1657–1737*, Cambridge, 1957, 2 vols.

Davies, *Worship and Theology in England from Watts and Wesley to Maurice*, 1690–1850, Princeton, U.S.A., 1961.

Carpenter, *Church and People*, 1789–1889, S.P.C.K., London, 1933.

Church, *The Oxford Movement, Twelve Years 1833–1845*, Macmillan, London, 1st ed., 1891, many reprints.

Brilioth, *The Anglican Revival*, Studies in the Oxford Movement, Longmans, 1925.

Smith, *Dean Church, The Anglican Response to Newman*, Oxford University Press, London, 1958.

Addison, *The Episcopal Church in the United States 1789–1931*, New York, 1951.

Chorley, *Men and Movements in the American Episcopal Church*, New York, 1950.

Herklots, *Frontiers of the Church, The Making of the Anglican Communion*, Bonn, London, 1961.

Lloyd, *The Church of England in the Twentieth Century*, London, 1946–50, 2 vols.

Bell, *Randall Davidson, Archbishop of Canterbury*, Oxford University Press, London, 3rd ed., 1952.

Lockhart, *Cosmo Gordon Lang*, Hodder and Stoughton, London, 1949.

Iremonyer, *William Temple, Archbishop of Canterbury, His Life and Letters*, Oxford University Press, London, 1948.

Jasper, *Arthur Cayley Headlam, Life and Letters of a Bishop*, Faith Press, London, 1960.

Higham, *Catholic and Reformed, A Study of the Anglican Church 1559–1662*, S.P.C.K., London, 1962.

Brook, *A Life of Archbishop Parker*, Clarendon Press, Oxford, 1962.

Booty, *John Jewel as Apologist of the Church of England*, S.P.C.K., London, 1963.

Welsby, *Lancelot Andrewes 1555–1626*, S.P.C.K., London, 1958.

285

————, George Abbot, The Unwanted Archbishop 1562–1633, S.P.C.K., London, 1962.

Babbage, Puritanism and Richard Bancroft, S.P.C.K., London, 1962.

Nuttall-Chadwick, From Uniformity to Unity 1662–1962, S.P.C.K., London, 1962.

Lewis, John Bangor, The People's Bishop, S.P.C.K., London, 1962.

Anglicanism and the Anglican Communion

Official Yearbook of the Church of England, latest ed., S.P.C.K., London. Contains information about the entire Anglican Communion.

Wand, Anglicanism in History and Today, Weidenfeld and Nicolson, London, 1961.

————, (ed.), The Anglican Communion; a Survey, Oxford, 1948.

Rawlinson, Current Problems of the Church, S.P.C.K., London, 1958.

Fairweather-Hettlinger, Episcopacy and Reunion, Mowbray, London, 1953.

Headlam, The Church of England, Murray, London, 1924.

Garbett, The Claims of the Church of England, London, 1947.

Williams, The Anglican Tradition in the Life of England, London, 1947.

Ratcliff, The Booke of Common Prayer; Its Making and Revisions 1549–1661, S.P.C.K., London, 1949.

Gasquet-Bishop, Edward VI and the Book of Common Prayer, London, 3rd ed., 1928.

Field, The English Liturgies of 1549 and 1661 Compared with Each Other and with the Ancient Liturgies, S.P.C.K., London, 1920.

Don, The Scottish Book of Common Prayer, S.P.C.K., London, 1949.

Dix, The Shape of the Liturgy, Dacre Press, Westminster, 4th ed., 1949.

Addleshow, The Architectural Setting of Anglican Worship, Faber, London, 1948.

Bicknell-Carpenter, The Thirty-nine Articles of the Church of England, Longmans, London, 3rd ed., 1955, new impr. 1961.

Canon Law Revision 1959, S.P.C.K., London, 1960.

Smethurst-Wilson, Acts of the Convocations of Canterbury and York, S.P.C.K., London, 1961.

More-Cross, Anglicanism, The Thought and Practice of the Church of England, illustrated from the Religious Literature of the Seventeenth Century, S.P.C.K., London, 1935.

286

BIBLIOGRAPHY

Mozley, *Some Tendencies in British Theology* from the Publication of Lux Mundi to the Present Day, S.P.C.K., London, 1952.
Ramsey, *An Era in Anglican Theology from Gore to Temple,* Scribner, New York, 1960. (Published also in England by Longmans, 1961, under the title *From Gore to Temple*). The last two works give information about Anglican theologians and their writings.
Alchin, *The Silent Rebellion,* S.C.M. Press, London, 1958.
Thornton, *English Spirituality,* S.P.C.K., London, 1963.
Tavard, *The Quest for Catholicity, A Study in Anglicanism,* Burns and Oates, London, 1963.
Ferris, *The Church of England,* Gollancz, London, 1962.
Vidler (ed.), *Soundings,* 1962.

A Few Recent Ecumenical Works

Van der Linde, *Wat is Oecumenisch?,* Roermond, 1961.
Rouse-Neill, *A History of the Ecumenical Movement,* S.P.C.K., London, 1954.
Brandreth, *The Ecumenical Ideals of the Oxford Movement,* S.P.C.K., London, 1947.
Bivort de la Saudée, "Anglicans et Catholiques," *Le Problème de l'union anglo-romaine,* Plon, Paris, 1948.
Latourette, *The Emergence of a World Christian Community,* New Haven, U.S.A., 1949.
Dumont, *Les voies de l'unité chrétienne,* Paris, 1954.
Sartory, *Die ökumenische Bewegung und die Einheit der Kirche,* Augsburg, 1955.
Thils, *Histoire doctrinale du mouvement oecuménique,* Louvain, 1955.
Garrison, *The Quest and Character of a United Church,* Abingdon Press, New York, 1957.
Mascall, *The Recovery of Unity,* Longmans, London, 1958.
Leeming, *The Churches and the Church,* Darton, Longmans and Todd, London, 1960.
Tavard, *Two Centuries of Ecumenism,* Burns and Oates, London, 1960.
Newbegin, *The Reunion of the Church,* A Defence of the South India Scheme, S.C.M., Press, London, rev. ed., 1960.
Torrance, *Conflict and Agreement in the Church,* Lutterworth, London, 1960, 2 vols.
Lambert, *Le problème oecuménique,* Ed. du Centurion, Paris, 2 vols.

287

Callahan-Oberman-O'Hanlon (ed.), *Christianity Divided*, Sheed and Ward, New York, 1961.

Lewis, *Toward Anglican-Roman Catholic Unity*, Anglican Book Centre, Toronto, 1962.

Brown-Scott (ed.), *The Challenge of Reunion*, New York, 1963.

Ehrenstrom-Muelder (ed.), *Institutionalism and Church Unity*, Associated Press, New York, 1963.

Index of Names

289

Index of Subject Matter

291

293